REDEFINING
THE MODERN

Joseph Wiesenfarth

REDEFINING
THE MODERN

Essays on Literature and Society in Honor of Joseph Wiesenfarth

Edited by

William Baker and Ira B. Nadel

Madison • Teaneck
Fairleigh Dickinson University Press
London: Associated University Presses

Associated University Presses
2010 Eastpark Boulevard
Cranbury, NJ 08512

Associated University Presses
Unit 304, The Chandlery
50 Westminster Bridge Road
London SE1 7QY, England

Associated University Presses
P.O. Box 338, Port Credit
Mississauga, Ontario
Canada L5G 4L8

The paper used in this publication meets the requirements of the American National Standard for Permanence of Paper for Printed Library Materials Z39.48-1984.

Library of Congress Cataloging-in-Publication Data

Redefining the modern : essays on literature and society in honor of
    Joseph Wiesenfarth / edited by William Baker and Ira B. Nadel.
        p. cm.
    Includes bibliographical references and index.
    ISBN 0-8386-4013-3 (alk. paper)
    1. English literature—19th century—History and criticism. 2.
Literature and society—Great Britain—History—19th century. I. Baker,
William, 1944– II. Nadel, Ira Bruce. III. Wiesenfarth, Joseph.
PR453.R43 2004
820.9′008—dc21   2003009806

Contents

6   CONTENTS

Preface

THIS MISCELLANY OF ESSAYS, RANGING IN TIME FROM JANE AUSTEN to Margaret Drabble and Richard Wright, is a tribute of friends, colleagues, and students of Joseph Wiesenfarth. His interests as a teacher and scholar are characterized by his focus on significant links between nineteenth- and twentieth-century literature and society and especially those forty years or so often referred to as the period of transition from Victorian to Modern (1880–1920). Several essays in this anthology illuminate this period, especially Joseph Kestner's "The New Woman and the Female Detective," which focuses our attention on two little-known novels by the author of *The Woman Who Did*, Grant Allen. These novels highlight feminist and other ideas of recent concern: *Miss Cayley's Adventures* and *Hilda Wade*—the latter completed by Arthur Conan Doyle.

Reflecting the greatly revived interested today in Oscar Wilde, James Nelson's "The Honey of Romance: Oscar Wilde as Poet and Novelist," reads both the poetry and *The Picture of Dorian Gray* from the perspective of the turn-of the-century controversy between romanticism and naturalism, offering an interpretation of the novel and, in particular, its memorable dénouement, which will strike the reader as completely wrongheaded or absolutely right. Linking both Victorian and Modern Literature, James R. Kincaid's sardonic, witty, and amusing "God Disappeared: Sing Tra, La, La, Tra, La La," is a shrewd commentary on the Victorians' sense of "God" (as well as the moderns). Kincaid is adroit and disarming at his task of placing his subjects in critical perspective, frequently introducing homely allusions and juxtaposing startling combinations (such as Aristotle with Clarence Thomas). Kincaid's approach is well illustrated in his "Valuable Summary" and his sole footnote explaining why his essay lacks footnotes!

Like Kincaid, Thomas H. Schaub, Max Saunders, and Ira B. Nadel further illuminate their readers about the close relationship between Victorian and modern literature. Schaub's essay on Richard Wright's *Native Son*, replete with diagrammatic representations, draws upon Wiesenfarth's *Gothic Manners and the Classic English Novel*. Schaub's fascinating structural analysis of the novel provides an excellent argument for Wright's sophisticated approach to both form and character. Saunders's essay on Ezra Pound and Ford Madox Ford combines an original and exciting analysis (which interacts at times with Wiesenfarth's Ford criticism) of the work of both Pound and Ford by paralleling the *Cantos* with *Parades End*. Similarly, Nadel in his "'Nightplots': *Our Mutual Friend* and *Finnegans Wake*," offers a careful examination of the parallels between the two novels to establish his view that Joyce specifically had Dickens's work in mind.

The highly significant and revealing conversation which Emily Auerbach had with Margaret Drabble in Madison and broadcast in February 1997 is reported here and provides the reader with a fascinating discussion of Jane Austen by a contemporary scholar and famous novelist. More specifically reflecting some of Wiesenfarth's particular interests are essays by William Baker, Paul Goetsch, Gareth Cordery, and Elizabeth Winston. In "Laughter in *Pride and Prejudice*," Goetsch examines various senses of laughter—the comic and associated terms—noting how "human growth may be described in terms of movement from critical laughter to sympathetic and amiable, though not complacent, smiles." Cordery's "Drink in *David Copperfield*" (which includes illustrations by "Phiz"), is a revealing study of the significant role Dickens's own personal drinking habits played in the novelist's frequent presentation of inebriation in his novels.

Baker's "New George Eliot and George Henry Lewes Letters" is a valuable compilation of previously unacknowledged primary materials that will prove indispensable to future Eliot scholars. In her amusing and insightful essay, "'Taking Off' the Neighbors: Margaret Oliphant's Parody of *Romola*," Winston examines the ways in which Oliphant's work parodies as well as parallels that of Eliot.

Acknowledgments

THE EDITORS WISH TO THANK THE FOLLOWING: JAMES A. KINCAID, James G. Nelson, Thomas M. Schaub, and all the contributors for their help and encouragement with this volume; Adam and Louise Halpin Wiesenfarth for answering questions and keeping the project a secret; Karen Blaser and Gina Unger of Northern Illinois University; Harry Keyishian, Director, Fairleigh Dickinson University Press; Christina A. Retz, Managing Editor, Julien Yoseloff, Director, Associated University Presses and staff for their advice and counsel; Emily Auerbach for all her most valuable help, Margaret Drabble, and Wisconsin Public Radio.

REDEFINING
THE MODERN

Introduction

IRA B. NADEL AND WILLIAM BAKER

THE OCCASION OF *REDEFINING THE MODERN: ESSAYS ON LITERATURE and Society* is to honor Professor Joseph Wiesenfarth, but it is more than a miscellany of tributes bringing fresh perspectives to nineteenth and twentieth century literary works. Rather, the volume examines the close and varied relationships between Victorian and modern literature through a set of redefinitions and realignments. The essays here reflect not only new approaches and readings based on cultural studies and literary theory but engage with the challenges that emerge from the sustained rewriting and rereading of nineteenth-century texts. Such revisions, which have been occurring for more than a generation, reinforce the link between literature and society, which the scholarship and criticism of Joseph Wiesenfarth has long encouraged.

Until recently, connections between the moderns and the Victorians had been denied or obscured; affiliations had to be established stealthily, much like those members of the India Survey of 1860 who, to map Tibet, had to disguise themselves as monks to foil the Tibetan government's ban on foreign geographers. Yet they accurately, if covertly, charted the land of this unknown country just as novelists and critics first clandestinely and then openly revealed the complex connections—not contradictions—between the modern period and the Victorian. For the last thirty years or so, an exploration similar to that which took place in Tibet has occurred through the historiographic metanarratives of novels like Jean Rhys's *Wide Sargasso Sea* (1966), John Fowles's *The French Lieutenant's Woman* (1969), A. S. Byatt's *Possession* (1989) and, more recently, Matthew Kneale's *English Passengers* (2000) and Michel Faber's *The Crimson Petal and the White* (2002).[1] A culture of austerity and prohibition no longer defines the Victorians who are now understood as anticipating many of the habits and concerns of the postmodern period, from sexuality to politics.

A little more than one hundred years after the term Victorian was first used—according to the historian G. M. Young 1851 was the year—Raymond Williams's *Culture and Society* (1958) and E. P.

Thompson's *The Making of the English Working Class* (1963) provided early revisionist critiques of Victorian history (Young 1936,
87). New work such as Simon Gunn's *The Public Culture of the
Victorian Middle Class* (2000), Kate Flint's *The Victorians and Visual Imagination* (2000), and Matthew Sweet's *Inventing the Victorians* (2001) continue to rewrite Victorian history. These, and other
works, have collectively broken up stereotypes and reshaped our
thinking of the Victorians to show that "most of the pleasures we
imagine to be our own, the Victorians enjoyed first" (Sweet, x).
Thought to be racist, for example, the Victorians had no anti-immi-
gration law and elected Britain's first Asian members of Parliament; thought to be religious, church attendance fell dramatically.
As Matthew Sweet importantly reminds us, "the Victorians invented us, and we in our turn invented the Victorians" (xii).

The condescension and reaction of Bloomsbury toward the Victorians, no doubt helped by "exposés" like Butler's *The Way of All
Flesh* (1903) and Gosse's *Father and Son* (1907), facilitated an
anti-Victorianism initiated before Strachey's *Eminent Victorians*
imaginatively outlined the hypocrisy of the period. Strachey's emphasis on the excesses and distortions of Florence Nightingale or
General Gordon provided the early moderns with reasons to rebel
against their predecessors. Soon, the habits of the Victorians were
comically stereotyped. By the 1930s and 1940s, the Victorian period was the favored setting for satiric, sentimental fiction and
drama such as *The Frozen Heart* (1935), a novel by Amy Strachey,
widow of Lytton Strachey's cousin, and *Don't Mr. Disraeli* (1940),
a play by Caryl Brahms and S. J. Simon.

Retro-Victoriana dominated cinematic reconstructions of the period as in the first Conan Doyle adaptation to portray Sherlock
Holmes in Victorian London, the 1939 film, *The Adventures of
Sherlock Holmes,* in which melodramatic acting best conveyed the
supposed criminality and sinister character of the age. With *Great
Expectations* (1944) and *Oliver Twist* (1948), David Lean heightened the dark atmosphere and mystery of Victorian life hedged in
by brick alleys and doorways jammed with the poor. The 1958
Hammer Studios *Dracula* extended the vamping of the Victorians
by setting the Transylvanian count in the center of a Victorian London dominated by sexual repression which he libidinously unleashed. The Gothic overtones of the late-Victorian world fed the
myths of Victoriana that were visually being undone on the screen.
The eastern European, old-world context of Dracula had been replaced by an urban, sophisticated, if dangerous, mise-en-scène with
an individual disfiguring (and deflowering) the confined young

women of the period. Dracula's release to prey on the corseted young punished the repressiveness of the Victorians. Only a vampire, it seems, could liberate the Victorians sexually.

Soon, studies like Steven Marcus's *The Other Victorians* (1966) and Martha Vicinus' *Suffer and Be Still: Women in the Victorian Age* (1972) began to correct the distortions attributed to the apparent sexual repression of the Victorians which Michel Foucault's *History of Sexuality* (1976) confronted. Foucault's reading of the nineteenth century called for a rejection of the repressive hypothesis; for Foucault, the century saw the increasing deployment and proliferation of sexuality in a series of discourses and institutions, mainly in medicine, psychiatry, and pedagogy. Later texts continued to revise alienating visions of the Victorians: Thomas Richards's *The Commodity Culture of Victorian England* (1990), Michael Mason's *The Making of Victorian Sexuality* (1994), Robert Douglas-Fairhurst's *Victorian Afterlives* (2002), and A. N. Wilson's *The Victorians* (2002) among the most notable. What their repositioning of the Victorians emphasizes is the ability of the age to live with contradictions without being destroyed by them; suppression and activism were in constant battle, their engagement a precursor of the modern in sexual, psychological, and cultural terms. The Victorians are no longer progenitors of the past but the present.

To repossess the nineteenth century is to confront the issue of historical continuity and disruption, two conflicting, if not contradictory, postmodern impulses. The former stresses the modeling aspect of Victorian life, understood as a homogenous society where respectability and virtues such as duty and industry sustain a kind of fable of the Victorians challenged by new historicist readings that reveal the age as its direct opposite. Paradox, not unity, characterizes the period, confronting rather than hiding issues of sexuality, materialism, and gender. The absorption of the contemporary novel, for example, with rewriting the Victorian past is not only a way of constructing a history of our present with elements of postmodern storytelling, but a revision of the nineteenth century. While narrative disruptions, irony, and doublings fashion many of these Victorian retellings, there is also a deep desire to reconstruct the visual and social dimension of the period. To reestablish that world reminds readers that the past was a physical as well as psychological space. When William Rackham, hero of Michel Faber's *The Crimson Petal and the White*, arrives at Mrs. Castaway's brothel in the company of the prostitute Sugar, he has traveled through a Dickensian world of darkness and dirt (Faber, 104). It is a sensual

experience for William and the contemporary reader more accus-
tomed to urban renewal than decay. The novel opens with the words
"watch your step," a narrative warning and physical guide: "The
cobblestones beneath your feet are wet and mucky, the air is frigid
and smells of sour spirits and slowly dissolving dung" (3–4). The
work then distills Sugar's ascent in Victorian society, a woman who
possesses not only sexual allure but business acumen and literary
ambition: throughout her challenging adventures she manages to
write a romance.

John Fowles's *The French Lieutenant's Woman* anticipated this
kind of fictional play, incorporating his reader into the story and
offering choices concerning the story's development. In chapter 55,
for example, he confides to his reader that he already thought of
leaving Charles, the hero, for eternity on a train on his way to London "but the conventions of Victorian fiction allow, allowed no
place for the open, the inconclusive ending." He had to decide what
to do, but as the narrator slips back to 1867, the time of the scene,
he acts defiantly, flipping a coin to determine the plot (Fowles, 317–
18). He makes his decision as the character, now awake, watches
the narrator, seated in the same train compartment, perform this
trick. The image of the novelist is no longer the omniscient Victorian voice maintaining a theological pose, but a critical spirit who
has freedom, not authority, as his first principle. And through reify-
ing the past, we defamiliarize but also clarify our present.

The conjunction of the Victorian and postmodern occurs not only
because of similar narratives of emergence but because of the understanding that concepts of twentieth-century culture began with
the Victorians. There is also a similar, if hesitant, identification of
equivalent losses and changes neatly expressed when the hero of
Pincher Martin asks, "how can I have a complete identity without
a mirror?" (Golding, 132). The editors of an influential collection,
*Victorian Afterlife, Postmodern Culture Rewrites the Nineteenth
Century* (2000), emphasize that the properties of the modern, which
organize time, and of culture, which organize space, "began with
the Victorians" (Sadoff, xviii). They further acknowledge that the
Victorian struggle with sexual repression was more a harbinger of
sexual self-realization than suppression. Our present sexualites are
post-Victorian rewritings.

The commodification of culture through consumerism further
identifies the postmodern with the Victorian which Oscar Wilde, in
a letter to the *St. James's Gazette*, recognized. Responding to an
article criticizing *Dorian Gray* that appeared in the magazine under
the headline "A Study in Puppydom," Wilde refuses to discuss the

merits or demerits of the remarks because he cannot understand "how any work of art can be criticised from a moral standpoint. The sphere of art and the sphere of ethics are absolutely distinct and separate," the first shot in what will be the modern critique of Victorianism. What he does object to, however, is the *Gazette*'s placarding "the town with posters on which was printed in large letters MR. OSCAR WILDE'S LATEST ADVERTISEMENT; A BAD CASE." What is offensive, he claims, is the word "ADVERTISEMENT," because "of all the men of England I am the one who requires least advertisement. I am tired to death of being advertised." His ironic objection to being commodified is the thrust of his letter, not the criticism of his book. What he perceptively understands is that "the real advertisement is your cleverly written article" since the English public takes no interest in a work of art "until it is told that the work in question is immoral and your réclame will, I have no doubt, largely increase the sale of the magazine" where *Dorian Gray* first appeared (Wilde, 237–38). Wilde's protest and then sly approval of turning his story into a commercial product reflects the Victorian recognition of consumerism's shaping taste, a process little different from our own time. Thomas Richards's study, *The Commodity Culture of Victorian England*, documents the evolution of his relation which, he argues, begins with the Great Exhibition of 1851. Advertising establishes its rhetoric and dominates the period, which the front page of the *Times* for 1 January 1861 confirms: it contains 179 advertisements on its cover (Sweet, 1). The "familiar imperatives of modern commodity culture" begin in the Victorian age (Richards, 71).

In the refiguration of the nineteenth century, with its sites of cultural emergence and literary innovation, there are parallels to today. If postmodernism has always been in search of tradition while pretending to innovation—history without chronology—then late-twentieth-century postmodernism has leaped over the modernist avant-garde to find a recent past that viably counters contemporary cultural exhaustion (Huyssen, 170). The postmodern focus on the provisional and unknowable, while the practices of deconstructionism concentrated on irony, disruption, and the absence of values, created a void which the structures of Victorian thought and culture filled—and found expression through—Victorian retellings. A vanishing past has been balanced by the recovery of the Victorians which is, itself, alternately subversive and comforting. The postmodern evocation of Victorian life opens up new directions for its evaluation at the same time that returning to the period corroborates our own sense of understanding our social and moral origins. The

Victorians, now understood to be like us in many ways through their similar engagement with spiritual, scientific, and moral crises, possess a dual position through their closeness and distance. They are both similar and different, sharing parallel dilemmas and challenges, whether suffocating under consumerism or perplexed by gender identities. The result is the freedom to reshape at the same time we respect the age.

Jean Rhys's shifting the time period of *Jane Eyre* in her retelling, *Wide Sargasso Sea*, to coincide with the emancipation of blacks in the West Indies is one example of how this dual process of remaking and respecting the Victorian past occurs. In setting her novel in 1839, rather than 1789–1808, the time of *Jane Eyre*, Rhys rewrites Brontë, revising the entire perspective and balance. Setting two thirds of the book in the West Indies, Rhys offers readers an entirely new and disorienting vision of the action. Suddenly, modernism, feminism, and postcolonial theory establish claims on the text in ways that seem more direct and demanding than *Jane Eyre* itself. Through her focus on the white Creole, Bertha, Rhys stimulated a rethinking of national literature and cultural territory in Victorian writing. The three divisions of the novel, with parts 1 and 3 narrated by Bertha (the first in the West Indies, the third from the attic room at Thornfield Hall; Rochester, newly arrived in the West Indies, narrates the second section), suddenly challenge the structural coherence and positivist conception of Victorian fiction and its reliance on omniscient narration.

Of course rewriting the nineteenth century did not begin in the late twentieth century. Oscar Wilde was one of the first to indite the age, commenting, for example, that Dickens never knew the limitations of his art: "When he tries to be serious, he only succeeds in being dull, when he aims at truth he merely reaches platitude." Wilde claims that Dickens could never satirize, only caricature; in later works Wilde goes on to overturn a series of Victorian precepts notably in *The Picture of Dorian Gray*, and in "Phrases and Philosophies for the Use of the Young" (Wilde, 47–48, 433–34). Henry James's "The Private Life," a hypothetical account about the relations between the private and public selves of Robert Browning, further criticizes the age, as does his novella *The Aspern Papers,* detailing a biographer's attempt to gain the letters of the nineteenth-century poet. Butler's *Way of All Flesh* (1903) established what would become a stereotypical view of Victorian moral life, restrictive and destructive, which Edmund Gosse in *Father and Son* (1907) continued.

Eleven years later, *Eminent Victorians* (1918) by Lytton Strachey enlarged the radical and ironic deconstruction of Victorian heroes and institutions, initiating a series of debunking works that capitalized on the excesses of Victorian life, especially religious intolerance, moral conservatism, and the sexual repression of women. The only place Victorianism was still upheld without question was in the late-nineteenth-century jingoist adventure stories of juvenile literature embodied in periodicals like *Boys' Own*. But soon the excesses of the Empire as expressed in Kipling and Rider Haggard came under scrutiny in Conrad. Other writers then began to undo the Victorians. Somerset Maugham in *Cakes and Ale* (1930) provided a composite, unflattering portrait of Hardy and H. G. Wells in the character of Edward Driffield whose marriages paralleled those of Hardy. *Flush* (1933), by Virginia Woolf, introduced a critical (if comical) perspective of Elizabeth Barrett Browning, seen through the eyes of her dog. Until the Second World War, interest was not so much in rewriting as unmasking the Victorians for their apparent hypocrisy and narrow-mindedness; however, as writers began to travel to the margins of the empire, literally as well as figuratively, coinciding with new historical understandings of the period, reconceiving the ethos of the Victorians was underway. Before A. S. Byatt could illuminate the life of Christable LaMotte in London, Jean Rhys had to tell the story of Bertha Mason at Coulibri and Granbois.

Contemporary writing illustrates this cultural repositioning most clearly, which many of the essays in this collection amplify. Revising the postcolonial narrative and unsettling the tropes of Victorianism, for example, is Peter Carey's *Oscar and Lucinda* (1988) which tests Victorian resolve and education against the sexual politics and religion of nineteenth-century Australia. Significantly, the novel underlines the increasing authority and direction of women, marked most noticeably by the cardplaying, cigarette-smoking, unconventional Lucinda who rises to be a factory owner in New South Wales, Australia, only to discover that her power threatens the male hierarchy: in one memorable scene, the workers refuse to talk to her, addressing only her companion, Oscar: "The men, her employees, had offered him a fellowship they had denied to her" Carey writes (374). Australia in 1859, the setting for a large part of the novel, reels with the issues of the working class, faith, and love, while the themes of technology, religion, and expansionism provide the core materials of the text. Early sections, set in Victorian Oxford and Notting Hill (to be visited again in Michel Faber's novel), resonate with the limitations of mid-Victorian moral life, from churchgoing to the natural sciences, although they are soon undermined by horse racing and gambling which will eventually, and ironically, unite Oscar and Lucinda. The beginning of the novel evokes the world of Gosse's *Father and Son*, the latter that of *Daniel Deronda* as Oscar's pursuit of his faith and the construction of a glass church parallels Deronda's pursuit of Zionism; Lucinda's gambling and power is parallel to Gwendolyn Harleth's attractions. George Eliot even appears in *Oscar and Lucinda* as a friend of Lucinda's mother who, in a clever play on texts, actually offers a comment on Carey's fictitious heroine (202).

In his elaboration of the contradictions of Victorian life—not only spiritually but in terms of the colonial attempt to dominate the wilderness of Australia through which the disassembled glass church must be perilously transported—Carey dramatically presents the very process of Victorian rewriting, but without the flourishes of postmodern fiction. Maintaining the nineteenth-century setting and narrative voice throughout, there is no need for the filigrees of intertextuality, narrative rupture, or interplays of textual politics. To tell the story of a life "riddled with sin and compromise" is for Carey enough (430).

The fiction of Sarah Waters similarly presents the politics of gender and empowerment of women whether in *Tipping the Velvet* (1999), a novel of late-Victorian lesbianism moving from music halls to female clubs (itself preceded by Jeannette Winterson's *The Passion* [1987] about a female cross-dresser in the Napoleonic Wars) to her more recent *Fingersmith* (2002). In this newest work, a Fagin-like group made up of orphans and artful dodgers plots a deceptive marriage to secure a fortune with the aide of the youthful but duplicitous narrator, Sue Trinder, who is herself deceived by the plotters yet manages to achieve revenge and a modest degree of love. When she, rather than the intended victim, is committed to a lunatic asylum, the novel moves from an indictment of marriages of convenience to a critique of Victorian medical practices. Waters's detailed account of treatment in a lunatic asylum is as frightening as it is powerful.

Another contemporary element in the novel is that the rare book library owned and carefully catalogued by the wealthy uncle, from which his niece, Maud Lilly, the "heroine" of the work reads to him every day, is devoted entirely to pornography. Bibliography crosses with flesh in the exchanges of arcane book details and pornographic rarities such as *The Whipping Milliners* with its irregular paging and punctuation (Waters, 245). By the end of the novel, echoing the end of Jane Eyre with Jane's return to Thornfield, Sue Trinder returns to an abandoned and partially damaged Briar, the country home of Maud's uncle, only to find Maud alive and writing—ironically and because of its economic value—pornography. An inheritance for Sue and Maud's writing career solidifies their independence and love for one another. Drawing equally from *The Woman in White*, as well as *Oliver Twist* and *My Secret Life*, Waters constructs a world with sympathetic heroes that alternates between petty thieves, lunatic asylums, and frustrated female lovers.

What both Carey and Waters also show in their work is the crisis in masculinity that occurred in late-Victorian culture. Oscar and the Gentleman, as he is called in *Fingersmith*, continue the lack of potency and confidence masculine figures like Rochester, William Dobbin, Franklin Blake, John Harmon, and Daniel Deronda exhibit. The erosion of masculinity and ascension of feminism in figures like Jane Eyre, Helen Huntington, Becky Sharpe, or Dorothea Brooke continues with Lucinda, Sugar, and Sue. "The fantasies of a pitched battle for sexual supremacy" as Elaine Showalter has written, "often concealed deeper uncertainties and contradictions on both sides." Masculinity, she reminds us, and as the rewritten Victorian novel emphasizes, is also "a socially constructed role, defined within particular cultural and historical circumstances" (Showalter, 8–9). Desire may drive a modern Victorian male—see Charles in *The French Lieutenant's Woman*—but the last active male hero in Victorian fiction may have been Disraeli's Sidonia in *Tancred* (1847). Few if any male Victorian heroes survive in twentieth-century fiction unless parodied as in the Flashman series by George MacDonald Fraser, popular in the 1980s.

Contiguous with the renewed emphasis on gender through the empowerment of women in the new Victorian novel are the issues of race and imperialism. Matthew Kneale's view of the English exploitation and mistreatment of the Aboriginals of Tasmania in the late 1850s in *English Passengers* (2000) and Daniel Mason's portrait of the English in Burma in 1886 in *The Piano Tuner* (2002) are two recent examples of reorganizing nineteenth-century legacies of political struggle and colonial repression that challenge Disraeli's 1847 assertion that "All is race; there is no other truth" (Disraeli, 149). Both *English Passengers* and *The Piano Tuner* foreground the politics of minority groups and non-Western cultures. In Kneale's novel, a group of religious Englishmen begin a quest for the Garden of Eden thought to be in the wilds of Australia. Their voyage on ship, captained by an irascible Manxman and his crew, tabulates the challenges of nineteenth-century sea travel to Van Dieman's Land. This is set against the fixed hostility and disparagement of the British toward the Aboriginals expressed most systematically by a Dr.

Thomas Potter, at one point writing "the dominating characteristic of the Black Type being barbarism, he has no comprehension of ideas, of enterprise, or time, and yet he cannot be regarded as harmless," a view echoing Dr. Robert Knox in *The Races of Men*, 1850 (Kneale, 406). Various narrative reports sent to London in the novel chart the sustained exploitation of the Aboriginals.

Peevay, the Aboriginal who narrates a portion of the story, carefully documents the increasing abuse of his people as his anger grows: "I WAS A FOOL TO LEARN WHITE SCUTS' WORDS AND GOD. . . . I SHOULD HAVE JUST SPEARED SOME AND GOT KILLED WHEN I HAD THE CHANCE" he thinks late in the novel (342). He also describes the powerful, almost mythical figure known as Mother who leads the Aboriginals to fight against the whites. Her prowess with a gun, knowledge of the bush, and ability to swear in English as she attacked made her a formidable figure. She was based on a real female rebel leader named Walyer captured by the British in 1831. After her arrest she immediately tried to organize fellow Aboriginals in a rebellion.

The journey of the religious zealots into the interior of Australia led by Reverend Wilson leads not to revelation but despair: "All at once I felt myself haunted by a terrible vision," confesses Reverend Wilson, "of a world without guidance: a land of emptiness, where all was ruled by the madness of chance" (370). Physical, as well as spiritual, disasters follow. Competing narratives, incorporating reports, journals, first-person narratives, and even Aboriginal dialogue, establish the historical voice of the novel that alternates between accounts of penal servitude, religious obsession, and the achievement of personal freedom. When, for example, Peevay boards the escaping English ship to recover a female Aboriginal specimen, he performs a dramatic act of recovery and independence against the Empire (399–400). A mutiny on the ship returning home further marks the crumbling authority of the British, although the wily Manxmen, temporarily prisoners, devise a way of saving themselves as the ship, ironically named *Sincerity,* begins literally to fall apart around them in a storm just off the English coast.

By a combination of good luck, ingenuity, and the help of nature, the sailors are miraculously saved, although they thought they might be arrested as smugglers and murderers. "It's never being right that matters, after all, it's being believed, which is another animal entirely" the Manx Captain Kewley states as rescuers meet them after their shipwreck on the English coast (442). Their survival has an ironic element, however: sometime later, when the captain attends an exhibit of strange and unusual artifacts from the "much lamented Dr. Thomas Potter" in London, the man who in fact instituted the mutiny on the return voyage, he spies the bones of a supposed Tasmanian Aborigine which he knows are those of the dead Dr. Potter, picked clean by the sea. (451, 454). In an epilogue, Kneale provides historical data to support his fictional recreation of imperial attitudes; one view he strenuously challenges is the late-nineteenth-century belief "that the most inferior of all races had been the aborigines of Tasmania . . . who were often depicted as being a kind of halfway house between men and apes" (456).

Set in 1886, Daniel Mason's *The Piano Tuner* provides a similar, recuperative view of colonial exploitation. Edgar Drake, a middle-aged London piano tuner with a speciality in Erard grand pianos, is asked by the War Office to fulfill an unusual commission: travel to a remote post in Burma at the request of a Surgeon-Major Anthony Carroll, botanist, physician, ethnographer, to repair his 1840 Erard that has been miraculously transported by ship, elephant, and man to the remote outpost of Mae Lwin. In a strange fashion, the doctor's playing is the source of peace in the Shan States, since his performances tame the fractious warring parties in the country; indeed, his political success for the British, in competition with the French for control of Burma, makes him an invaluable officer, so much so that his bizarre request for a piano tuner is met.

The journey to Burma by ship and train across the Mediterranean, Red Sea, India, and Burma presents Drake with a series of unusual encounters from storytellers to religious fanatics. As he travels, he also reads Carroll's unusual history of life in the Burmese jungle, a history that counters the "official" reports of order and political control. Ethnography, politics, culture, and history, filtered through a lengthy narrative written by Carroll—sympathetic to the Burmese and anti-imperial in outlook—prepare the hero and the reader for arrival. The man, not the piano, of course, holds the interest of the traveler and the War Office. Even before he arrives, the piano tuner likens himself to Dr. Carroll, noting the difference between being needed versus being accepted. Welcomed into the homes of the wealthy to repair their pianos, Drake never felt an equal, just as Dr. Carroll, needed to aid those of the Shan States, struggles to be accepted and establish peace among competing factions. Yet the initial mystery remains: What is wrong with the piano in the jungle? No one seems to know, although they honor the doctor's request. To counter the absence of information about the piano, Mason has Drake interpose a history of the Erard piano and its innovations as he justifies to himself the nature of his mission. The Erard in Burma, he rationalizes, "merits not only respect and attention. It should be defended as one would protect an objet d'art in a museum" (78–80).

Drake's arrival in Rangoon in chapter 6 begins the exotic phase of the novel, distant from the world of nineteenth-century Europe. Natives with tattooed bodies greet him while remarkable pagodas perched above the harbor echo their welcome. In the fifteen paces from the dock to his carriage, Burma collapses in around him, from beggars pressing up against his leg to others thrusting garlands and food. Workers carry crates of spices and women, whose faces are painted white with ground sandalwood called thanaka, who stare out at him (84). The irregularity of the streets and dress of the people in the tropical climate—at one moment there are saffron-covered monks, the next a group of children in rags—contrasts with the drab orderliness and cold of London. Ironically, in the town square the British have erected a statue of Mercury, the Roman god of merchants, as a symbol of their regulated commerce, but all Drake witnesses is the disorder of street vendors and beggars. Drake's first venture out is as a pilgrim to the golden Shwedagon Pagoda. But as the white tiles and gold merge in the heat, he hears music and discovers four remarkable musicians playing Burmese instruments that enrapture him. He then descends to encounter a gilded woman begging, a sight that startles and mystifies him (91). A tragic accident on a tiger hunt, however, soon initiates him into the colonial abuse of others, the English believing that they could cover up the mishap with coins and the payment of fines. Concentrating on the sights and sensuality of Burma, Mason rewrites not just the image of Victorian London but imperial conceptions of a tropical, inescapable city on the edge of the unknown.

As Drake journeys further inland, his sense of destiny and loss increase. From Prome to Mandalay, Drake hears stories of the magnificent Dr. Carroll and his ability to establish peace in the Shan States. The cultural details also grow from the street theater Drake observes in Mandalay to the fascinating music. Indeed, much of the contrast between the imperial attitudes of the British and the resilience of the Burmese culture expresses itself in the difference between the music of Liszt or Bach and that of the folk music and original songs of the Burmese. Late in the novel, to satisfy a visiting warlord and evoke themes of friendship and peace, Drake performs (at Dr. Carroll's request) a piano recital, playing part of Bach's Prelude and Fugue in C-sharp Minor in the jungle camp of Mae Lwin. The music that personally saves Drake, however, is either the natural sounds of the Burmese jungle or the native songs that he hears others play. But when he teaches the Burmese beauty Khin Myo to play, he turns first to Bach, a section from *The Well-Tempered Clavier*, but integrated with the sounds of the night. "Music, like force, can bring peace" the politically savvy Dr. Carroll tells Drake, but in the end betrayal by the British rather than the natives brings conflict and death, ironically ending what might have been the first steps not only to peace but gradual autonomy for the Burmese (257).

The reassertion of colonial power at the end of the novel leads to disaster, and for Drake—ordered to remove the piano from the danger at Mae Lwin—death, but a death which occurs as he fruitlessly returns to join the inhabitants of the now overrun outpost. For all of the culture Dr. Carroll has brought to the jungle, to the people of the Shan States, civilization cannot survive misunderstanding, deception, and gunfire. Of course, colonialism is shown to be itself dying, but not before it manages to undo any efforts to improve the political and moral conditions of the people. The rotting of colonialism from within is one of the striking themes *The Piano Tuner* records, while the representation of the culture and beauty of nineteenth-century Burma is one of the powerful notes in its recuperation of the marginal.

Fictionally untroubled by the historical distortions of late Victorians, in an author's note Daniel Mason nonetheless defensively explains that "what Victorians thought to be fact at the turn of the century is more important to me than what is known to be fact today" (318). The statement justifies many of the distortions of colonialism ca. 1886–87, while acknowledging its shortsightedness. *The Piano Tuner* records the deterioration and violence of imperialism, while glimpsing the emergent drive for freedom from British domination. And ironically, both this novel and *Oscar and Lucinda* focus on importing a symbol of western culture—the piano in Mason, the glass church in Carey—into an unregulated and unknown world.

These rewritings collectively emphasize the issues of literature and society which this volume highlights. Ranging from Austen through Richard Wright and Margaret Drabble, the essays here construct a cultural narrative of nineteenth- and twentieth-century writing which redefines our understanding of both the Victorian and modern period. Whether it is parody, as in Elizabeth Winston's article on Margaret Oliphant's imitation of Eliot's *Romola*, or Joseph Kestner's detailed and historical analysis of the female detective set against the reconstruction of genders instituted by educational and legal reforms of the Victorian period which improved opportunities for women, the contributions concentrate on the remaking of the

Victorians and moderns. James Kincaid's sardonic review of the loss of faith is an acute, and at times, witty account of this dilemma. His discursive commentary on the Victorians' sense of God— compared to the moderns—is equally witty and insightful. Many of the essays in the volume focus on relationships, on new pairings of Victorian and modernist texts that illuminate connections previously unnoticed: Ira B. Nadel examines associations between *Our Mutual Friend* and *Finnegans Wake*, arguing that Joyce had Dickens's text in mind when he wrote his complex work; Max Saunders explores new bonds between Ford Madox Ford's *Parade's End* and Pound's *Cantos*, showing that Pound's interwar poems, *Hugh Selwyn Mauberley* and *The Cantos*, can be read as a dialogue with the four novels that comprise Ford's tetrology. Margaret Drabble, in conversation with Emily Auerbach, outlines her literary indebtedness to the nineteenth century and attachment, in particular, to Jane Austen. The process of reconnecting is paramount but more than thematic linking are the revisions and intersections of modern writers with nineteenth-century predecessors.

A number of the essays here also reevaluate the divide (more metaphor than fact) between late-nineteenth- and early twentieth-century literary culture. Reflecting the greatly revived interest, for example, in Oscar Wilde, James Nelson's—the author of a noted trilogy on the literary publishers of the 1890s—"'The Honey of Romance': Oscar Wilde as Poet and Novelist," reads both the poetry and *The Picture of Dorian Gray* from the perspective of the turn-of-the-century controversy between romanticism and naturalism, offering an interpretation of the novel and in particular its memorable denouement, which will strike readers as completely wrongheaded or absolutely right. Other essays explore canonical figures: Paul Goetsch, a preeminent German authority on nineteenth-century English literature, moves through various concepts of comedy and humor in his essay "Laughter in *Pride and Prejudice*." Gareth Cordery examines the social practice of drink in Dickens's *David Copperfield*, outlining cultural attitudes, Dickens's own behavior, and literary usage of alcohol. William Baker enlarges the Victorian archive in "New George Eliot and George Henry Lewes Letters," providing a set of fresh documents that expand the corpus of primary materials. But not all the contributions focus on the British tradition. Thomas H. Schaub investigates Richard B. Wright's *Native Son* to document the structuring of the novel through an analysis of the home in which Bigger Thomas works.

Appropriating the Victorians and early modernist writers is no longer an act of colonization but renewal. The essays in this volume demonstrate how revisiting prose fiction from *Pride and Prejudice* to *Native Son* implicates our Victorian identity still further, establishing a cultural narrative that not only reveals its past configurations but contests its contemporary forms. The essays also question totalizing concepts like modernity and culture, while registering a consensus that the nineteenth century, with its doubts, diversity, and divisions, is the century for conceiving ideas of the modern.

But a question remains, one that A. S. Byatt sharply posed: Why is the Victorian past the subject of so much modern fiction (Byatt, 92)? Is it the desire to rewrite the Victorians in our own image? Or is it the recognition that our own values and concepts are empty of meaning and that the contemporary absorption with existentialism, modernism, and materialism have not answered challenges of history, value, or faith and that possible solutions may be rooted in the literature and culture of the nineteenth century? For Byatt, rewriting the Victorian past resuscitates it, but for others revisiting the Victorians is the means through which postmodernism attempts to think its own cultural identity. The essays in this collection, many of which grow out of the criticism and scholarship of Joseph Wiesenfarth, provide additional resources to perform that act.

NOTES

1. Other titles of what has become the literary practice of revisiting the Victorians include Brian Moore, *Great Victorian Collection* (1975), Charles Palliser, *The Quincunx* (1989), Lindsay Clarke, *The Chymical Wedding* (1989), and William Gibson and Bruce Sterling, *The Difference Engine* (1991). Two additional works are John Keates's *The Strangers' Gallery* (1987) set in 1847 and Graham Swift's *Ever After* (1992) about a Cambridge scholar editing the notebooks of a Victorian ancestor. *Jack Maggs* (1997) by Peter Carey is a rewrite of *Great Expectations*. Forthcoming is Lillian Nattel's *Theatre of Consolation* (2003) set in London's Jewish East End in the late nineteenth century. Sometimes these reconstructions are fanciful as in William J. Palmer's *The Detective and Mr. Dickens* (1990) and the rewrite and completion of Dickens's *The Mystery of Edwin Drood: The D. Case, Or The Truth about The Mystery of Edwin Drood* by Charles Dickens, Carlo Fruttero, and Franco Lucentini (1993).

REFERENCES

Byatt, A. S. *On Histories and Stories: Selected Essays.* London: Chatto and Windus, 2000.

Carey, Peter. *Oscar and Lucinda.* 1988. Reprint, London: Faber and Faber, 1990.

Disraeli, Benjamin. *Tancred.* 1847. Reprint, Westport, Conn.: Greenwood, 1970.

Faber, Michel. *The Crimson Petal and the White.* Toronto: Harper Flamingo, 2002.

Fowles, John. *The French Lieutenant's Woman*. 1969. Reprint, New York: New American Library, 1970.

Golding, William. *Pincher Martin*. London: Faber, 1956.

Huyssen, Andreas. *After the Great Divide: Modernism, Mass Culture, Post-modernism*. Bloomington: Indiana University Press, 1986.

Kneale, Matthew. *English Passengers*. London: Hamish Hamilton, 2000.

Mason, Daniel. *The Piano Tuner*. New York: Knopf, 2002.

Richards, Thomas. *The Commodity Culture of Victorian England: Advertising and Spectacle, 1851–1914*. Stanford, Calif.: Stanford University Press, 1990.

Rhys, Jean. *Wide Sargasso Sea*. Edited by Judith L. Raiskin. New York: Norton, 1999.

Sadoff, Dianne F., and John Kucich, eds. *Victorian Afterlife: Postmodern Culture Rewrites the Nineteenth Century*. Minneapolis: University of Minnesota Press, 2000.

Showalter, Elaine. *Sexual Anarchy*. New York: Viking, 1990.

Sweet, Matthew. *Inventing the Victorians*. London: Faber and Faber, 2001.

Waters, Sarah. *Fingersmith*. London: Virgo, 2002.

Wilde, Oscar. *The Artist as Critic: Critical Writings of Oscar Wilde*. Edited by Richard Ellmann. New York: Vintage 1970.

Young, G. M. *Portrait of An Age: Victorian England*. London: Oxford University Press, 1936.

Laughter in *Pride and Prejudice*

PAUL GOETSCH

ELIZABETH BENNET DEARLY LOVES A LAUGH (AUSTEN, 57). SO DOES Jane Austen. She invites us to laugh with Elizabeth and her father at fools like Collins and more intricate characters like Darcy.[1] She does not, however, exempt those who like to laugh at other people from her criticism and shows how Elizabeth learns to check her laughter in the course of the novel. In contrast with her *Juvenilia* and *Northanger Abbey*, Austen restrains her comic and satiric bent in *Pride and Prejudice*[2] and reflects on laughter's psychological, moral, and social implications. Hence, as Patricia Meyer Spacks points out, "As readers, we too must be careful not to laugh too much. When we accept the narrator's invitation to feel superior to the novel's characters, we find ourselves unable to comprehend those characters' emotional lives. We thus resemble Mr. Bennet, who at first cannot see Elizabeth's passionate love for Darcy, and Elizabeth, who long fails to recognize Darcy's feeling for her. While Elizabeth preserves her mocking stance, she perceives in Darcy only corresponding mockery. Laughter, protecting frail mortals, can also distort their vision" (75). Laughter is thus linked to the central problem of perception, signaled by the novel's title.[3] But it is also an important theme in its own right. Jane Austen distinguishes between various kinds and functions of laughter and uses the theme for dividing her characters into groups and illuminating questions of manners and morals.

In the following discussion I take up the suggestion made by Alistair Duckworth that the eighteenth-century debate on laughter is relevant to an understanding of the novel ("Jane Austen," 46f.). This debate considered laughter as a bodily phenomenon, a form of aggression, an expression of a feeling of superiority, or as a sign of good nature and benevolence; it centered on the question of how to discipline laughter by invoking norms of propriety, morality, and reason. In the course of this debate, as Stuart M. Tave has demonstrated, the "seventeenth-century concept of humor as an aberration

demanding satiric attack" was increasingly replaced by the prefer-
ence for an amiable kind of humor, which, based on good nature,
promotes "the values of cheerfulness and innocent mirth" and restrains "raillery, satire and ridicule, the several expressions of 'ill-
natured' wit" (chap. 8). In *Pride and Prejudice* Jane Austen does
not fully break with the older tradition, but she illustrates some of
its dangers and problems. The mortifying experiences of Elizabeth
as a self-appointed wit suggests that human growth may be described in terms of a movement from critical laughter to amiable,
though not complacent, smiles.

LAUGHTER AND ANIMAL SPIRITS

Hobbes and other thinkers of the seventeenth and eighteenth centuries believed that laughter and joy went together. They did not,
however, agree upon how to define and evaluate joy. While Hobbes
explains it as the "sudden glory" of feeling superior to someone
else (4:46), other critics emphasize the bodily basis of pleasure.
James Beattie, for instance, describes "*Animal* Laughter" as one
"which arises from some bodily feeling or sudden impulse acting
on the animal spirits, like tickling or gladness, and which may vary
from the gentle excitement raised in a child by moderate joy to
painful excess" (Tave, 80). Whereas such laughter is sometimes
seen as "a very good Counterpoise to the Spleen" (Addison and
Steele, 2:465), it also gives rise to much concern and criticism. This
is reflected in Jane Austen's treatment of Lydia, Mrs. Bennet, and
Elizabeth. Even more than Elizabeth, Lydia likes to laugh. As a
well-grown girl of fifteen, "with a fine complexion and good-
humoured countenance," she has "high animal spirits, and a sort of
natural self-consequence, which the attention of the officers . . . had
increased into assurance" (45). Naively self-reliant and indifferent
to social conventions, she is too impatient to listen to Collins's
reading of Fordyce's sermons or to keep his proposal to Elizabeth
a secret from Charlotte Lucas. "[T] here is such fun here," (112)
she tells Charlotte, and fun for her means dancing, flirting, men,
sexuality, and marriage. Lydia laughs at recalling a scene involving
a man dressing up in women's clothes (221); she regards her elope-
ment and marriage as jokes which will make people laugh (291),
and explains to her family later, "When I went away, I am sure I
had no more idea of being married till I came back again! Though
I thought it would be very good fun if I was" (316). She is insensible to her family's reactions and indulges her "good spirits" by

boasting of her marriage even before the servants (317). If any-thing, her laughter is immoderate. She thinks that she could have died of laughter at the cross-dressing incident or, later, at the thought of men and women having to be crammed into the same coach. She reports her merry homecoming as follows: "we talked and laughed so loud, that any body might have heard us ten miles off" (222). Her experiences leave her unchanged. After her mar-riage, Austen states, "Lydia was Lydia still; untamed, unabashed, wild, noisy, and fearless" (315). Lydia is her mother's daughter. Mrs. Bennet is never actually described as laughing, but her out-bursts and cries of delight—her "tumult of joy" and "raptures" at Bingley's arrival in the neighborhood (7f.), her exuberance at Lyd-ia's marriage (306), her fear of getting distracted by the news of Darcy's proposal (378)—surely involve laughter and carry Lydia's "wild giddiness" (213) to a hysterical extreme. Lydia's sense of fun and her desire for sexual pleasure are replaced by Mrs. Bennet's delight in matchmaking, an obsession that drives her, like Lydia, to flout social conventions and disregard people's feelings.Treating both mother and daughter as representatives of desire in a society that tries to control and channel the same, Jane Austen draws upon some traditional arguments concerning bodily laughter and sensual pleasure. John Mason observes in *Gentlefolk in the Making*: "the polite world desired to impose restraint of behavior. This restraint included the control of such natural actions as laughter" (216). As Chesterfield writes in a letter, "Frequent and loud laughter is the characteristic of folly and ill manners: it is the manner in which the mob express their silly joy at silly things; and they call it being merry. In my mind there is nothing so illiberal, and so ill-bred, as audible laughter. True wit, or sense, never yet made anybody laugh; they are above it: they please the mind, and give a cheerfulness to the countenance. But it is low buffoonery, or silly accidents, that always excite laughter; and that is what people of sense and breed-ing should themselves be above." (quoted in Berger, 101).

Correspondingly, eighteenth-century conduct books criticize im-moderate laughter as vulgar and warn women neither "to break out into violent loud laughter" nor to laugh "without any Occasion, like a Country Milk-Maid" (quoted in Fritzer, 64). Other critics and moralists remind their readers, "Fools are always painted laughing" (Fritzer, 68), and argue, "Laughter, while it lasts, slackens and un-braces the Mind, weakens the faculties" (Addison and Steele, 2:466). Steele summarizes the contemporary discussion as follows: "Mirth to a prudent Man should be accidental. . . . That Mind is dissolute and ungoverned, which must be hurried out of it self by

loud Laughter or sensual Pleasure, or else be wholly unactive"
(2:268). Accordingly, Austen creates a number of situations in
which Lydia and Mrs. Bennet's behavior appears to be vulgar, in-
considerate, mindless, and foolish to other people, especially to
Elizabeth.

Elizabeth has inherited her father's intelligence, but in some respects she resembles her mother and Lydia. Apart from enjoying
laughter, she shares her sister's energy and vitality and has a similarly lively temperament.[4] Her spirits are frequently high and have
"seldom been depressed" before (213). She has "a lively, playful
disposition" which delights "in any thing ridiculous" (12). Like her
mother and sister, she misjudges other people; like Lydia, she is
attracted to Wickham for some time; and like Lydia, though to a
lesser degree, she disregards social conventions. Ironically, Mrs.
Bennet, who does not curb Lydia's wildness, at one point tells Elizabeth: "remember where you are, and do not run on in the wild
manner that you are suffered to do at home" (42).

In the course of events Elizabeth comes to see her mother and
Lydia critically. Thus she also learns something about herself. At
Netherfield Park, long before Darcy criticizes her relations, she
blushes at the stupid and loud remarks made by her mother. At the
Netherfield ball she suffers because she believes that her family has
made "an agreement to expose themselves as much as they could"
(101). Later, she accepts the justice of Darcy's objections to her
relations. Consequently, she is no longer diverted by Kitty, Lydia,
and her mother's lamentations over the departure of the regiment
from the neighborhood: "all sense of pleasure was lost in shame"
(299). She and Jane frequently unite "to check the imprudence of
Catherine and Lydia" (213), but because the younger sisters are
supported by their mother's indulgence, there is no chance of improvement. Lydia simply laughs at Jane and Elizabeth's "formality
and discretion" (220). So when Elizabeth notices Lydia's violent
joy at being invited by Mrs. Forster, she feels obliged to advise her
father to restrain Lydia's "exuberant spirits" (231). Her effort is in
vain. Later, she can only distance herself from both her mother and
Lydia; she is sick of her mother's folly (307) and disgusted by her
sister (316). The parallels and differences between Lydia and Elizabeth are illustrated by the letters they write on the occasion of their
imminent weddings. Lydia's letter to Harriet is mindless, emotion-
ally shallow, and unconcerned about the future: "You will laugh
when you know where I am gone, and I cannot help laughing myself at your surprise tomorrow morning, as soon as I am missed. I
am going to Gretna Green, and if you cannot guess with who, I

shall think you a simpleton, for there is but one man in the world I love, and he is an angel. I should never be happy without him, so think it no harm to be off. You need not send them word at Long-bourn of my going, if you do not like it, for it will make the surprise the greater, when I write to them, and sign my name Lydia Wick-ham. What a good joke it will be! I can hardly write for laughing" (291). Lydia's references to laughter characterize her as someone who blindly assumes that everyone will enjoy her anarchic flouting of social norms and her grasping "at instant, total pleasure" (Allen, 437). Elizabeth promptly condemns her thoughtlessness.

By contrast, Elizabeth's letter of gratitude to Mrs. Gardiner testi-fies to the writer's self-awareness and her ability to discriminate and mock herself: "I am the happiest creature in the world. Perhaps other people have said so before, but not one with such justice. I am happier even than Jane; she only smiles, I laugh. Mr. Darcy sends you all the love in the world, that he can spare from me" (382f.). Unlike Lydia's laughter, Elizabeth's laughter is a "gift of joyfulness" (Spacks, 74) which she has earned. According to Den-nis W. Allen, the logic of desire in *Pride and Prejudice* is "gov-erned by an ascetic logic based on an economy of pleasure: Repressing desire and renouncing satisfaction, one experiences the necessary amount of unhappiness. Repression is then magically lifted, one's desire automatically satisfied, and the endless *glisse-ment* of desire halted" (437). Lydia, who continually seeks immedi-ate gratification, is left unsatisfied at the end of the novel, "condemned to eternal want, both romantic and financial" (Allen, 437). Elizabeth achieves happiness because she has learned to disci-pline desire and suffer when Lydia's misalliance had appeared to shatter her hope for a marriage with Darcy.

LAUGHTER AND RIDICULE

Elizabeth has to distance herself not only from her mother and Lydia but also from her father. Deeply disappointed in his unwise marriage, Mr. Bennet is prepared "to meet with folly and conceit" in every room of his house except his library (71). Usually, he ei-ther withdraws from family life to his library or seeks refuge in the maxim, "For what do we live, but to make sport for our neighbours, and laugh at them in our turn?" (364). Thanks to his intelligence, he has a keen sense of the ridiculous in other people and, like his daughter Elizabeth, serves Austen as a fairly reliable guide to some of the characters of the novel. The narrator's characterization of him as an odd "mixture of quick parts, sarcastic humour, reserve, and caprice" (5) is, however, an early warning not to trust his judgment entirely. In fact, Mr. Bennet is eventually found wanting both as a wit and a father, especially by his favorite daughter. Elizabeth shares her father's appreciation of the ridiculous and his pride in being able to assess people critically. Like her father, she often uses wit and ridicule as a defensive strategy.[5] When she is mortified by Darcy's remarks at the Meryton assembly, she tells the incident "with great spirit among her friends" (12). In her later conversations with Darcy she wants to resist his "assumption of control over her, a control which he exercises through the expression of critical judgments" (Newton, 77). She tells Charlotte, "He has a very satirical eye, and if I do not begin by being impertinent myself, I shall soon grow afraid of him" (24). The pose of ironic detachment empowers her to express herself more freely and wittily than decorum allows. Though there are some hints that she could become as cynical as her father, she is still young and spirited enough to learn. Her growing insight into her father's limitations points to changes in herself and can best be understood in the context of the eighteenth-century debate on wit, ridicule, and satire.

Partly as a reaction to restoration comedy and neoclassical satire, many contemporary writers had misgivings about the functions and effect of ridicule. Laughter, some believed, had to have a serious purpose, for instance the correction of weaknesses, the critique of deviations from moral and social norms, and the reformation of character and society. Addison, for one, asserts, "I would not willingly Laugh but in order to Instruct . . ." (Addison and Steele, 2:205). In his "Essay on Conversation" Henry Fielding defends ridicule if it is directed against affectation, selfishness, and ill-nature; he hastens to add, however, that the well-bred man should use ridicule sparingly and try "to cultivate the Good-humour and Happiness of others, and to contribute to the Ease and Comfort of all his Acquaintance, however low in Rank . . ." (152). In "Hints towards an Essay on Conversation" Swift defends raillery as the finest part of conversation, provided that it does not mean "to run a Man down in Discourse, to put him out of Countenance, and make him ridiculous, sometimes to expose the Defects of his Person, or Understanding" (quoted in Berger, 227). Francis Hutcheson proposes to restrict ridicule to those imperfections which one can amend and recommends the combination of criticism with "Evidences of good Nature, and Esteem" (7:129).

In the light of these views Mr. Bennet's behavior is questionable. He exposes the ignorance and folly of his wife to his family and enjoys Collins's foolishness as well as that of his daughters. Although he manages to amuse himself, he is too resigned and embittered to attempt to reform, help, or warn others. When Elizabeth asks him to intervene for Lydia's sake, he does not act responsibly and misjudges the situation entirely. Mr. Bennet disqualifies himself as a satirist and wit not only by his abnegation of responsibility but also by his want of delicacy. John Fielding argues, "Wit and delicacy should be inseparable" (quoted in Fritzer, 64). Mr. Bennet's lack of tact is the result of his inability to empathize with people and consider their emotional needs. He has hardened himself to the wishes and nerves of his wife and enjoys fooling and surprising her. Caring little about his daughters' actual feelings, he, for instance, jokes at Jane's being crossed in love. Later, he hurts Elizabeth with his mocking comments about Darcy; finding it extremely difficult to join in her father's pleasantry, she forces "one most reluctant smile" (363). When he asks why Lady Catherine called, she tries defensively to laugh the question away: Elizabeth had never been more at a loss to make her feelings appear what they were not. It was necessary to laugh, when she would rather have cried. Her father had most cruelly mortified her, by what he had said of Mr. Darcy's indifference, and she could do nothing but wonder at such a want of penetration, or fear that perhaps, instead his seeing too *little*, she might have fancied too *much*" (364). When she can speak openly about Darcy at last, Mr. Bennet displays a momentary concern for her future. But after hearing that she loves Darcy, he mockingly reminds her of her previous embarrassment and then plays the eccentric again by asserting that he will like Wickham best of all his sons-in-law.

Such a willful and capricious evaluation is, as Elizabeth has known for some time, one of the dangers the satirist and wit lives with. Eighteenth-century commentators regularly point out that satirists like to exaggerate and distort reality. Writing about literary critics, Addison claims, "a Man who has the Gift of Ridicule is apt to find Fault with any thing that gives him an Opportunity of exerting his beloved talent" (Addison and Steele, 3:37). He also asserts that the satirist's penchant to "pass over all the valuable Parts of a Man, and fix our Attention on his Infirmities" is simply absurd and disqualifies him as a man of good sense: "The Talent of turning Men into Ridicule, and exposing to Laughter those one Converses with, is the qualification of little ungenerous Tempers" (2:466). That Elizabeth is made to suffer from her father's insensitivity, blindness, and cynicism is the fitting climax of a development in which she overcomes her prejudices, tempers her pride, and grows apart from her family and her father's kind of wit. It is not necessary to describe Elizabeth's learning process and her relationship with Darcy in detail. In the present context it suffices to outline what Elizabeth and Darcy learn from each other about laughter, ridicule, love, and humor.

FROM LAUGHTER TO SMILES

Early on in their acquaintance, Elizabeth seeks protection under the mask of the self-appointed wit. To take such a stance is, as the previous discussion has shown, problematic and potentially offensive. This is even more so, because Elizabeth is a young woman. Eighteenth-century conduct books are agreed that women "should not be forward to exhibit their wit and knowledge" (Fordyce, 80). Women are told: "Wit is the most dangerous talent you can possess. It must be guarded with great discretion and good-nature, otherwise it will create you many enemies. Wit is perfectly consistent with softness and delicacy; yet they are seldom found united. Wit is so flattering to vanity, that they who possess it become intoxicated and lose all self-command." (Gregory, 35). Still stricter commentators admonish the young lady to beware of the "Reputation of being Witty, for fear of the Invitation it may give her of Intriguing and turning critic" (Fritzer, 63).

Violating such rules and refusing to display the modesty and reserve expected of young women, Elizabeth risks appearing as a model of bad behavior in society.[6] This is made clear by the reactions from the Bingley sisters and Darcy. The Bingley sisters, who are "not deficient in good humour when they were pleased" (15), pronounce Elizabeth's "manners to be very bad indeed, a mixture of pride and impertinence" and maliciously claim that she has "no conversation, no stile, no taste, no beauty" (35). While Darcy sees through Miss Bingley's attempts to denigrate Elizabeth and her relations, he is also somewhat irritated at Elizabeth's behavior. Unlike the Bingley sisters, he does not ridicule or sneer at her behind her back. Instead, he attempts to come to know and influence her by drawing her into serious conversations which focus, for instance, on female accomplishments, the concept of the intricate character, and the legitimacy of ridicule. At this stage of their acquaintance Darcy, it is true, appears as a somewhat pompous representative of the upper classes, who wish, as they did in the Augustan age, to distinguish themselves "from the rest by their gravity, decorum, and deportment" (Duckworth, "Jane Austen," 46). For one thing,

Darcy never laughs, not even at Mrs. Bennet and Collins. He seems to have internalized Chesterfield's belief that open laughter and mirth are signs of ill-breeding.[7]

At the beginning of the novel, then, an arrogant, overly grave representative of traditional good conduct appears to be faced with a fascinating anti-conduct-book heroine. This relationship changes quickly, in spite of what Elizabeth may think. Darcy begins to smile at her witticisms (45, 58, 91) or simply to look at her with a friendly or loving smile (91, 174, 176, 179). And Elizabeth begins to speak archly to him (52, 91, 174), smile at him (26, 52), and check her laugh in order to avoid offense (51), or hide a smile, rather than mock at his pride openly (57). Darcy loses some of his gravity, and Elizabeth ceases to laugh openly at him.This movement toward each other, which leads to the first proposal, is of course riddled with misunderstandings. Elizabeth is not fully aware of the fact that her "resistance to Darcy is undermined by a lingering susceptibility to his attentions and by a lingering desire to please" (Newton, 78). Nor does she realize that her behavior may be interpreted as flirting. Darcy himself tries to resist her attraction. And both characters are still proud and prejudiced and do not know their own characters well enough. For all these reasons their Netherfield Park discussion of their attitudes toward laughter does not represent their mature views though it contains arguments whose importance is revealed later. Miss Bingley initiates Darcy and Elizabeth's exchange of opinions by asserting flatteringly that Darcy is not a proper subject for laughter. Convinced that the opposite is true, Elizabeth exclaims that she dearly loves a laugh and expresses the ironic hope that Darcy will remain an exception among her acquaintances. In the ensuing discussion Elizabeth and Darcy use standard arguments from the contemporary debate on ridicule.[8] Elizabeth defends ridicule as laughter directed against "Follies and nonsense, whims and inconsistencies" and hopes that she never laughs at "what is wise or good" (57). She thus defines herself as a satirist who intends improvement and instruction and indirectly claims to be different from her father, "an ironist who lacks the moral fibre of a satirist" (Paulson, 300). That her self-definition sounds defensive in character and fails to adequately describe her attitudes is indicated by the contradictions she catches herself in. Though she is convinced that Darcy is too proud and stands in need of correction, she does not laugh at his statement about well-regulated pride, but turns away to "hide a smile" (57). Out of tact, a sense of respect for the man and his arguments, or because of a still unconscious attraction to Darcy, she does not openly turn him into the object of her ridicule. She still loves a laugh, though, and soon vents her desire for laughter on Collins, thus moving back to her father's position.

Since Darcy is not alienated or wounded by an open attack, he uses the discussion to state his opinions on ridicule and laughter, reveal his character, and instruct Elizabeth about proper behavior. He emphasizes the transgressive nature of ridicule and echoes the standard warning that a person "whose first object in life is a joke" (57) may render the wisest and best of men ridiculous and may, like Elizabeth, willfully misunderstand other people (58). Self-critically, he adds another argument familiar from the eighteenth-century debate: He says it is a weakness not to forget the follies and vices of others as soon as one ought. He thus accuses himself of being too severe and resentful rather than generous. At Hunsford he uses still another conventional argument by telling Elizabeth, "you find great enjoyment in occasionally professing opinions which in fact are not your own" (174). The truth of these warnings strikes Elizabeth only much later. It is confirmed by the ill-behavior of her father and her realization that her own conduct has been faulty. Both Mr. Bennet and Darcy love Elizabeth for the same reason, her "lively talents" (376) or "liveliness of mind" (380).[9] Elizabeth's movement from her father to her husband-to-be is symbolized by her rejection of her father's type of ridicule and her acceptance of Darcy's criticism of the same. In an intimate conversation about the development of their love relationship, she gratefully acknowledges Darcy's generosity in helping the family and overcoming his resentment of Wickham. She criticizes what Darcy calls her liveliness as impertinence, thus using the term she and the Bingley sisters applied to her behavior at the beginning of their acquaintance: "You were disgusted with the women who were always speaking and looking, and thinking for *your* approbation alone. I roused, and interested you, because I was so unlike *them*. Had you not been really amiable you would have hated me for it; but in spite of the pains you took to disguise yourself, your feelings were always noble and just; and in your heart, you thoroughly despised the persons who so assiduously courted you" (380). Elizabeth here realizes that the very behavior that aroused Darcy's interest might easily have alienated him and spoiled her chances of happiness. In her *Strictures on the Modern System of Education* Hannah More explains this ambivalence by calling wit a basically "dangerous talent," which will increase a woman's chances only if it is employed properly: ". . . the temperate exercise of this fascinating quality throws an additional lustre round the character of an amiable woman" (1:69).

Of course Elizabeth's self-criticism is excessive. Toward Darcy she has been less impertinent than she makes it appear, because she has largely repressed her laughter and penchant for ridicule. When after the second proposal she longs to criticize Darcy's influence over Bingley, she checks herself once again: "She remembered that he had yet to learn to be laught at, and it was rather too early to begin" (371). As Darcy's wife she seems to practice her "dangerous talent" again, but in a way that protects her from harm: "Georgina had the highest opinion in the world of Elizabeth, though at first she often listened with an astonishment bordering on alarm, at her lively, sportive, manner of talking to her brother. He, who had always inspired in herself a respect which almost overcame her affection, she now saw the object of open pleasantry. Her mind received knowledge which had never before fallen in her way. By Elizabeth's instructions she began to comprehend that a woman may take liberties with her husband, which a brother will not always allow in a sister more than ten years younger than himself" (388). Though this description is rather vague, one can assume that this pleasantry, which may go along with laughter and smiles, is chiefly informed by love and good nature. It demonstrates, to use Hutcheson's terms, that "Laughter is none of the smallest Bonds of common Friendship . . ." (97). And if such pleasantry is intended critically, it probably fits in with Hutcheson's definition of good-natured ridicule: ". . . we may, by testifying a just Esteem for the good Qualities of the Person ridiculed, and our Concern for his Interests, let him see that our Ridicule of his Weakness flows from Love to him, and then we may hope for a good Effect" (7:129). In any case, Elizabeth's behavior as a wife is quite unlike her father's stance towards her mother. It probably also differs from Jane and Bingley's complacent attitude toward life, which is, in Darcy's words, mirrored in Jane's smiling too much. All in all, Elizabeth may not be able to laugh Darcy out of his solemnity,[10] but she is likely to make him unbend and smile occasionally or even frequently.

Tensions in the Comic Vision of the Novel

In one of his studies of *Pride and Prejudice* Joseph Wiesenfarth cogently argues that the main plot issuing in the happy union of the protagonists expresses "the values of the novel" and "dramatizes the possibility of an ordered world" in which "people who see reality and act reasonably in relation to it find fulfillment and happiness" (*Errand*, 82f.). In the light of how Lydia, Mrs. Bennet, sexuality, and the Dionysian elements are treated, Wiesenfarth justly remarks that the god symbolically presiding over this novel as well as other comedies of manners is Apollo ("Austen," 62). Yet tensions in Jane Austen's comic vision remain. What the author grants her protagonists—love, mutual tolerance, good-natured criticism, and a measure of equality—she refuses her other characters. Her portrayal of Bingley and Jane suggests that she judges good nature skeptically as a form of naivete. And her caricatures of the Bingley sisters, Lydia, Mr. and Mrs. Bennet, and Lady Catherine indicate that the world is largely peopled by ill-natured or foolish people. The exceptional development of the protagonists and the stasis of the minor characters point to a tension between the ideal values Jane Austen wishes to advocate and the reality she creates in her novel. One problem that results from this conflict between Austen's moral conservatism and her comic realism is an aesthetic one. While many readers will find Darcy and Elizabeth's education psychologically interesting and didactically meaningful, they may nevertheless prefer the comic and satiric passages and the sequence of misunderstandings the protagonists have to pass through. Many critics prefer the early Elizabeth[11] and wonder whether she does not dwindle into a wife who is forced to impose on herself "many and more serious checks and repressions . . . as she takes her place in the social group" (Tanner, 137).[12]

The tension between the moralist and the comic realist is also rendered problematic, because Austen's Apollo is after all a male god. Lionel Trilling once said about the relationship between Darcy and Elizabeth: ". . . a formal rhetoric, traditional and rigorous, must find a way to accommodate a female vivacity which in turn must recognize the principled demands of the strict male syntax. The high moral import of the novel lies in the fact that the union of styles is accomplished without injury to either lover" (222). From the perspective of gender criticism this conclusion appears dubious in that it veils the conflict between patriarchal values and female rebellion. Regina Barreca writes "Austen struggles, according to Gilbert and Gubar, to 'combine her implicitly rebellious vision with an explicitly decorous form' . . . Austen illustrates this double-talk by calling attention to, while at the same time denying, the presence of unacceptable behavior. The split lies between the articulation of rebellion and the denial of the desire, and is at the heart of much of women's humor; it doubles the irony of a woman's apparent submission to her assigned role even as she re-writes it from within" (45).[13]

It is very well possible that women and men like *Pride and Preju-*

dice for different reasons: women for Jane Austen's sensitivity to the position of women in society and the moments of autonomy and freedom from social restraints the Elizabeths and Lydias of her world enjoy; men because the fascinating, defiant female protagonist can be tamed after all. It is of course equally possible that both women and men like to read the novel for the same or some of the same reasons.

NOTES

1. The family resemblance between Jane Austen and Elizabeth is overemphasized by Mudrick, 94 f. Butler rightly argues, "The trouble with *Pride and Prejudice* is that many readers do not perceive just how critical the author is of Elizabeth's way of thinking" (216).

2. See Bilger, 55, 203; Paulson, 291.

3. For the theme of perception see, for instance, Morgan and Satz (quoted in Todd).

4. See Duckworth, "Prospects," 8 f.; Poovey, 194 ff.

5. See Harding; Hirsch; Mudrick; Paris; Poovey, 196 ff.

6. See also Fritzer, 64 ff.; Moler, 104; Waldron, 41 ff.

7. A point made by Bradbrook, 31 f.

8. Duckworth suggests that Elizabeth defends raillery in a way reminiscent of Shaftesbury's arguments in *Characteristics* (*Improvement*, 136). For a somewhat different reading of Darcy and Elizabeth's discussion see Bilger, 71 ff.

9. For Mr. Bennet and Darcy see Polhemus, 34–40.

10. In Julia Barrett's *Presumption*, a sequel to *Pride and Prejudice*, Elizabeth gives birth to a male heir: "Geoffrey Fitzwilliam Darcy was a good-natured and comely infant, but oddly solemn, which his mother proudly attributed to a sagacity uncommon in babyhood, and which she made it her particular business to laugh him out of, ere he had reached his fifth year" (237).

11. See, for instance, Brower, 75; Moler, 102; Mudrick, 119 f.

12. Priestley believes that she will "laugh at Darcy—for his own good and her pleasure" (122). While Bilger (72), Brownstein (67), and Paris (102) agree, Barreca (56) dissents.

13. For further studies of Austen's humor from a feminist perspective see Bilger, Brownstein, Gillooly, Glage, and Sulloway.

REFERENCES

Addison, Joseph, and Richard Steele. *The Spectator*. 1711–12. 5 vols. Edited by Donald F. Bond. Reprint, Oxford: Clarendon Press, 1965.

Allen, Dennis W. "No Love for Lydia: The Fate of Desire in *Pride and Prejudice*." *Texas Studies in Literature and Language* 27 (1985): 425–43.

Austen, Jane. *Pride and Prejudice*. Edited by R. W. Chapman. London: Oxford University Press, 1959.

Barreca, Regina. *Untamed and Unabashed: Essays on Women and Humor in British Literature*. Detroit: Wayne State University Press, 1994.

Barrett, Julia. *Presumption: A Sequel to Jane Austen's Pride and Prejudice*. London: Michael O'Mara Books, 1993.

Berger, Dieter. *Die Konversationskunst in England, 1660–1740: Ein Sprechphänomen und seine literarische Gestaltung*. München: Fink, 1978.

Bilger, Audrey. *Laughing Feminism: Subversive Comedy in Frances Burney, Maria Edgeworth, and Jane Austen*. Detroit: Wayne State University Press, 1998.

Bradbrook, Frank W. *Jane Austen and Her Predecessors*. Cambridge: Cambridge University Press, 1967.

Brower, Reuben A. "Light and Bright and Sparkling: Irony and Fiction in *Pride and Prejudice*." In *Jane Austen: A Collection of Critical Essays*, edited by Ian Watt. Englewood Cliffs, N.J.: Prentice-Hall, 1963.

Brownstein, Rachel M. "Jane Austen: Irony and Authority." *Women's Studies* 15 (1988): 57–70.

Butler, Marilyn. *Jane Austen and the War of Ideas*. Oxford: Clarendon Press, 1975.

Duckworth, Alistair M. *The Improvement of the Estate: A Study of Jane Austen's Novels*. Baltimore: Johns Hopkins University Press, 1971.

———. "Prospects and Retrospects." In *Jane Austen Today*, edited by Joel Weinsheimer, 1–32. Athens: University of Georgia Press, 1975.

———. "Jane Austen and the Conflict of Interpretations." In *Jane Austen: New Perspectives*, edited by Jane Todd, 39–52. New York: Holmes & Meier, 1983.

Fielding, Henry. "An Essay on Conversation." In *Miscellanies*, edited by Henry Knight Miller, 9:119–52. Oxford: Clarendon Press, 1972.

Fietz, Lothar. "'Versuche' einer Theorie des Lachens im 18. Jahrhundert: Addison, Hutcheson, Beattie." In *Semiotik, Rhetorik und Soziologie des Lachens*, edited by Lothar Fietz, Joerg O. Fichte, Hans-Werner Ludwig, 239–51. Tübingen: Niemeyer, 1996.

Fordyce, James. *The Character and the Conduct of the Female Sex, and the Advantages to be Derived by Young Men from the Society of Virtuous Women*. 2nd ed. London, 1776.

Fritzer, Penelope Joan. *Jane Austen and Eighteenth-Century Conduct Books*. Westport, Conn.: Greenwood Press, 1997.

Gillooly, Eileen. *Smile of Discontent: Humor, Gender, and Nineteenth-Century British Fiction*. Chicago: University of Chicago Press, 1999.

Glage, Liselotte. *Jane Austen: "Pride and Prejudice."* München: Wilhelm Fink, 1984.

Gregory, Dr. *A Father's Legacy to His Daughters*. 1774. A new e. London, 1814.

Harding, D. W. "Regulated Hatred: An Aspect of the Work of Jane Austen." *Scrutiny* 8 (1940): 346–62.

Heydt-Stevenson, Jill. "'Slipping into the Ha-Ha': Bawdy Humor and Body Politics in Jane Austen's Novels." *Nineteenth-Century Literature* 55 (2000): 309–39.

Hirsch, Gordon. "Shame, Pride and Prejudice: Jane Austen's Psychological Sophistication." *Mosaic* 25, no. 1 (1992): 63–78.

Hobbes, Thomas. 1966. *The English Works*. Edited by William Molesworth. Aalen: Scientia Verlag, 1966.

Hutcheson, Francis. *Collected Works*. Hildesheim: Georg Olms, 1971.

Mason, John. *Gentlefolk in the Making*. Philadelphia: University of Pennsylvania Press, 1935.

Moler, Kenneth. *Jane Austen's Art of Allusion*. Lincoln: University of Nebraska Press, 1968.

More, Hannah. *Strictures on the Modern System of Female Education*. 2 vols. London, 1799.

Morgan, Susan. *In the Meantime: Character and Perception in Jane Austen's Fiction*. Chicago: University of Chicago Press, 1980.

Mudrick, Marvin. *Jane Austen: Irony as Defense and Discovery*. Princeton: Princeton University Press, 1952.

Newton, Judith Lowder. *Women, Power, and Subversion: Social Strategies in British Fiction, 1778–1860*. Athens: University of Georgia Press, 1981.

Paris, Bernard J. *Character and Conflict in Jane Austen's Novels: A Psychological Approach*. Detroit: Wayne State University Press, 1978.

Paulson, Robert. *Satire and the Novel in Eighteenth-Century England*. New Haven: Yale University Press, 1967.

Polhemus, R. M. *Erotic Faith: Being in Love from Jane Austen to D. H. Lawrence*. Chicago: University of Chicago Press, 1990.

Poovey, Mary. *The Proper Lady and the Woman Writer*. Chicago: University of Chicago Press, 1984.

Priestley, J. B. *English Humour*. London: Heinemann, 1976.

Satz, Martha. "An Epistemological Understanding of Pride and Prejudice: Humility and Objectivity." In Todd, 171–86.

Siebers, Tobin. "Jane Austen and Comic Virtue." In *Morals and Stories*, 135–57. New York: Columbia University Press, 1992.

Spacks, Patricia Meyer. "Austen's Laughter." *Women's Studies* 15 (1988): 71–85.

Sulloway, Alison G. *Jane Austen and the Province of Womanhood*. Philadelphia: University of Pennsylvania Press, 1989.

Tanner, Tony. *Jane Austen*. London: Macmillan, 1987.

Tave, Stuart M. *The Amiable Humorist: A Study in the Comic Theory and Criticism of the Eighteenth and Early Nineteenth Centuries*. Chicago: University of Chicago Press, 1960.

Todd, Jane, ed. *Jane Austen: New Perspectives*. New York: Holmes & Meier, 1983.

Trilling, Lionel. *The Opposing Self*. New York: Viking Press, 1955.

Waldron, Mary. *Jane Austen and the Fiction of Her Time*. Cambridge: Cambridge University Press, 1999.

Wiesenfarth, Joseph. *The Errand of Form: An Assay of Jane Austen's Art*. New York: Fordham University Press, 1967.

———. "Austen and Apollo." In Todd, 46–63.

God's Disappeared:
Sing Tra, La, La, Tra La La

JAMES R. KINCAID

SOME TIME AGO,[1] J. HILLIS MILLER PROVIDED STUDENTS OF THE VIC-
torian period (of which I am one) with the wittiest and most produc-
tive metaphor for understanding the period since Walter Houghton
told us the Victorians had a "frame of mind." What Hillis said, in
his justly celebrated book (and title), was that God had disappeared
for the Victorians. He said that this disappearance of God was not
only a central feature of the Victorian cosmological landscape but
the central feature we must take into account in understanding how
Victorians, writers, and other intellectuals especially, saw their
world and located their place in it. Without God, how could one
understand language or what it did? Suspended in dark uncertainty,
how could they locate a geography of the mind? Where could one
find structure, continuity, coherence, stability? How did one know
how to fashion a plot or a cravat, take council or tea, conduct business or trains, entertain royalty or ideas?

What made the matter all the worse, in every sense, was that God
hadn't really died or anything like that, just gone away—on vacation or something. Indisposed, out of the office, nowhere to be located just now. For Miller, then, this God haunted the Victorian
world without offering it assurances, left behind traces that could
neither be made into solids nor sucked into an exhaust fan. In such
a world, everyone was on a melting iceberg—if it indeed was melting, if it indeed was an iceberg. Nothing could be certain, including
a certain uncertainty. Miller's finest point is that the Victorians
were denied the relatively simple clarity of the modernists, who
could declare God and the world he presumably structured van-
ished, irrelevant; and then make much of their rather gratuitous
boldness in saying so. The smug ease and redundancy of modernist
pronouncements on their own fragmented and foundationless world
were denied the Victorians, not because they could not see that
world but because they could see so much more; the world that had

been there just yesterday, might even, somehow and somewhere, still be there. The layered, anguished complexity of the Victorian vision, Miller argued, rests on precisely their unwillingness to release themselves from a structure of knowledge and vision they also know is not only inadequate, but often poisonous.

The enormous influence of Miller's idea rests, it is true, partly on its timing—it came along just when Victorian scholarship needed some bracing in the way of being a little less softheaded—and on its ability to speak to what we all, in some fuzzy way, had bought previously when we subscribed wholeheartedly to the idea of "Victorian doubt." Miller's book was, then, both brilliantly argued and sweetly unoriginal; it took what we all suspected and gave us reason to be proud of it. He also supplied superbly formulated arguments, both historical and philosophical, to use in the presence of scoffers. There were and are, however, no scoffers. Take my word for it. A now-you-see-it-now-you-don't deity was a convincing inciter of the "doubt" we had been talking about; and it colored the Victorians dark, somber, and serious. Dark, somber, and serious were good. Still are, unfortunately, but you'll have to wait a bit to get to see me demonstrate that. For now, let's be sure we have straight the influence of this idea of a poof-up-in-smoke God on the business of recent Victorian scholarship.

The illustrations Miller offers of his thesis are well known; I think they include Browning, Pater, Emily Brontë, and others. These are his illustrations, however, and this is not his essay; so we'll use mine. My illustrations of the disappearance of God idea are, as it happens, much better than Miller's anyhow, though his are no doubt very good. Mine are drawn from Hardy; but as I've already published them (as you know), I will not repeat them here. Well, I will repeat them, actually, but only in a very sketchy form, as you need only a reminder anyhow and as I do not remember them well. Hardy, I have argued, bases his world always on what is not there, this what-is-not-there constituting always in Hardy the strongest presence. What is not there is practically everything: reason for hope, justice, kindness, causality, love, and nice weather. It's never there, but Hardy's characters, and clearly Hardy himself, are not about to take their absence lightly. They continue to expect some fairness somewhere. It doesn't come, of course (because nobody comes); but that inevitable failure to show up is treated each time as if it were a tragic shock, justifying suicidal thoughts (or actions), writhing anguish, and (best of all) delicious resentment (look at "A Broken Appointment").

You see the point. Hardy would have nothing to write about and no effects to produce were God safely dead. God ought to be there and isn't: that's the basis of everything he wrote and basis of the considerable pleasures we have in reading him—or so I proclaimed. Not very imaginative of me, you'll be saying; kind of mean-spirited and narrow, bullying and spit-in-the-face/knee-in-the-groin. I agree.

I'm with you entirely that the idea of a disappearing God, like that of a disappearing schoolteacher or prison guard or parent, need not cause anguish. When the teacher leaves the room, trilling, "Tend to your workbooks. I'll be back in a bit" who feels paralyzed with horror? "I've got to run out for a while. Don't break anything!" is not a prompter of tears and torment. A few paranoid Victorians, here and there, may have found God's disappearance alarming, just as some students like workbooks and some of us relish the idea of wardens and keepers. But nearly all Victorians—and it's important that you take this on trust—knew it was time for the fun and the art to begin. They didn't, mind you, feel relief or anything so simple. The teacher might come back at any time, which added a tension to the frolic, a spice of danger: you might get sent to the principal's office or, in the case of God, to Hell. But art thrives on taking risks, especially comic art, which springs into any wedge it can find—Dad's gone to the grocery store!—to invent a world outside of wedges.

It is important first to secure a correct understanding (my understanding) of comedy. To start with, it is an independent thing, not relational or some reflex of seriousness. It is not the opposite of tragedy; it is not a momentary relief from something; it is not even a "view" of the world. It does not define itself over and against anything, including "the world" or "real life." When we're inside it, comedy constitutes the real and the way we think of the world we suppose we're in. More on this later, of course. For now, if you'll grant the independence of comedy, you'll see that God's departure opened up new possibilities not dependent on God at all. God out of the way, fools rush in—and the comic centering that allows the fools their necessary stage and equipment.

"Doubt" was certainly not the dominant mode, since doubt is a dependent term; it takes for granted that God is still at the center and that the question of his existence or status still controls the show. But once offstage, God's forgotten, last week's trash. The Victorians, then, didn't *doubt*—once God took her leave, they frolicked. (As I mentioned earlier, there were probably a few people who missed the old God or couldn't let go or didn't get the word, but I'm talking about the mass of people here and don't intend to offer this qualification every time I want to make a grand assertion, so here it is for the last time.) The Victorians managed then, for the first time since the Enlightenment (when God also was sent away), to find comedy. The Enlightenment didn't manage much, though, being a quarrelsome people anxious to force God out. All too often, they turned to satire, a feeble wanna-be comic gesture that still acknowledges the importance of the old center and simply wants to whack at it. The romantics were even feebler, allowing only conservatives like Byron to continue the satire, while liberals put God back into nature or the general atmosphere and lost comedy altogether. It was only with the Victorians and God's slipping out the door that comedy was possible.

As for literary history necessary to my essay, that is all ye know on earth, and all ye need to know.

Which brings us, first, to a negative question:

WHY DOES GOD HATE COMEDY?

Let's look closely at the way that question is formed, at the direct and even childish linearity of that sentence. True, the grammatical form of the sentence is that of a question (you noticed), but actually there's a resounding affirmation here. It affirms not only that God hates comedy but that such hatred—a strong noun, a good noun—goes only in one direction. God's hatred for comedy is not reciprocated. The idea of "God," in fact, is a relational, really an oppositional, not an independent, notion. God comes into being in reference to a rejection of the comic. God can only exist by keeping the police active in the pursuit of comedy, imagining always that somewhere, someone is having fun, laughing, seeing things too rambunctiously. Comedy, on the other hand, is blithely indifferent to God, isn't even aware of the hatred or where it's coming from. God's hatred of comedy, then, is like your hatred of Tom Hanks or mine of the guy who stole my gal. It never touches the object of its wrath, leaves Tom Hanks, the rat who did me in, or comedy just where they were. So the title is crucial. We'll explicate it, you and I, from back to front.

Let me first say that explicating my title is not the same thing as defining terms. Only an idiot would define terms, as Aristotle said—Aristotle and Justice Clarence Thomas too in several of his recent and celebrated commentaries.

The last term in my title is Comedy. Comedy is, you'll be glad to hear, neither a formal property nor a property of form; it is not something residing IN a work or an action, nor is it an experience. It is a posture, a way of presenting oneself to the world so as to make visible one's own grace and expose to the max one's own foolishness. That means standing unguarded, face forward, uncovered, ready not just to observe pratfalls but offering one's own pratt for a fall. Resiliency, infinite hope, infinite skepticism, never judging, eschewing fixed principles or principles, of any sort: that's what comedy is. Mrs. K, make that Ms. K, for instance, is a gloriously comic person and the cause of comedy in others, not least because she is, through and through, resolutely unprincipled. Comedy doesn't make principled stands—it ducks. Comedy doesn't live free or die; it lives free and lives. Comedy doesn't make plans, doesn't live for the future, doesn't look to power—it knows that the best plans are for yesterday, as we dress up our pasts so as to glide in the present. We plan what we were to make room for what we want to be now, which is certainly not what we'll want to be tomorrow. Most of all, *most* of all—comedy allows us to exist outside the monolithic paranoid horrors of power, the metaphysical claims made by what is simply a word—power.

Power has no more right to control things than does Pluralism or Pragmatism or Peanuts or Play. They are all words, and if we cease to bow down to them, then they shrivel and take up their proper positions, serving us, which is the way it should be. Comedy allows us not to be knowing, not to know—not to know anything—always to be surprised and to spring surprises on those we care about, which is everybody. As Miss Bates says, "It's such a happiness when good friends get together—and they always do."

The modes of critical operation we most honor these days all reverence Power, as if Power could offer anything more than confirmation of Power, telling us, gee, things are really Powerful. Set up a metaphysical center and, sure enough, it will confirm itself. Inside power, we will, voilà, spot the operations of power and its victims. Of course, there *is* sometimes reason to be able to spot the victims and Power is good for that. That's important. But all that means is that Power is a useful tool to do some things for us—find the victims of oppression. But it isn't a good tool for *all* things and it is downright horrible for some. It is, for one thing, unable to see any relationship that is open, trusting, and fun. Openness, trust, and fun are rendered by Power into illusions. Power will always spot enemies, even when there are none. Turn power loose on Miss Bates or The Wife of Bath or Falstaff or Roseanne or Mae West and all power can do is tell us they are victims or victimizers, which means Power has nothing to say and should shut up.

Most of human experience is made scanty and wizened by Power explanations, which is one reason our current models of critical operation teach graduate students a disastrous game of cynical one-upsmanship, a sanctimonious exercise in excluding others from the camp of the true believers. *Comedy* has no true believers, no truth, and no belief. It is agnostic to the core—worse, a pickpocket, a blasphemer, one you wouldn't want your sister sleeping with.

OK, the next term, working backward, is "Hates." "Hate" is a terrible word, but that's because of the subject of the sentence, which we're coming to. Comedy doesn't hate but God does. By hate here I mean getting all steamed up and defensive because something is presented to us that is outside our ken. Hate is the spilling over of fear, but hate actually means in my title really bad posture. Comedy, as I say, makes one graceful and lithe, gives one the body of—well, a body like mine, like Plastic Man, like The Artful Dodger. The body of hate, on the other hand, is the body of an offensive guard on a pro football team—neck and waist the same dimension—one immobile block of flesh.

Hate is what happens to our body when it is fed by too much agreement and knowingness, when it is flattered into thinking its paradigm—in this case Power (or God)—makes some necessary contact with what it thinks is the world. The stubbiness of the hate-filled body is the result of living inside Power (or God). Living there, we cannot but assume that the world provided to us is the only one, and that it allows us easily to understand and assume analytical control of the way it operates. Hate is the expression of some shadow anxiety about this world, an eagerness to defend it that, ironically, is the consequence of too steady a diet of self-assurance. But hate doesn't require us to think about any of this, just react. One thing you can say about living inside Power or God: it doesn't take much in the way of smarts. Once there, we are cemented in and moving out doesn't occur to us. We do not, in fact, have to stir at all, except to disable any accidental attempt to liberate or frolic that comes along. Even that disabling effort doesn't take much, just—and a few routine ritual gestures: you're complicit; you're naive; read Foucault. That's what hate is.

God now. My last key term. (My last key term should be "Why"—the first word in my title. And I have some fine things to say on that subject—but I don't want to write a really long essay here. That's not called for. I also don't want to use all my limited material in one go. Therefore, I will save my explication of the word "Why" for another occasion, perhaps an MLA Convention address.)

I don't want to offend anyone. Many good people—or at least some good people—put a lot of stock in that word, "God." I've never met any of these people, but I've been told it's so, and, in the spirit of comedy, am willing to go along. So, I mean to clarify myself right off and remove from the darkness those who have a special relationship to that word. As a friend of the family (not my friend, my parents') used to say, his own personal relation to God had taken his feet from out the miry clay and put them on solid rock. I don't want any readers to be in the miry clay on my account.

First, what I do not mean by "God." When I use that word, I do not refer to nor do I mean to insult the general idiom, the useful, if fuzzy, term employed in common phrases like "God help us!" or "My God!" or "God damn you, you lousy bastard!" I heard in the elevator one old friend say to another, obviously meeting after several years, "Lord God Almighty but you've gotten ugly!" I wouldn't want to lose such intensifiers of affection. We'd be the poorer without the God of curses, execrations, and whammie, the God of satire and lampoons, of burlesques and scurrilous cartoons, of obscenity and happy pornography. That's a "God" who loves comedy and the feeling is mutual.

The God who hates comedy is the big power broker, the Mafia boss, the bully in the sky. The unmovable mover, that which changeth not, that which is, art, and ever will be. Given that such eternal immobility and resistance to change is supposed to be admirable, comedy's fluid dynamism is bound to present a threat. God is aloof; comedy's by your side, in your face, at your elbow, tripping you up. Comedy wants us in on the joke; God is that which passeth understanding. But of course the God who hates comedy only passeth the understanding of those who ask questions or want something. Ask about bad things in the world or ask, as Huck does, for fishing equipment, and you'll be told you wouldn't be asking about such things if you knew how far God passeth your ability to understand. On the other hand, if you're among the faithful, God does not really passeth understanding at all—the reward you get for walking the line and offering a lot of praise is a perfect understanding of God and what he wants. You also are offered the ability to excoriate every other human being for her or his imperfect understanding of your God who hates comedy.

The God who hates comedy demands faith, obedience, stupefying reverence, unthinking loyalty, inflexible virtue. It is the deity in whom our Nation trusts, who gives us the thing that we are under (as in THE PLEDGE—"One nation under—"). He is our help in

Ages past, our hope in years to come—always the same rock of ages, the one from whom all blessings flow and all tribulations, curses, and horrors as well. I once was lost but now am found—once and for all, the same thing. This God is the Father we all fear and must placate, though placate we never can: the proper attitude is submission or, what is much the same, groveling fear. This steady God is like any other unquestioned but questioning entity we set up as a center to make our world cohere. This God is a bulwark, quieting our fears that maybe there are no explanations, that things do not cohere. This God is like any other stiff and defensive abstract concept—like nation, or manhood, or consciousness, or the university, or whiteness, or steely virtue. As Oscar Wilde says, virtue is a myth invented by good people to account for the curious unattractiveness of others. He actually said the reverse about wickedness, but it comes to the same thing. Oscar presented himself to the world as a bobbing and weaving performance, uncovered and unafraid. We couldn't stand his blitheness and ease, so we did him in—but his words still worm themselves into us—in matters of grave importance, style, not sincerity, is the important thing.

And this God who hates comedy need not be useful to us any more than Power is. We can sacrifice him for the God of fun. Maybe we can convert him, comedy not being big on sacrifices. Anyhow, do we really need *this* god?

A mighty fortress is our God, a bulwark never failing. Our helper he amid the flood Of mortal ills prevailing. For still our ancient foe doth seek to work us woe. His craft and power are great, and armed with cruel hate. On earth is not his equal.

Well, if that's true—if we really are surrounded by craft and power aimed at ruining us—we'd better get whatever help we can at whatever price. But what if the world is not Martin Luther's paranoid nightmare? What if there is no ancient foe, but a random mix of this and that, the uncaused and causeless, without past or future—no memory and no power to predict? Well, things could be worse—in fact, comedy suggests, things are pretty good. At least we can find more opportunities for invention without cringing before fixed principles. We can find opportunities to move—even move toward the things we love, as Eve Sedgwick says.

The Victorians saw and can instruct us in how much we do not need the God who hates comedy. After all, send that God packing, make him disappear, and we can see that it's only our fearful and feebleminded need for protection that creates both hate and the God who hates it when comedy comes along with pies to throw at Power. We need that God about as much as we need rectitude, which, as my wife reminds us, we are better off without. The Victorians anticipated, in their frolic after the Bully left, the Guide to Good Living offered by Groucho Marx, who always gives us nice lines. Speaking of his deepest and most firm beliefs, Groucho said, with tears in his eyes, "Those are my principles—and if you don't like them, well I have others." We all have others—and we shouldn't be shy of using them, especially if it's in the service of pleasure and the big buffoon God who really likes comedy.

VALUABLE SUMMARY

So, just to summarize, for those who have gotten lost along the way (bored): "God" was a structuring metaphysical center that made necessary a set of assumptions. These assumptions were so ingrained that they seemed to come not from above, a set of commandments or even beliefs, but a set of taken-for-granteds. Inside this world, it was not a matter of conscious "faith" that serious things were serious and that solemnity was the order of the day; that's just the way the world seemed to be. Since it seemed to be that way, it was. Similarly, this world was, if you could understand justly, consequential: it was ordered by a firm, if sometimes complex or obscure, causality. Acts had meanings, were caused by past acts and were themselves the cause of future acts. This God-world, in other words, was linear, mysterious, but potentially explicable (riddled with meanings), a serious matter, causal, consequential. The God who authorized these characteristics could be said to be the product of the metaphysical needs as much as the author: God and the world coincident with the idea of God have a symbiotic relation. Thus God was figured, as I suggested, as permanent, changeless, reasonable (if we but knew it), and so forth; thus figured, God functioned as proof of that state of things, as well as cop and bogeyman, policing the borders for escapees and scaring the rest into true belief.

None of this, by the way, has any very necessary relation to what we think of as "religion," which is only a kind of loud and irritating manifestation of obedience to the center. God could do fine without religion and religion without God, as in the case of New Age practices, Unitarians, and Shirley Maclaine. People who lived before God (what is taken for granted) disappeared may or may not have thought of themselves as religious. It didn't make a dime's worth of difference: they all breathed in the same smog, whether it was credulous or rationalist, faithful or doubting. Some, for instance, called this solemn meaningful God "Nature"; but it made no difference.

It wasn't until God went away that it became possible to see, if even for an instant, that there had been a wholly arbitrary center we had set up to structure the world and all that happens in it. It had been one sort of center and not another, as it might have been. It really had been wholly arbitrary, without any connection to "things as they are," since "things as they are" shifted to fit the center. Victorians living in this heady time sniffed freedom and found within their reach this sense that one center can do for us some things and not others, that the old solemn center was both old and solemn and more than a little dreary, and that, even if we couldn't get along with no center at all, we could take a ride to a new one that would give us new things to see and do. Also new things to be, of course. It isn't that a new center would see things differently or explain things differently: there were no "things" independent of the center that brought them into being. That being the case, many Victorians, feeling somewhat stiff in body and mind after such a long time inside a God of meaning and order, saw a different land and transported themselves to it: hauled ass, would be a phrase more befitting their plopping into comedy.

The new comic center was not formed as a reaction to the old order, God, but simply as a different place. It was and is in no way dependent on the old order or merely satiric of it. Satire, in fact, is not comedy at all. Like "doubt," satire takes up residence inside the old order and substantiates it by saying to us, "This is the best that can be done. Accept the rules and point out their deficiencies." Comedy not only does not accept the old rules; it is not even conscious of them. O Brave New World. Comedy and Us: A Homily.

Without doubt, we have slipped a little out of the comic center provided by the Victorians, the one that was inconsequential, nonlinear, noncausal; the one that was eager to expand chances, to keep the game going, to open up what seemed closed. We still live now and then within that world, even if we are uncomfortable, worried that someone might come along and designate it in classical (or stupidly snobbish) terms as "low." The true and wild comic sophistication these days is found almost exclusively among the low. Comedy is a low form, living a robust existence among the people but droned against by the new godly in our culture: critics, Rotarians, and university types. The most awesome writers in our midst— Sherman Alexie, Percival Everett, T. C. Boyle, David Sedaris, Toni Morrison—are all blasting out new comic territory, but we have some trouble reading them that way. Sedaris is reduced to a stand-up comic in prose; Alexie is easily packaged as an angry Indian; Everett is an extraordinarily smart writer, especially considering he's black, but everlastingly solemn; Boyle is funny but dead serious underneath; Morrison gets prizes because she is, within this way of seeing, never ever comic. The high in our culture see comedy as froth. Imagine one of them saying something is drearily solemn on top but profoundly comic underneath. Meanwhile, the people read comic writers like Thomas Harris, Alice Walker, Terry MacMillan, and Stephen King.

Other forms of art show this slipping even more ominously. The finest television drama by far is found in the subtle play on originality-within-repetition found in sitcoms. There we find the best writing, most intricate acting, most subversive and generous vision of the world. Yet even the television industry is half ashamed of this form and tries to compensate with some of the high-minded—though not much. The movies are worse, ashamed of their own greatest works. Spinning out dozens of first-rate comedies every year, the industry still gives its official attention to the drearily high-minded, pretending it really wants to honor (or watch) such tributes to shallow solemnity as "The English Patient" or "Philadelphia." One "Rushmore" has more to offer than a dozen "Schindler's List"s, and a wise viewer (that is, virtually all of us) will find ourselves thinking richer thoughts about "Waiting for Guffman" than about "Dances with Wolves."

One might, of course, say that comedy has, right now, a profound and undisturbed existence, whatever we might suppose, that it runs wildly beneath the solemn surface pretenses of the culture. I'd say that myself, but I think there is cause to worry about the rigid inflexibility of that official line and its direct hostility to comic ways of being and knowing. As it is, prigs and true believers and "A" students, those who live earnestly inside officialdom, may find themselves immune to comedy. We wouldn't wish that on anybody.

The best cure is to turn to the Victorians, to find in their writings voices we can no longer hear, questions we cannot raise ourselves, currents that have dried up under us. It will take some vigorous misreading, that is, reading aslant the doctrinal interpretations of these writers and texts. We have been taught to read them well, that is, to read them as pursuing their life inside an intense anxiety about God's disappearance. We must summon the energy and the wit to read real bad, to think of these writers not as more constrained than we but wilder, not as seeing less but more, not as paralyzed by doubt but playing with it.

Victorian Comedy

All Victorian writings are comic, exist inside a world constructed as discontinuous, graceful (sometimes) and bumbling (often), non-causal, absurd, forgiving, and open. You might not want to read them that way, but there's no reason you wouldn't want to, it seems to me. It's all a matter of how you station yourself. Move from here to over there and you see and hear altogether different sights and sounds. There's nothing implicit in any text or literary movement requiring that it be understood or even that it is best understood inside a particular paradigm. Paradigms for reading can be called genres; and, as E. D. Hirsch has demonstrated, all genres are really contractual matters, established not by texts but by readers and the institutions which issue instructions to readers on what contracts to sign. So, let's repeat it: All Victorian texts are comic, given your willingness (right?) to sign that reading agreement. You might want to sign all sorts of different agreements, of course, and to violate them at will. Sure. It's just that there's nothing outside the authority of the good-reading directions that requires us to sign anything for any one reading experience. Other contracts will look very odd, it is true, since our agreements have been naturalized. But there's great pleasure in oddity.

I do not mean here to parade at length and analyze the usual suspects in the Victorian comic lineup, those texts which we are right now instructed to read as comic. It is, however, instructive to ask why we get this list and not another and why the list we get is so wizened. Power (God) gives us a very slim allowance. Let's see: we are offered Thomas Hood, Robert Surtees, William Aytoun, Douglas Jerrold, Charles Stuart Calverley, A. C. Hilton, and a few others of that sort, there to swell the list, since no one will ever read them anyhow. Other than that, we get early Dickens (and even that is "really" serious), the bits of Thackeray we wave at in passing, Carroll and Lear (half-mad perverts), a bit of Browning (a very little bit), W. S. Gilbert and Wilde, both of whom we turn into satirists, that is, serious moralists hiding behind a comic disguise.

This is pathetic. Within Power, we are bound to see comedy as nonessential, providing occasional holidays from the serious ("comic relief"), merely another perspective within Power and a strategy by which Power achieves its already-established goals ("satire"). We must admire the way this metaphysical center maintains itself. Power does not argue the case for comedy's triviality, rather assures us that comedy is alive and well, doing its janitorial and remotely serviceable work: they also serve who only stand and chuckle. We come to believe that Power's interested version of comedy is the only one; but Power can only see comedy within Power. It's not really a strategy of Power to reduce comedy or a matter of recognizing an enemy or competitor: Power simply is that way. With centrality comes the stupidity born of smugness; and Power should not be faulted for imagining that comedy is either serving it directly or allowing little refreshing escapes from Power's rigors.

Now, one of the ways Power operates, moronically but persuasively, is to make us think that comedy resides inside texts, that it's loaded in there like prizes in Cracker Jacks. Comedy is an ingredient in something else, and that something else is always Power. Power cannot conceive of comedy as an independent way of reading and being; for Power it is a matter of form and content read through Power, something Power allows to be and to be THERE. This ruse makes it seem as if the reading practices authorized by Power were natural and universal, and that Power were opening us up to what is, what IS. And in terms of Victorian comedy, what Power says IS isn't much: a little bric-a-brac on the wall, an occasional sniff of air, a rare walk in the woods.

Inside comedy, however, we are provided with different lenses and different allowances. We have a different world and thus different ways of being. Thus, it is not just W. S. Gilbert and Edward Lear who present us with comedy, but Thomas Hardy, Emily Brontë, George Eliot, G. M. Hopkins (those "terrible sonnets"), then gloomy Arnold, the severe James, Kipling, Newman, Tennyson, Marx, Engels, Gaskell, and "The Song of the Shirt."

Since I see that I'm almost out of time and space, illusions as they may be, and that my editor here is becoming impatient, I'll just conjure up a couple of examples that you will be able to row in better than me, once I've rented you the leaky craft and set you adrift in the water. "There's a lake of stew, and whiskey too, in the Big Rock Candy Mountain!" Take *Emma* and *The Way of All Flesh*. The first is usually read as excess (pride, vanity) tamed; the second as satire. These readings, like any other readings under the sun, are not wrong of course, just faithful to the center dictating them. My quarrel with them is that they have become as predictable as what comes out when you put a quarter in any machine. Plug in Power, feed her, and she'll give you a reading of any text or discourse whatever, a reading that will feel right. It will feel right because it will confirm, for the billionth time, that Power can reward the faithful by providing an explanation, an interpretation, that will account for all the details and tidily show us that there's nothing Power cannot explain. These explanations, when we give them plenty of time to roll over us, tend to be—well, Powerful.

Comedy, however, affirmeth not, or affirmeth differently. It opens up new beings, new ways of seeing, new reading practices. It might also, I suspect, allow us to do more than endlessly interpret texts, as if interpretation were all we were good at or wanted to do. I'm not sure about you, but I haven't yet become very good at interpreting. I may become good in time, just as I may also run a three-minute mile or join a rock group (drums, I think, and some solo vocal work, ballads). Also, I would like to do things other than interpret, such as asking why we interpret so much, as if we were dogs able only to fetch. I think I can roll over and speak too, if given the chance.

Emma, for instance, might become a carnival by this reading, the triumph of a mistress of Eros over the tight little, timid little restrictions of conventional rationalism and social organization. We would see what now is buried so deep as a subtext it suffocates. Emma's plans for the world are organized around a fertility festival. Harriet Smith becomes a Rubenesque erotic playground for minds and hands, and men like Mr. Elton, she knows, may think they are sensible but cannot, in the long run, resist a "pretty face" (code for a roll in the hay, a roll so fine men never want to stop rolling and will marry to keep the ferris wheel of delights spinning). Similarly, the world conforms to our pleasures and never asks that the greater term (pleasure) submit to the lower (the measureable) anymore than Kant's higher Reason should submit to the Understanding. It's an absurdity and comedy finds it a matter for giggles. "You have made her too tall," Mr. Knightley says of Emma's artful portrait of Harriet. Look again.

Then at Box Hill, we find not pain and humiliation but triumph. Miss Bates is not permanently scarred by Emma's wit, since there are no scars and nothing is permanent. She bounces back like Falstaff, glad for the game. Her good nature cannot be squelched by a joke on her capacity to bore. She knows that she is an inexhaustible source of warm good feeling, a fountain of mild love. It will take a lot more than a joke to dry it up; better, it finds jokes a source of renewal. And Mr. Knightley is, as always, idiotic to reprove Emma and to cite lots of irrelevant and quite static constructs, such as Miss Bates's poverty and "station," as if those things were immutable or in any way to the point. At the end, Emma beds Mr. Knightley and takes him under her pedagogical wing. We can be sure he'll learn to see things her way, to learn to measure not only Harriet's stature but the stature of all human absurdity and fluidity by very different means. His fixed beliefs and pleasure-dimming assertions will expand into comic uncertainty, writ on water, and turning that water into wine for a Bacchanal.

Not to be predictable or turn comedy into another producer of mechanical interpretations, let's look at how a bounteous book like *The Way of All Flesh* could be reduced to a satire. Why would we ever feel the need to read it that way, as if Butler had some ax to grind and depended on the world-as-it-is for his grinding? Why do we insist that this book is relational only, playing off of a fixed world that it ridicules? Instead, think of it as a primer for readers, leading us not into but out of satire. We exorcise our resentments and angers, produced by the mistaken notion that others have done us wrong. We have made that mistake by assuming we were in a world of consequences, laws, powers. But, as Butler tickles and gooses us into seeing, there is a sublimity in being grandly indifferent, finding pleasure in church attendance just as in being faithful to the brothel. In Ernest's world as he comes to see it, doing what comes naturally and very easily is the best road to success and certainly to fun. Take nothing seriously and it'll return the favor. Be ye lukewarm, says this gospel—but it doesn't enforce that principle at all, doesn't argue us into it.

It gets us drunk with comedy and asks us how we like it. That's what comedy does all over Victorian landscape. Once we're drunk, of course, we're hardly in a position to answer responsibly. I mean, we can scarcely think straight of antecedents and possible consequences, of what we owe to God or to standards of decency or to Mother. We can scarcely stagger well, much less take a stand. Those are only some of the benefits offered by Victorian comedy, only a sampling of the gifts it holds out in its old bawdy generous hands.

NOTES

1. Everybody knows about when that was, so there's no need to get fussy. In fact, I have found that footnotes seldom serve a useful purpose. What I have found—surveys, personal experience, conversation with the best scholars—is that they never ever serve a useful purpose. However that may be (probably somewhere at some point some scholar found a footnote serviceable), I won't bother you with them here in this essay. Not that I couldn't if I wanted; but I know what you like, which is not footnotes, and I'm here to minister to your pleasures. Joe Wiesenfarth, possessed of the most hospitable of minds and hearts, will approve, I feel sure.

Drink in *David Copperfield*

GARETH CORDERY

As long ago as 1961 Roland Barthes wrote that food, includ-ing drink, is "a system of communication, a body of images, a pro-tocol of usages, situations and behavior" (167), yet most discus-sions of drink in Dickens focus on what is consumed, how much or how to make it. This approach gives us a taxonomy of drinks in Dickens but there have been few attempts to view drink as part of the symbolic economy of Dickens's fiction or to situate it in its his-torical and cultural context as a site where religious, social, and moral issues are played out.[1] Merrett's contention that Dickens's representation of drink "tends to be journalistic" and its "goal topi-cal satire" (110) may be partly true for early newspaper pieces such as "Gin-Shops" (1835), but when we come to *David Copperfield*, written at midcentury but dealing largely with events a generation earlier, we may view drink as a discursive field for interrogating the radical changes that took place during that period. I want first, then, to examine the cultural significance of drink in the novel as it emerges from its historical and material circumstances, especially in relation to the Temperance Movement and to George Cruikshank, who highlights Dickens's public attitude and whose iconography of drink is reworked by Hablot K. Browne in *David Copperfield*.[2] Secondly, I want to view drink in *David Copperfield* as it relates to Dickens's personal circumstances. Because the novel draws upon the autobiographical fragment and is thus as close a fictionalizing of Dickens's own experience as we have, it betrays his own anxie-ties about his origins and his class, as David-Dickens looks back from the security of middle-class respectability to the trauma in the 1820s of the bottling-blacking warehouse. The key scenes in reveal-ing these fears are David's "Magnificent Order at the Public-House" (the title of Phiz's illustration) in chapter 11, and his "first dissipation," the title of chapter 24, at his Adelphi chambers. Thus drink is at once a mark of a society in transition and an index for Dickens's own uneasiness about class.

But before examining these crucial scenes, a word about Dickens's personal drinking habits. While the almost "endless succession of splendid public banquets and private parties" (Watt, 173) that marked his life and the 185 dozen bottles of various wines, champagnes, and spirits he possessed at his death may suggest he was a heavy drinker, nothing could be further from the truth. The contents of his cellar were simply "commensurate with his station in life, the size of his household, and the scale of his entertaining" (Hewett and Axton, 177) and there is no evidence that Dickens himself ever became drunk. Indeed, despite that substantial cellar and those lavish parties Dickens was, according to his daughter Mamie, "abstemious in both eating and drinking" while his reading tour manager, George Dolby, wrote: "Never once can I call to mind a single instance of his having dulled his brain or made his tongue speak foolishly by such a vice" (quoted Holt, 170). So despite his knowledge and appreciation of fine wines and spirits "the idea," in the words of Annie Fields, wife of Dickens's American publisher, "of his ever passing the bounds of temperance is an absurdity not to be thought of for a moment" (169). Which is not to say that he acted like Mrs. Pardiggle, as a kind of moral policeman to his friends who did, it would seem, not infrequently pass those bounds, friends such as Collins, Egg, Sala, Leigh Hunt, and especially George Cruikshank, whose escapades were legendary.

Cruikshank's conversion to teetotalism in 1847 together with the flourishing Temperance Movement bring into focus Dickens's publicly and confidently expressed attitude to drink, while in *David Copperfield* a less certain, more ambiguous representation of the same topic is evident. Dickens's public position is unequivocal. Firstly, he opposed teetotalism while advocating moderation. He wrote: "I am a great friend to Temperance and a great foe to Abstinence" (*Letters*, 3:404), and drink *"moderately used*, is undoubtedly a cheerful, social, harmless, pleasant thing—often tending to kindness of feeling and openness of heart" (4:31). In his journalism he attacked teetotalism for what he was later to call its "whole hoggism," which denied the poor in particular the right to some enjoyment and relaxation in their drab lives.[3] Secondly, Dickens carefully distinguished the causes and effects of drunkenness in, for example, his letter to Theodore Compton, secretary of the National Temperance Society, attacking its "monstrous doctrine which sets down as the *consequences* of Drunkenness, fifty thousand miseries which are, as all reflective persons know, and daily see, the wretched *causes* of it" (4:31), and in his 1848 review in *The Examiner* of Cruikshank's "The Drunkard's Children" whose message that drunkenness and family ruin are caused by one fatal slip is firmly opposed by Dickens who asserts its causes as "misery, neglect and despair" (Slater, 2:105). But in *David Copperfield* the purchasers of the August 1849 number would have read in chapter 11 that the orphan boy who endured all these things did not become drunk on Genuine Stunning Ale, and that in chapter 24, published in December, the educated young man, comfortably settled in his middle-class chambers in the Adelphi buildings, becomes as drunk as a lord (I use the term deliberately) in the company of Steerforth and his aristocratic friends. It is in *David Copperfield*, which draws so heavily upon the autobiographical fragment, where Dickens betrays his anxieties about his social origins. In other words, drink in the novel is the site where class issues are played out and where the seemingly seamless ideology of moderation as publicly expressed and personally practiced becomes fractured.

In chapter 11 David Copperfield, enjoying a half-hour "tea" break from his demeaning work with common boys at Murdstone and Grinby's warehouse, strolls around the streets close to the Thames. A genuine working-class lad would have gone to the pub, identified as the Fox-under-the-Hill, situated near the mysterious "dark arches" of the Adelphi, where on a previous occasion he had observed some dancing coal-heavers. The Adelphi Arches, memorably portrayed in the third of Augustus Egg's triptych "Past and Present" (1858), were "described by one near-contemporary as 'malodorous caverns where . . . ragged forms huddled against the curving bulkheads of the blackened slimy brick walls'" (Ackroyd, 94). The Arches and the Fox-under-the-Hill were frequented by coal-heavers who were hired, organized, and exploited by the "undertakers" (often dockside publicans) who forced them "to take part of their pay in drink" (George, 295).[4] Consequently, as Mayhew notes, "none but the most dissolute and intemperate obtained employment" (Quennell, 534) and as coal-heaving[5] was the dirtiest and most physically demanding of laboring jobs it was performed by immigrants, mainly the Irish (Flinn, 276). Now Dickens clearly knew all this: as a boy he used to play "on the coal-barges at dinner-time with Poll Green and Bob Fagin" and the Fox-under-the-Hill was "one of his favourite localities" (Forster, 1:28), but in the novel the drunkenness and violence endemic to the coal-heavers are conspicuously absent.[6] Instead they are probably dancing an Irish jig. Dickens may well be celebrating here, as he does elsewhere, the vitality of working-class culture, but in romanticizing the dancing coal-heavers he is also censoring his distaste for and fear of the very lowest of that class. Cruikshank, no doubt, would have joined in the dancing, for in one escapade described by Dickens "He was last seen, taking Gin with a Waterman" (*Letters*, 3:264) and in another the artist, attracted by music, entered a "low public house . . . frequented by coal-heavers" (Jerrold, 2:59–60), but in the novel Dickens allows David, that fictionalized version of his younger self, to observe them from the safety of a bench. "I wonder what they thought of me!" (215) ponders David. More to the point we wonder what he thought of them.

Harboring a "sense of unmerited degradation" for having to work with "common companions" (223) and resenting his descent to the level of a "common drudge" (229) at Murdstone and Grinby's one evening David turns his back on the wharfside Fox-under-the-Hill and enters an unnamed public house identified as the Red Lion in Parliament Street, close to the seat of power. Soon he will flee the degradation of the wine warehouse for the security and domesticity of Aunt Betsey's middle-class cottage at Dover and will eventually settle in chambers, located *above* the Adelphi Arches. His journey toward bourgeois respectability is here foreshadowed and the scene at the Red Lion encapsulates David's desire for and eventual rise to gentlemanly status. As Orwell once observed, Dickens's attitude to class often emerges incidentally when he is writing about something else.

> I remember one hot evening I went into the bar of a public-house, and said to the landlord:
> "What is your best—your *very best*—ale a glass?" For it was a special occasion. I don't know what. It may have been my birthday.
> "Twopence-halfpenny," says the landlord, "is the price of Genuine Stunning ale." "Then," says I, producing the money, "just draw me a glass of the Genuine Stunning, if you please, with a good head on it." The landlord looked at me in return over the bar, from head to foot, with a strange smile on his face; and instead of drawing the beer, looked round the screen and said something to his wife. She came out from behind it, with her work in her hand, and joined him in surveying me. Here we stand, all three, before me now. The landlord in his shirt-sleeves, leaning against the bar window-frame; with his wife looking over the little half-door; and I, in some confusion, looking up at them from outside the partition. They asked me a good many questions; as, what my name was, how old I was, where I lived, how I was employed, and how I came there. To all of which, that I might commit nobody, I invented, I am afraid, appropriate answers. They served me with the ale, though I suspect it was not the Genuine Stunning; and the landlord's wife, opening the little half-door of the bar, and bending down, gave me my money back, and gave me a kiss that was half admiring and half compassionate, but all womanly and good, I am sure. (216)

David orders the very best ale with an air of insouciance and superiority in keeping with his assumed gentlemanly status: "Just draw me a glass of the Genuine Stunning, if you please, with a good head on it." The phrases "my good man" and "look sharp about it" hover nearby. And he specifies a glass of ale and not a pot of porter. The latter, also known as "heavy wet," was the working-man's beverage and named after the porters who drank it. It was served by potboys in pewter pots and it was not until 1845 when the excise tax on glass was repealed did lighter ale, pleasing to the eye, begin to displace porter (Hewett and Axton, 131). So both drink and vessel confirm David's sense of himself as the "little gent" (218) his fellow workers call him. But David, in his conversation with the landlord and his wife, is suitably evasive about his laboring background, inventing "appropriate answers" to the landlord's questions so that he might "commit nobody," least of all himself of course. There is a little game of deception being played out here because David pretends to be something that he is not but wants to be, and pretends to be able to afford the very best ale, which he can't: twopence-halfpenny from the six shillings a week he earns at Murdstone and Grinby's is a fifth of his daily wage. Earlier he had spent sixpence on a meat pie and nothing on drink as he washed the pie down with "a turn at a neighbouring pump" (212). But the landlord sees through David's pretensions: he will not serve the false gentleman with the Genuine Stunning which, as David suspects, is not at all genuine, having been probably adulterated or diluted (or both).[7] However, the landlord's motherly wife takes pity on David and gives him back his money, thus signaling the end to David's fantasy and his return to the reality of the wine warehouse, a return emphasized by the insistent repetition of "I know" in the next paragraph.

When we turn to the illustration (fig. 2) we can see that Phiz, as in so many of his illustrations, elaborates and extends the meaning of the verbal text, even at the expense of literal accuracy. Thus the landlord is not in his shirtsleeves but wears a jacket, which adds an air of respectability to his character, and the bar window-frame is missing, which lessens the barrier between David and the proprietor and his wife. His mother dead, expelled from Blunderstone Rookery, and away from the Peggotys, David continues his search for surrogate parents, and here the amiable landlord and his good, compassionate wife, rejecting his role as the "little gent," offer themselves as just that, and the public house, with the parlor door opening directly into the bar becomes, for a brief moment, a refuge and a home for the orphan boy.

Figure 2. Browne's "My Magnificent Order at the Public-House" (from *David Copperfield*, August 1849)

Phiz underscores this by alluding to the illustration's visual pre-decessors, namely Cruikshank's "The Gin Shop" of 1829 (fig. 3) and the illustration of the same name he did for *Sketches by Boz* (fig. 4) in 1836. The earlier version itself draws upon Hogarth's fa-mous "Gin Lane" (1751) and Thomas Rowlandson's "The Dram Shop" (1815) and we read it as we would those, for the embedded

Figure 3. Cruikshank's "The Gin Shop" (from *Scraps and Sketches II,* 1829), by permission of The British Library

written text, the emblematic detail, the visual puns, and the allegorical narrative. My focus is not here[8] but on its relation to the 1836 version and its reworking by Phiz, but it is worth noting its general content and structure: the barrels at the back, the disreputable and poorly dressed customers separated from the skeletal barmaid by the bar, and the spirit vaults through the doorway.

Before Dickens and Cruikshank parted ways over the latter's taking of the pledge, as working professionals they were at one in their condemnation of excessive gin drinking, in their registering of changes in drinking practices, especially the rise of the flashy new gin palace,[9] and in their celebration of colorful working-class life. Cruikshank's illustration for Dickens's "Gin-Shops" is more realistic and less emblematic than the 1829 print. The barrels are no longer coffins but are massively heavy, threatening to crush the drinkers beneath, who are individualized and distinguished by their dress. The focus of the earlier print was on the deadly consequences, both physical and spiritual, of drinking gin, but here allegory is transformed into realism in keeping with Dickens's interest in the social interaction of the customers, watched over by a beefy landlord.

Phiz relies upon Cruikshank's iconography but exploits it to

Figure 4. Cruikshank's "The Gin Shop" (from *Sketches by Boz,* 1836)

stress David's desire for respectability and need for a family. The
barrels in the background are not coffinlike nor hugely threatening;
they are labeled "nectar," not with the names of gin; the pendulous,
chandelier-like gas lamp is more ornate and stylish than those in
Cruikshank's; "the death's head Bacchus above the gin taps"
(James, 164) of the 1829 print has become a playful, naked figure

holding a bunch of grapes (wine, then, not gin) astride a small cask, moved from center stage to window as a kind of advertisement; the door opens into the domestic parlor revealing neither a spirit vault of dancing fiends nor a pugnacious proprietor; the well-dressed "little gent" in the public house has replaced the filthy and the ragged of the gin shop and the chattering and the argumentative of the gin palace; the friendly, parental figures of the landlord and his wife have taken the place of the tarty barmaids. And there is no actual drinking in either Dickens's text (David is merely served), or in Phiz's illustration, and thus no possibility of drunkenness. The novelist's and illustrator's interests lie not in drinking and its possible consequences but in how certain values may be conveyed through the kinds of drinks on offer and where they are consumed. Phiz's illustration, endorsed by Dickens, gives us a drinking establishment that is a respectable family home. Rather than gin destroying the home, which was the major thrust of Cruikshank's "The Bottle" and "The Drunkard's Children," wine, ale, and soda water help to establish and confirm it. As we have seen, this number of *David Copperfield* was published in August 1849, a year after Dickens's review of "The Drunkard's Children" and two months before his *Examiner* article "Demoralisation and Total Abstinence." At one level, then, David's order at a public house, both text and illustration, may be seen as the writer's and the artist's collaborative response to the Temperance Movement in general and to Cruikshank's conversion in particular.

At another level it reveals that drinking in a particular kind of pub is an index of social change. Much of the action of *David Copperfield* takes place in the 1820s such that the superimposition of the past on mid-century London highlights the radical changes in drinking habits and social attitudes during this period. If "by the 1850s no respectable middle-class man would enter a public house" (Thompson, 308) then David on his journey toward respectability is halfway there. The middle classes forsook the pub and increasingly took to drinking at home, as David does in his comfortable chambers at the Adelphi, but at this stage he has some way to go. And the Red Lion is a halfway house in another sense: the early Victorian pub was "mid-way between the more regulated and formal contexts such as work, and more private and intimate inter-personal contexts, such as the family" (Smith, 383). Thus David's brief visit to the Red Lion can be seen as an intermediate stage between Murdstone and Grinby's and Aunt Betsey's and the Strongs. In the new age of industrial capitalism pubs were strategically placed to offer workers refreshment on their way home: not for nothing were the old terms like alehouse, inn and tavern replaced by the catch-all "public house."[10] Drink, then, played its part in mediating the separation of spheres as David moves from working hind to domestic writer.[11] Even the architecture of the Red Lion keeps David "outside the partition" while the open door simultaneously invites him into the couple's home. As Clark wrote of the eighteenth-century alehouse, the pub is "a private dwelling house but also a public meeting place. It is an extension of the family but a rival to it" (341). This complex interaction between public and private is seen nowhere more clearly than in the relation between the streets and the pub. Sen has argued that "within the nineteenth-century experience of urbanization, a tension always existed between the known world of the home and the chaotic, unpredictable streets" and quotes Benjamin on how the arcade addresses that tension by extending "the threshold of the interior into the streets to such an extent that the streets themselves become interiorized" (493–94). Examples of such interactions are Cruikshank's "Gin-temple turn-out at Church-time" (1833) and Dickens's prose equivalent "Sunday Under Three Heads" (1836) where drunks spill onto "the open streets" (483). But if the Fox-under-the-Hill encourages, the Red Lion resists this "breaching of the domestic threshold" (Sen, 493) as it carefully shuts out the chaotic and unpredictable streets to allow David a peaceful moment of domestic security.

Finally, at a third level, David's magnificent order, both text and illustration, is psychologically as well as culturally significant. The quarter century between the incident at the Red Lion and its rewriting highlights not only changes in drinking practices but also Dickens's retrospective response to his childhood experiences. The text is almost identical to Forster's account of Dickens's autobiographical fragment: the slight changes in the fictional version are that the ale is specified as Genuine Stunning, it costs a halfpenny more, and David is given his money back, which may be Dickens wishing for David the compassion and charity his own mother, who was "warm for [his] being sent back" (Forster, 1:32) to Warren's, failed to show him. But the illustration (fig.2) significantly adds to the text in the way that Phiz foregrounds David's gentlemanly pretensions: he has turned his back on his menial task of washing and labeling wine bottles, as J. Philpot's wine list suggests; a heap of pots lie symbolically at his feet; his pose, as he stands nonchalantly against the bar, having carelessly thrown his twopence-halfpenny on the counter, perfectly captures the insouciant superiority of his order; and most important of all his clothes are in keeping with his idea of the little gent. In the autobiographical fragment Dickens describes how he frequently entered pubs dressed in his "poor white hat, little jacket, and corduroy trowsers" (Forster, 1:29), exactly what David is wearing, though this is omitted from the text. It is well known that Dickens closely supervised the illustrations and for the earlier "The Friendly Waiter and I" he gave Browne instructions about what David should wear: "I think the enclosed capital. Will you put Davy on [*sic*] a little jacket instead of this coat, without altering him in any other respect?" (*Letters*, 5:536). Browne, unaware of Dickens's childhood experiences, thus expresses the novelist's (and David's) aspirations toward respectability, domestic security, and gentlemanly status (the jacket is an Eton jacket). Chapter 11 of *David Copperfield* was perhaps the most personal and painful of any chapter Dickens had written or was ever to write. So painful in fact that he could not bear to have in the form of an illustration a powerful visual reminder of the "secret agony of [his] soul as [he] sunk into [the] companionship" (Forster, 1:22; *David Copperfield*, 210) of common laboring boys labeling pots (bottles) of boot black-ing (wine). A fine topic for an illustration one would have thought. When Warren's moved from Hungerford Stairs to Covent Garden Dickens as he tied up the pots before a window, was in full view of passers-by, so that "the people used to stop and look in" (For-ster, 1:32). Displayed in the window like some public freak and having to cross one of those chaotic and unpredictable streets, in fact Chandos Street, to buy his ale from some low public house, Dickens-David retreats to the privacy and security of the Red Lion. The magnificent order at the public house, both text and illustration, is the novelist's simultaneous remembrance, distancing, and recre-ation of his childhood trauma and aspirations. In short, Dickens re-imagines his past experience as David's escapist fantasy.[12]

By chapter 23, thanks to the generosity of his aunt, the little gent finally makes it into the middle class: Betsey engages for him, from the redoubtable Mrs. Crupp, a "compact set of chambers, forming a genteel residence for a young gentleman" in Buckingham Street in the Adelphi" (413), an "imposing complex of dignified streets" built by the Adam brothers, the central feature of which was "a great terrace of houses . . . raised on arches and fronting the river" (Bentley, 1–2). Former inhabitants included Garrick, Fielding, George IV, and Dickens himself who briefly lodged there in 1831. The symbolic import of his rise in status is not lost on David as he remembers roaming "about its subterranean arches" and ponders "on the happy changes which had brought [him] to the surface" (415).

Yet those middle-class values so carefully nurtured by his aunt,

Agnes and Dr. Strong, are challenged by the aristocratic world of Steerforth in whose company he indulges his "first dissipation," the title of the following chapter. It is instructive to compare this scene with Kit Nubbles's "extraordinary dissipation" (378) in *The Old Curiosity Shop* because it brings out so clearly Dickens's uncertainties and anxieties regarding class. Chapters 39–41 describe the Nubbles's visit to Astley's, their subsequent supper at an oyster bar, and Kit's return to work the next day for his employers, the benevolent Garlands. The latter have given Kit a half holiday (and five shillings to spend), a clear illustration of Dickens's belief in the working class's natural right to entertainment and enjoyment which includes not only the play followed by oysters and beer but also "a glass of something hot to finish with" (379), most likely gin. The next day Kit is full of a "vague kind of penitence" (379) for this extraordinary dissipation and he absolves himself of his sins by his "punctual and industrious conduct" (380) in rubbing down the pony and (I especially like this touch) trimming the grapevine (381). Historically Kit's half holiday represents a temporary release from the controls of his employer Mr. Garland, no factory owner but a benevolent patriarch who lives in rural Finchley where Kit, the agricultural worker, tends his garden and horse. Dickens stands back and meditates on the temporary release from the Protestant work ethic that holidays provide, the ambivalence expressed, significantly, in the discourse of drink: "why will they [holidays] hang about us like the flavour of yesterday's wine, suggestive of headaches and lassitude" (380). Kit's momentary dissipation is approved and forgiven because Astley's and oysters are no threat to the established social structure, for the lord of misrule reigns only temporarily, and the return to orderly middle-class values is swift and punctual; and because Kit works for a benevolent, paternalist landowner and not for a capitalist entrepreneur. The discipline demanded by the factory whistle has not yet replaced the traditional master-servant relationship (382) where each is bound to the other by benevolence and deference respectively.

If Kit's dissipation is approved and forgiven, David Copperfield's is not. David, "flushed with the . . . dignity of living in [the Adelphi] chambers" (413) high above its arches feels, when he closes his outer door, "like Robinson Crusoe, when he had got into his fortification, and pulled his ladder up after him" (415): he shuts himself off from his former working-class life and temporarily shuts out his new middle-class existence. After visiting Highgate and Rosa Dartle he returns to imagine "what delightful company she would be in Buckingham Street"; next day Steerforth admires his chambers, calls David "a rare old bachelor" and suggests making "a town-house of this place" (417). As Markham says, "a man might get on very well here" (419). David fantasizes about being a man about town, with his own chambers where he can entertain his bachelor friends and make love to women like Rosa Dartle. For the dinner he hosts for Steerforth and his two friends, he orders wine (not ale), oblivious to the irony that he will become intoxicated from bottles he formerly labeled. The menial laborer at Murdstone and Grinby's warehouse becomes, albeit temporarily, as drunk as a lord: he is "absolutely frightened" at the "numerous" bottles of wine "drawn up in a square on the pantry floor" (419) not only because of the quantity but because he is stepping into a class that is, in its own way, as terrifying as the one he has stepped out of. David wishes to be like Steerforth but can only act out these desires when the moral values drummed into him by Aunt Betsey and Dr. Strong are suspended. As he says, "I abandoned myself to enjoyment" (420). Like Kit he visits a theater, most likely in Covent Garden or Drury Lane but clearly not Astley's, and there confronts middle-class morality in the shape of Agnes. Full of "remorse and shame" (423) the repentant David next day seeks out his good angel to ask forgiveness for his sinful dissipation. David's feelings are of a different order and intensity from the "vague kind of penitence" experienced by Kit who views the events of the previous night as an opportunity to indulge the harmless cheerfulness and good humor Dickens celebrates.

Dickens's radical unease with his own place in society leads him to condone Kit's dissipation but condemn David's. Kit, as we have seen, is no threat to the social hierarchy, and after the half holiday allowed him by his employers, willingly submits to their middle-class values. On the other hand Steerforth and his way of life *are* a genuine threat to David and *his* way of life, and it takes the good angel to eventually defeat the bad one. Under the tutelage of Agnes David returns to those values that he later identifies as the basis for his success: "punctuality, order, and diligence" (671). But David's foray into the world of aristocratic dissoluteness can be seen also as a parallel to Kit's, a momentary escape from the discipline imposed by Betsey and Agnes and from the demands of his own work.[13] The dissipation in chapter 24 simultaneously expresses David's desire to join the aristocracy and to repudiate the work ethic that his new bourgeios morality and position demand.

The symbolic economy of drink in *David Copperfield* exists within a matrix of historical and material circumstances such as the Temperance Movement and changing drinking patterns and practices. Dickens's relationship with Cruikshank provides a focus for the novelist's public response to these circumstances while Phiz, drawing upon the iconography of his predecessor but closely supervised, enables Dickens to engage them at a more personal level. Based upon the autobiographical fragment of David's rejection of the Fox-under-the-Hill in favor of the Red Lion, his move to his Adelphi chambers and his first dissipation there, especially when contrasted to Kit Nubbles's, are socially and psychologically significant. Drink in the novel, then, is not only a forum for interrogating shifting attitudes and social relationships during a crucial period of nineteenth-century history, but also the site where Dickens's radical unease with his own place in society is displayed.

NOTES

1. The classic example of the former approach is Hewlett and Axton's *Convivial Dickens* where each chapter, devoted to a particular kind of drink, is followed by recipes for Grandfather's Nightcap, Dog's Nose, etc. A rich mine of information on the subject, it does not pursue its implications for a reading of Dickens's novels—nor was it intended to. The studies by Hardy, Watt, and more recently by Edwards are more in line with the approach taken here.

2. I ignore Wickfield's alcoholism which is merely a plot device to allow Heep to inveigle his way into the household, and Micawber's ritualistic making of punch, a Pickwickean celebration of conviviality and friendship, though even here we may see an affirmation of those values in response to the threat posed by the Temperance Movement.

3. Dickens's journalistic writings on drinking, drunkenness, and temperance are conveniently surveyed and summarised by Pope, 71–77, 117–22, and by Schlicke, 199–200.

4 . See also Flinn (275–77) for an account of the coal-heavers, and Dickens's atmospheric description in *Little Dorrit* of the lighters as "long and broad black tiers . . . moored fast in the mud as if they were never to move again, [which] made the shore funereal and silent after dark" (586).

5. Dickens specifies coal-heaving, which involved shoveling by hand coal from the holds of colliers rather than coal-whipping, a relatively easier process, using buckets, ropes, and pulleys, and which Dickens mentions in chapter 54 of *Great Expectations*.

6. In chapter 42 of *Pickwick Papers* Mr. Roker reminisces about how Tom Martin the butcher "whopped the coal-heaver down Fox-under-the-Hill by the wharf there" (680) but David's account is no comic anecdote.

7. Hewlett and Axton note that "'Stunning' was another term for strong ale, as 'genuine' was for home-brewed" (122). For the adulteration of drink see Burnett (91–95) who states that adulteration reached "a peak in the middle of the nineteenth century" (91). Dickens may have known John Mitchell's *A Treatise on the Falsifications of Food and the Chemical means to Detect Them* published just before *David Copperfield* in 1848. Thomas Wakley had begun a campaign against

adulteration in *The Lancet* in 1850 and an article on the subject, "Our Commission," appeared in *Household Words*, 11 August 1855.

8. See James (163–64) for a detailed analysis.

9. See Girouard, 26–29.

10. See chapter 1 of Clark who distinguishes various drinking establishments in terms of their size and status. The term "public house," in the restricted sense of "a house of which the principal business is the sale of alcoholic liquors to be consumed on the premises; a tavern" (*Oxford English Dictionary*), first appeared in 1768.

11. See Poovey (122) for a discussion of the collapsing of the spheres as David engages in true domestic labor, as a writer at home.

12. I find, then, Andrew Sanders's comment that "Dickens's account of his precocious order . . . is directly transferred to David" (857) misleading.

13. For the disciplining of David by his middle-class mentors see my "Foucault, Dickens and *David Copperfield*."

REFERENCES

Ackroyd, Peter. *Dickens*. London: Minerva, 1991.

Barthes, Roland. "Towards a Psychosociology of Contemporary Food Consumption." In *Food and Drink in History*, edited by Robert Forster and Orest Ranum, 166–73. Baltimore: Johns Hopkins University Press, 1979.

Bentley, Nicholas, Michael Slater, and Nina Burgiss, eds. *The Dickens Index*. Oxford: Oxford University Press. 1988.

Burnett, John. *Plenty and Want: A Social History of Food in England from 1815 to the Present Day*. 3rd ed. London: Routledge, 1989.

Clark, Peter. *The English Alehouse: A Social History, 1200–1830*. London: Longman, 1983.

Cordery, Gareth. "Foucault, Dickens and David Copperfield." *Victorian Literature and Culture* 26 (1998): 71–85.

Dickens, Charles. *David Copperfield*. Edited by Trevor Blount. Harmondsworth: Penguin, 1966.

———. "Gin Shops." In *Dickens' Journalism*. Vol. 1. Edited by Michael Slater. London: Dent, 1994.

———. *The Letters of Charles Dickens*. Pilgrim ed. Vols. 3–5. Edited by Madelaine House, Graham Storey, et al. Oxford: Clarendon Press.

———. *Little Dorrit*. Edited by John Holloway. Harmondsworth: Penguin, 1967.

———. *The Old Curiosity Shop*. Edited by Angus Easson. Harmondsworth: Penguin, 1972.

———. *The Pickwick Papers*. Edited by Robert L. Patten. Harmondsworth: Penguin, 1972.

———. Review of "The Drunkard's Children." In *Dickens' Journalism*. Vol. 2. Edited by Michael Slater. Columbus: Ohio State University Press, 1996.

———. "Sunday Under Three Heads." In *Dickens' Journalism*. Vol. 1. Edited by Michael Slater. London: Dent, 1994.

Edwards, Simon. "Anorexia Nervosa versus the Fleshpots of London: Rose and Nancy in *Oliver Twist*." *Dickens Studies Annual* 19 (1990): 49–64.

Flinn, Michael W. *The History of the British Coal Industry*. Vol. 2. Oxford: Clarendon Press, 1984.

Forster, John. *The Life of Charles Dickens*. Vol. 1. Edited by A. J. Hoppe. London: Everyman, 1969.

George, Dorothy M. *London Life in the Eighteenth Century*. 3rd ed. London: Kegan Paul, 1951.

Girouard, Mark. *Victorian Pubs*. London: Studio Vista, 1975.

Hardy, Barbara. "Great Expectations." *In The Moral Art of Dickens: Essays*. London: Athlone, 1970.

Harrison, Brian. *Drink and the Victorians: The Temperance Question in England, 1815–1872*. London: Faber and Faber, 1971.

Hewett, Edward, and William Axton. *Convivial Dickens: The Drinks of Dickens and His Times*. Athens: Ohio University Press, 1983.

Holt, Alfred. "The Dickens of a Drink." *The Dickensian* 27 (1931): 169–76.

James, Louis. "An Artist in Time: George Cruikshank in Three Eras." In *George Cruikshank: A Revaluation*, edited by Robert L. Patten, 157–68. Princeton: Princeton University Press, 1974.

Jerrold, Blanchard. *The Life of George Cruikshank*. Vol. 2. London: Chatto and Windus, 1898.

Merrett, Robert J. "Port and Claret: The Politics of Wine in Trollope's Barsetshire Novels." In *Diet and Discourse: Eating, Drinking and Literature*, edited by Evelyn. J. Hinz, 107–25. Winnipeg: University of Manitoba Press, 1991.

Poovey, Mary. *Uneven Developments: The Ideological Work of Gender in Mid-Victorian England*. London: Virago, 1989.

Pope, Norris. *Dickens and Charity*. London: Macmillan, 1978.

Quennell, Peter, ed. *Mayhew's London*. London: Pilot Press, 1949.

Sanders, Andrew. "Appendix A." In *David Copperfield*. Oxford: Oxford University Press, 1997.

Schlicke, Paul. *Dickens and Popular Entertainment*. London: Allen and Unwin, 1985.

Sen, Sambudha. "*Bleak House, Vanity Fair*, and the Making of an Urban Aesthetic." *Nineteenth Century Literature* 54 (2000): 480–502.

Slater, Michael, ed. *Dickens' Journalism*. Vol. 1. London: Dent, 1994.

———. *Dickens' Journalism*. Vol. 2. Columbus: Ohio State University Press, 1996.

Smith, Michael A. "Social Usages of the Public Drinking House: Changing Aspects of Class and Leisure." *British Journal of Sociology* 34 (1983): 367–85.

Thompson, F. M. L. *The Rise of Respectable Society: A Social History of Victorian Britain, 1830–1900*. London: Fontana, 1988.

Watt, Ian. "Oral Dickens." *Dickens Studies Annual* 3 (1976): 165–81.

"Nightplots": *Our Mutual Friend* and *Finnegans Wake*

IRA B. NADEL

Is THERE A PARADIGMATIC VICTORIAN NOVEL FOR *FINNEGANS WAKE*? One laughs at the question, thinking "how ludicrous, impossible, unthinkable—a game only for textually challenged Joyceans!" Reflection, however, suggests some contenders: Lewis Carroll's Alice books, Sheridan Le Fanu's *House by the Church-Yard*, and Wilde's *Portrait of Dorian Gray*. Casual references in the *Wake* to Thackeray, Mrs. Braddon, Conan Doyle, Stevenson, and Trollope hint at additional nominees. But the work with the most serious claim to the title is Dickens's last completed novel: *Our Mutual Friend*, published in 1865.

The possibility of *Our Mutual Friend* as *the* Victorian novel for the *Wake* begins with the analogous use of setting—an urban metropolis—as well as theme (identity) and character (multiple). Expanding the connection is the emphasis on linguistic worlds in flux, if not decay. The similar use of night and the importance of water further reinforce the argument that *Our Mutual Friend* is the quintessential nineteenth-century fictional antecedent of the *Wake*. A compressed example of this mutuality is the repetition of King George III when he mistakenly knights Sir Thomas Tippen in Dickens's novel: "What, what, what? Who, who, who? Why, why why?" In the *Wake*, this collapses into "whowitswhy" (164; 272.2). The Dickensian echo is but one of many illustrations of the sustained textual and linguistic union between the two books.

Among English novelists, Joyce admired Dickens the most. The subject of his 1912 essay written in Padua for an Italian teaching certificate, Dickens stood proudly on Joyce's shelves in Trieste in five separate volumes. Allusions to Dickens appear in every chapter of *Ulysses* and Joyce's 1923 notebook for the *Wake* contains a reference to "Dean Hercules Dickens" whose name appears in the text at 157.27. Contrary to Stanislaus's remarks on his brother not caring for Dickens, Carola Giedion-Welcker states that Joyce "loved to carry on a dialogue about Dickens with some unknown attendant at the post office window" (S. Joyce, 78; cf. 94; Giedion-Welcker, 272). Nonetheless, stylistic similarities between Joyce and Dickens remain unanalyzed, although Beckett first identified such parallels in 1929, which Frank Budgen repeated in 1933. More recently, Philip Herring has noted Joyce's use of *David Copperfield* for sections of "Oxen," but all of these comparisons remain descriptive and incomplete (Beckett, 15; Budgen, 72; Herring, 33, 261–62).[1]

Direct references to *Our Mutual Friend* occur throughout the *Wake*, from citations of its title to the names of its characters. At 65.35, during the tangled discussion of Humphrey Chimpden Earwicker's (HCE) scandal, a banging is heard and a comment made about "Our Mutual friends the fender and the bottle at the gate." Reference to the fender suggests Lizzie Hexam who perpetually sits and dreams at the fender before the fire at her waterside home, while the bottle directly alludes to Dickens's novel: Boffin locates John Harmon Sr.'s last will in a Dutch Bottle (bk. 3, chap. 6; bk. 4, chap. 14). But a bottle also contains Anna Livia Plurabelle's (ALP) letter (63.32–35; 623.24–30; 624.1), an echo of Bloom's thoughts of maps in bottles recorded in "Nausicaa" (13.1246–52). A later reference to "your meetual fan" appears at 434.28, while Joyce mentions Jenny Wren, the crippled dolls' dressmaker, at 278.12. He borrows the nickname of Nicodemus Boffin, "Noddy," and uses it at 24.2. "A dustman nocknamed Seven-churches" (59.16–17) also alludes to Boffin whom Dickens later calls the "Golden Dustman." The Porters in the *Wake* (560.22) evoke the Six Jolly Fellowship Porters, the central pub of *Our Mutual Friend* and locale for a number of crucial discoveries and revelations. The proprietoress is Miss Abby *Potter*son (emphasis added). The most extended parallel between Dickens's novel of night and the river and Joyce's occurs at 447.10–24, epitomized in the phrase "compost liffe in Dufblin" (447.23).

The passage begins with a reference to "my jolly young watermen," possibly an ironic comment on the watermen Gaffer Hexam and Rogue Riderhood of *Our Mutual Friend*, neither of whom are very jolly. The narrator then refers to a "drawadust jubilee along Henry, Moore, Earl and Talbot Streets. Luke at all the memmer manning he's dung for the pray of birds . . ." (447.13–15). The passage contains a set of key terms drawn from Dickens's novel: dust, dung and "pray of birds," an inversion and vowel shift of "Birds of Prey," cited in book 1, chapter 3 (65) and the partial title of book 1, chapters 13 and 14, and book 2, chapter 12. The narrator uses the term for Gaffer Hexam, Rogue Riderhood, and others associated with the body snatching from the Thames. The phrase occurs when Shaun, as Jaun, lectures the twenty-nine girls from "Benent Saint Berched's national nightschool" (430.2) and warns them of impending dangers as he prepares to depart by sea. The entire chapter ends at 473 with the anticipation of return and resurrection, one of the fundamental themes of both the *Wake* and *Our Mutual Friend*.

In his *Book of Memoranda* for 1862, Dickens seemingly anticipated Joyce when he wrote "LEADING INCIDENT FOR A STORY. A man . . . feigns to be dead, and *is* dead to all intents and purposes external to himself, and for years retains that singular view of life and character" (19). The return of John Harmon from the dead (actually drowned and then reborn from water) in the novel, one of several characters who perform this feat, anticipates not only the Finn McCool myth but the actions of HCE, the slumbering—or is he dead?—giant of a man in the *Wake*. The comic reference to Pierce Egan's *Real Life in Dublin by a Real Paddy*, stated as "Compost liffe in Dufbin" (447.23), alludes to the life generated by the dust mounds of *Our Mutual Friend* which symbolize the origin and meaning of wealth in the novel, a wealth built up of refuse, dung, and letters. The narrator of the *Wake* summarizes this as the "litters from aloft, like a waast wizard all of whirlwords . . . now all . . . tombed to the mound, isges to isges, erde from erde" (17.28–30). For Dickens and Joyce, Jute's reference to Cedric Silkyshag (Sitric Silkenbeard who led the Danes at the battle of Clontarf) as the one who "dumptied the wholeborrow of rubbages on to soil here" is figuratively true of each author's texts while suggestive of each writer's method (17.4–5). For Dickens and Joyce, the rubbish heap is history and functions metaphorically through signifying images: dust mounds for Dickens and the "middenhide hoard" for Joyce (19.8).

More important than specific references or borrowings from *Our Mutual Friend* is the structure and function of language in the novel which confirms the claim of its centrality in understanding the *Wake*. The parallels between Wegg and Mr. Venus's searching the dust mounds (354–57) for anything of value and discovering a document, as Biddy Doran searches her mound for the letter, is obvious (110.22–111.36) and crucial. Appropriate to both novels is the title of a chapter in a book Wegg reads to Boffin, "Treasures of a Dunghill" from Merryweather's *Lives and Anecdotes of Misers* (543). Not only does the title express the value of discarded stories, styles, and even words used by both novelists, but it expresses the notion of the text as a repository and reconstruction of such items. The question Joyce asks, "What is to be found in a Dustheap, / The Value of Circumstancial Evidence?" (307.23–24), actually encapsulates the textuality and plot of *Our Mutual Friend* and the *Wake*. The discovery of John Harmon Sr.'s will in a Dutch bottle, hidden and retrieved by Boffin, confirms the transmission of the mounds and proper rights of the former servant, thwarting the nefarious Wegg; the recovery and reading of ALP's letter performs a similar function, solving the mystery of inherited texts and values in Joyce's novel. As Joyce summarizes, "From the litter comes the letter as from the dump" (18.14).

Beyond the significance of the mounds, the river settings, or the night world as the central locus of the action in *Our Mutual Friend* (from Gaffer's discovery of a body in chap. 1 and Wrayburn's nighttime sojourns about London deliberately misleading Bradley Headstone [bk. 3, chap. 10], to the violent night attack on Wrayburn in bk. 4, chap. 6)—transformed into Joyce's "book of the dark" (251.24)—is the novel's use of the life-in-death motif and the complex power of words.

Book 3, chapter 13 of *Our Mutual Friend* contains John Harmon Jr.'s famous interior monologue, an effective psychological explanation of why the hero maintains the fiction of his death. The need to bury his former self is explicit as the passage emphasizes the struggle and rebirth of the character through the life-in-death theme which dominates a good deal of the novel. The narrator describes this dilemma clearly as Rogue Riderhood, injured in a boating accident, recovers: "like us all, when we swoon—like us all, every day of our lives when we wake—he [Rogue Riderhood] is instinctively unwilling to be restored to the consciousness of this existence, and would be left dormant, if he could" (bk. 3, chap. 3 [505]). "The living dead man," the term for Harmon-Rokesmith (430), applies with equal force to the protagonist of the *Wake*. Early in the novel, Harmon, then disguised as Julius Handford, actually identifies his own body (i.e., that of the supposedly drown John Harmon Jr.[bk. 1, chap. 3]), as HCE at times seems to disassociate and yet identify himself in his bodily form in a manner similar to that of Bloom in "Circe."

Ascent in both novels, however, is no guarantee of salvation. "Come up and be dead" Jenny Wren cries out to Fascination Fledgeby, referring to the heavenlike power of her rooftop garden (335). To "rise afterfall" (78.7) requires knowing "the hingeworms of the hallmirks of habitationlesnes, buried burrowing in Gehinnon" (78.8–9). These paradoxes, linking the two novels through their constant set of metonymic worlds, underscore such additional themes as sex, fathers, and spying. But it is the treatment of language that dominates and unites both texts.

The constant references to texts and titles in both novels fashions each as a heteroglossia of books and documents which makes Dickens's choice of a paper mill as the industry which employs Lizzie Hexam, the location of Betty Higden's death and the source of the polluted landscape, triply ironic (bk. 3, chap. 8). Echoing Dickens, Joyce labels such absorption with the oxymoron "paperspace" (115.7–8) in a parallel section of the *Wake* devoted to the history and use of paper (114.21–36).[2] This, Joyce puns in the novel, "is a perfect signature of its own" (115.7–8), a signature in printing a folded sheet that is one unit of a book. Whether it is the reading sessions between Wegg and Boffin, with Gibbon's *Decline and Fall of the Roman Empire* their principal text of misunderstanding, or the innumerable titles and passages taken from other works in the *Wake*, such as the Quinet sentence at 281.4–13, reference and citation to other books is self-conscious and constant, merging with the presentation of characters as literal texts to be inscribed. Yet texts and documents are frequently misunderstood; and the progenitor of this distorted reading practice are those comic reading sessions in *Our Mutual Friend* between Wegg and Boffin where texts are disrupted through their oral transmission.

The inscription of literal texts on the body in the *Wake* is a commonplace observation in the book which Shem famously enacts at 185.34–186.8, creating a "dividual chaos, perilous, potent, common to allflesh, human only mortal" (186.4–6). *Our Mutual Friend* is, again, the pretext as characters become enigmas as well as texts: Wegg at his corner near Cavendish Square is hemmed-in on all sides by his ballads "like so many book-leaf blinkers" (93), while print itself is physical. Wegg tells Boffin that there isn't a piece of English print that "I wouldn't be equal to collaring and throwing"—on the spot (93)! Eugene Wrayburn, the indolent lawyer, calls himself "an embodied conundrum" linking riddles with the self (339), while late in the book, Jenny Wren's father has "a strange mysterious writing on his face" (800), literally becoming a text as Shem has done. *Our Mutual Friend* is a principal source for Joyce's concept of the textualized self, both novels articulating the presence and use of "letterish fragments" (66.25).

Our Mutual Friend displays the constant decomposition and recombination of language recorded in the *Wake*. In Dickens, words are compartmentalized and fragmented in an effort to educate the reader to recognize "Tokens . . . Marks . . . Signs . . . Appearances—Traces" (179). "Ours is a Copious Language, and Trying to

Strangers" Mr. Podsnap announces to the foreign gentleman who is his dinner guest (179). The "tissues and textures" of language become paramount with names, at times, the only text for an individual (357). What readers and characters alike discover in *Our Mutual Friend* is that there are "No Thoroughfares of speech" (303) and that we are all ventriloquists who can only mimic meaning. Or as Betty Higden says of the literate young reader of newspapers, Sloppy, "he do the Police in different voices" (246). Characters are in constant fear of words (see Gaffer Hexam, 64) and made anxious by the inability of language to convey any meaning as Georgiana Podsnap displays in a conversation with Mrs. Lammle. It begins with "What I mean is" and concludes with "I say it very badly—I don't know whether you can understand what I mean" (186).

Joyce in the *Wake* treats language in a similar fashion, constantly altering names and identities. Dickens does the same. Not only are there the obvious shifts—John Harmon Jr. becomes Julius Handford and then John Rokesmith—but Jenny Wren is actually Fanny Cleaver. In the *Wake* name changes are constant as Shem and Shaun become Kevin and Jerry, Nick and Neck, Mutt and Jeff. The process of naming, of attempting to identify and to discern personalities attached to names, is a constant struggle; indeed, characters would prefer to borrow only names as Twemlow in *Our Mutual Friend* makes clear when he asks if he could secure his cousin's name as an endorsement for Veneering's political campaign: "I don't go so far as to ask for his lordship; I only ask for his name" (296).

In advance of Joyce, Dickens explores the comic ambiguities of language in the midst of his narrative. This exchange between Mr. Alfred Lammle and the moneylender Fascination Fledgeby is but one example:

> "What did you think of Georgiana [Podsnap]?" asked Mr. Lammle.
> "Why, I'll tell you," said Fledgeby, very deliberately.
> "Do, my boy."
> "You misunderstand me," said Fledgeby. "I don't mean I'll tell you that. I mean I'll tell you something else."
> "Tell me anything, old fellow!"
> "Ah, but there you misunderstand me again," said Fledgeby. "I mean I'll tell you nothing."
>
> (321)

The confusion and indirect exchange suggests how words lose their meanings at various moments in the novel. It is not surprising, then, that so many characters cannot read, from young Charley Hexam to Gaffer Hexam, Boffin, and Rogue Riderhood. Nonetheless, they have a strange, oral sense of language. Visiting the lawyer Wrayburn, Rogue Riderhood mutters "Alfred David."

> "Is that your name?" asked Lightwood.
> "My name?" returned the man. "No; I want to take a Alfred David."
> (Which Eugene, smoking and contemplating him, interpreted as meaning Affidavit.)
> "I tell you, my good fellow," said Lightwood, with his indolent laugh, "that I have nothing to do with swearing."
> "He can swear *at* you," Eugene explained; "and so can I. But we can't do more for you."
>
> (195–96)

Such exchanges indicate the verbal play and evasiveness of language that would have appealed to Joyce as a model for what he created in the *Wake*.

What the above exchange also reveals is the way both texts structure themselves as riddles. For Joyce this is not news. The *Wake* is a riddling book, all of chapter 6, for example, taken up with twelve riddles. The work, furthermore, contains "the first riddle of the universe: asking, when is a man not a man?" (170.4–5). The question, repeated in various guises throughout the novel, is not answered until late in the text. The so-called prankquean riddle appears at 21.18: "Mark the Wans, why do I am alook alike a poss of porterpease?" From this query, the "skirtmisshes" begin in the entire book (21.18–19). This core riddle of Shem—"when is a man not a man?"—finds an echo in his second: "Was liffe worth leaving?" (230.25), which is also repeated throughout the work. That riddles underscore the *Wake*'s most crucial themes such as the concept of individual duality, the theme of brothers and sex has long been understood.[3] The role of riddles in *Our Mutual Friend* has not.

Riddles in Dickens join puns, word games, acrostics, and enigmas in his writing. The emergence of serial publication contributed to their prominence. *Punch*, *Bentley's Miscellany*, and Dickens's *All the Year Round* featured them. Contributors posed riddles to be solved by the next issue, the answer to one serial riddle frequently becoming the source and text for the next. Dickens even included riddles in his letters. As one critic has noted, Dickens begins *Our Mutual Friend* with a riddle, a tipped-in slip that overlapped the opening paragraph of the serial and first edition version, telling the reader he or she will understand the title "on arriving at the Ninth

Chapter."[4] The reader then must lift the slip to begin the first chapter proper of the novel which itself contains a series of riddles: who are the figures in the boat, what are they doing, how old is the girl? The reader becomes the riddlee. To understand the book, the reader must answer a set of riddles dealing with identity, language, and action. For Dickens as well as Joyce, riddles interrogate language.

More exactly, characters in the novel become riddles or conundrums. Rokesmith is Harmon, while Wrayburn is, in his own words, "an embodied conundrum" who bored himself "to the last degree by trying to find out what I meant." He gives up, unable to answer the riddle of himself until he is "found drowned"; only then does he confront his identity (339, 807–8). Other characters seem only to speak in riddles, such as Wegg whose fondness for riddles characterizes his reading and ballad offerings. But the novel also contains "articulators" who solve riddles, such as Mr. Venus or Jenny Wren who makes dolls out of scraps, giving meaning to waste. In Dickens's text, riddles manufacture meaning, despite their constant exposure that things, particularly words, are unstable. As the grand riddler, Dickens chops up or inverts the continuity of his narrative, description, and plot (in France, a Riddler is one who twists inverted champagne bottles to reduce their sediment and increase their fizz as they age).

Like Joyce, Dickens drives his readers to despair in their search for order in a heap of fragments. Slips of paper, however, form a key and throughout the novel such slips establish not only the plot but its resolution, as slips from the manuscript letter dug up by Biddy Doran from the midden heap (and falsely claimed by Shaun) form order in Joyce. Late in Dickens's novel, as Wegg is "beset by polysyllables" and a "perfect archipelago of hard words" (639) while reading, Mr. Venus passes a scrap of paper into Boffin's hand and he suddenly learns of Wegg's designs on his fortune. Earlier, when John Harmon raises a cup to his lips offered by George Radfoot and Rogue Riderhood, a "small folded paper" appears in the bottom of the cup which contains a drug which causes him to collapse (425) and then nearly drown. Slips of paper, which are themselves riddles, shape the narratives of both novels.

Two other linguistic features of importance for Dickens are the fragmented rendition of words and his use of initials. A sign of the first are the fragmented titles of the four books that make up his novel: they are all broken off or incomplete maxims. The fractured proverbs, beginning with "The Cup and the Lip," part of "There is many a slip 'twixt the cup and the lip," signal the transformation of language into fragments, repeated in visual and verbal signs throughout the text where words are broken down into their sylla-bles and then reproduced on the page. "Neg-lected!" is Boffin's ex-planation for his lack of education (96). At the Veneerings for the wedding celebration of the Lammles, the "Buffers are . . . over-heard to whisper Thir-ty Thou-sand Pou-nds!" (166) concerning a rumored dowry. Later, Bella Wilfer tells her father she has had an offer of marriage from "Mis-ter Roke-smith," separating the sylla-bles for emphasis (519), while Boffin reacts to Wegg's narrating the life of Robert Baldwin and his wills by concluding "see what men put away and forget, or mean to destroy, and don't! He then added in a slow tone, 'As-ton-ish-ing!'" (547). In the next chapter, Wegg prepares Venus for news of finding a will by Harmon in a pump among the mounds by exclaiming "I wanted to give you a delight-ful sap-pur-IZE!" (554). And finally, when Bella angrily denounces Boffin for his mistreatment of Rokesmith, he reacts with "HUL-LO!! . . . in an amazed under-tone" (661). Typography acts to em-body the division of language which projects the divisions within individuals between the outer and inner selves, and between the ex-pression and meaning of words (see further 503, 565, 577).

Our Mutual Friend demonstrates the breakdown of language and its inability to convey meaning through another form: misspellings. Often associated with the uneducated and illiterate, they neverthe-less become important semiotic signs of the weaknesses of lan-guage Dickens sensed and Joyce elaborated. Whether it is Wegg commenting on the "atomspear" (721) or Dickens imitating the jerky speech of one trying to talk in a rattling carriage— "Doyouknow-Mist-Erboff-in?" (98)—Joyce could see here the possibilities of linguistic wordplay that would control the *Wake*. Metathesis, the intentional misspelling of words to pack more meaning into their sounds, occurs constantly in Joyce and periodi-cally in Dickens. "Shovelling and sifting at alphabeds" is *not* Joyce's, but Dickens's phrase, yet it is a practice essential to both writers (94).

Another linguistic feature, possibly borrowed by Joyce from Dickens, is the use of initials. The examples of HCE and ALP are the most obvious, shorthanded references to his major characters. Throughout *Our Mutual Friend*, Dickens relies on various initials as metonymic devices. The most consistent is "M.R.F." First used in book 1, chapter 12 by Eugene Wrayburn to identify his "most respected father," it stands as an ironic epithet throughout the novel (193). "Let me shorten the dutiful tautology by substituting in fu-ture M.R.F.," Eugene tells Mortimer who comically respects the shift. Later, reintroducing the term (765), Dickens develops its

value and borrows the technique for Mrs. Veneering, calling her
"W.M.P.," "wife of Member of Parliament" (683). Such coding of
names may have prompted Joyce to extend the process to his title;
often in letters and other sources he referred to his text only as
"W.I.P."

A further Dickensian feature of language is the use of visual
texts. By this I mean the presence at three distinct moments in the
novel of visual signs that disrupt the prose (88, 335, 497). The first
reproduces the placard hanging on Wegg's signboard at his stall and
states his willingness, for a fee, to act for others. It reads

> *Errands gone*
> *On with fi*
> *Delity By*
> *Ladies and Gentlemen*
> *I remain*
> *Your humble Servt:*
> *Silas Wegg*
>
> (bk. 1, chap. 5, 88)

The vertical presentation of the words as they appear on Wegg's
sign creates a comic juxtaposition visually displaying the fragmentation of language orally present in the book. The passage anticipates moments of textual fragmentation duplicated in the *Wake* as
in the margins of the Study Hours section (275.25–27). One marginal notation reads

> FROM CENO-
> GENETIC DI-
> CHOTOMY
> THROUGH
> DIAGONISTIC
> CONCILI-
> ANCE TO
> DYNASTIC
> CONTINU-
> ITY.
>
> (275.3–12)

Visual form determines syntactic expression and semantic understanding.

The second visual text of *Our Mutual Friend* occurs in book 2,
chapter 6 (335) as we read the sign on the door of the new chambers
inhabited by Wrayburn and Lightwood. The reproduced hand in the

parenthetical line spatializes the text and shows the reader the ways language can perform within a prose narrative. Joyce parodies this image at page 308 on the bottom left margin. Additional visual disruptions in the text of the *Wake* include ellipses, songs, musical scores, and diagrams (94, 272 L, 293).

The well-noted sigla of the *Wake* (re the "Doodles family" at 299 n. 4) are further visual statements in the text which literalize the phrase "scriptsigns" (118.28), establishing visual puns and semiotic clues to the work. An additional visual sign in *Our Mutual Friend* is the business card of Jenny Wren. Not only does it announce a surprising occupation but it emphasizes the unique behavior of a singular character. Even when there is no visual sign apparent to correlate a verbal statement, visual elements interpret the event; traveling in a boat piloted by Rogue Riderhood, Eugene tells Mortimer that "the staring black and white letters upon wharves and warehouses looked . . . like inscriptions over the graves of dead businesses" (219). The importance of these elements is to show that Dickens's work contains the seeds of the visual signs and sigla Joyce was to include.

Perhaps no element linguistically links the two texts more directly than the fragmentation of the body in Dickens's novel, a projection of the fragmentation of language, history, and the city. As characters in the book speak elliptically, without connectives or prepositions, vigorously short-circuiting syntax and meaning (see Lightwood's speech, 135), so, too, are physical descriptions and bodies truncated or segregated. Joyce performs a similar task in his dream text. In the dark, only parts, not the whole, can be seen or felt. Hence, *Our Mutual Friend* begins by emphasizing the upper half of a human form (44) dragged from the Thames and continues to concentrate on patchwork figures such as that found in Mr. Venus's taxidermy shop. There, among many fragmented forms, he has "a Beauty . . . one leg Belgian, one leg English" and "the pickings of eight other people in it" (124). Throughout the novel, Dickens treats the individual body in its individual parts: hands (223, 456), arms (180, 269–70, 759), legs (re Wegg and his wooden leg), eyes (790), heads, hearts (135), noses (327), and ears (134) become the means of expressing the fragmentation not only of words but of human reality. This Joyce develops into descriptive passages on his own characters, often itemizing private parts or individual portions of the human body such as the Russian General's rump, or ALP's hair.

Joycean anatomy finds its model in Dickens which this description of Rogue Riderhood drinking highlights:

It [the wine] was given him. Making a stiff arm to the elbow, he poured
the wine into his mouth, tilted it into his right cheek, as saying, "What
do you think of it?" tilted it into his left cheek, as saying "What do *you*
think of it?" jerked it into his stomach, as saying "What do *you* think
of it?" To conclude, smacked his lips, as if all three replied, "We think
well of it." (bk. 1, chap. 12, 196)

Like Mr. Venus, Dickens and Joyce have "the patience [and skill]
to fit together on wires the whole framework of society" (540).
Dickens and Joyce are the "articulators of human bones" (128) and
as Joyce inscribed his text on parts of the body, so too did Dickens,
who provided him with a vibrant and dramatic anatomical model.

On many levels *Our Mutual Friend* is a sourcebook for the *Wake*.
From its exploration of language to its nightworld, the novel provides a fictional paradigm of Joycean wordplays and scenes. It contains a "perfect archipelago of hard words" that possesses a reality
as startling and disturbing to its characters as to its readers (639). It
teaches that "all Print is open" (93) and can enclose contradictory
elements but it also shows that "No Thoroughfares of speech"
(303) disorient and bewilder characters and readers alike. The presentation of reading as a subject in Dickens prepares for its exploitation in the *Wake* and his awareness of its limitations makes his
text a primer for the treatment of the experience of reading in Joyce.
In the "nightmaze" of the two texts, where "black looking white
and white guarding black" (66.19–20) occurs, language is a "constant fluxion" (297.28). It may only be fancy, but the "Night-
Inspector with a pen and ink . . . posting up his books" observed
by Wrayburn and Lightwood early in *Our Mutual Friend* may be a
prophetic glimpse at Joyce (48).

What *Our Mutual Friend* exhibits is an awareness of two critical
issues for Joyce: the procedure of composing a text and the problem
of understanding it. Mr. Venus in *Our Mutual Friend* comments on
this issue when he remarks that "putting the same meaning into
other words" (642) is his goal in order to achieve understanding.
This describes much of what occurs linguistically and self-con-
sciously in both texts. And when Wegg expatiates the qualifications
of Mr. Venus, he not only celebrates his "skill in piecing little
things together" but the "likelihood" of "small indications leading
him on to the discovery of great concealments" (357). This identifies not only the activity of the reader of both novels but the very
process of Joyce who, in his refashioning of language, creates
something new, often through concealment. Lady Tippins in *Our*

Mutual Friend pinpoints the method when she refers to "the spontaneous thingummies of the incorruptible whatdoyoucallums" (301). And as Mr. Venus precedes Shem, Lightwood predates Shaun, and Lizzie Hexam prefigures Issy, Dickens anticipates Joyce with *Our Mutual Friend* rightly standing as his model Victorian text.

NOTES

1. Of interest on Dickens as an intertext for Joyce, however, is Jay Clayton, "Londublin: Dickens' London in Joyce's Dublin," *Novel* 28 (1995): 327–42. Clayton also points out that the model of the one-legged sailor of "Wandering Rocks" is Silas Wegg of *Our Mutual Friend* (10.238).

2. In canto 14, Pound draws on similar images, reflecting his encounter with Dickens's world and anticipating, perhaps, Joyce's concerns when he writes that the loudest noise in hell seems to be "howling, as of a hen-yard in a printing-house, / the clatter of presses, / the blowing of dry dust and stray paper." Ezra Pound, *The Cantos*, 13th printing (New York: New Directions, 1995), 61–62.

3. On the question of riddles in the *Wake* see the following: Bernard Benstock, *Joyce-Again's Wake* (Seattle: University of Washington Press, 1965), 205–8 and passim; Patrick McCarthy, *The Riddles of Finnegans Wake* (Rutherford, N.J.: Farleigh Dickinson University Press, 1980), and John Bishop, *Joyce's Book of the Dark: Finnegans Wake* (Madison: University of Wisconsin Press, 1986), 310–14.

4. On *Our Mutual Friend* as a riddle, see Gregg A. Hecimovich, "The Cup and the Lip and the Riddle of *Our Mutual Friend*," *ELH* 62 (1995) 955. The entire article is a detailed account of the novel as a riddle.

REFERENCES

Beckett, Samuel. "Dante . . . Bruno. Vico . . . Joyce." In *Our Exagmination*, 3–22. 1929. Reprint, New York: New Directions, 1972.

Budgen, Frank. *James Joyce and the Making of Ulysses*. 1933. Reprint, Bloomington: Indiana University Press, 1967.

Dickens, Charles. *Charles Dickens' Book of Memoranda*. Edited by Fred Kaplan. New York: New York Public Library, 1981.

———. *Our Mutual Friend*. Edited by Stephen Gill. Harmondsworth: Penguin, 1987.

Giedion-Welcker, Carola. "Meetings with Joyce." In *Portraits of the Artist in Exile*, edited by W. Potts, 256–80. Dublin: Wolfhound Press, 1979.

Herring, Phillip, ed. *Joyce's Ulysses Notesheets in the British Museum*. Charlottesville: University Press of Virginia, 1972.

Joyce, James. *Finnegans Wake*. 1939. Reprint, New York: Viking, 1966.

———. "*Finnegans Wake*: Holograph Workbooks." In *James Joyce's Manuscripts and Letters at the University of Buffalo*, compiled by Peter Spielberg, 129–30. Buffalo, N.Y.: University of Buffalo, 1962.

———. *Ulysses*. Edited by Hans Walter Gabler et al. 1922. Reprint, New York: Random House, 1986.

Joyce, Stanislaus. *My Brother's Keeper*. Edited by Richard Ellmann. London: Faber, 1958.

New George Eliot and George Henry Lewes Letters

WILLIAM BAKER

THE ANNUAL CHRISTMAS "ENGLISH LITERATURE AND HISTORY" SALE on Tuesday, 19 December 2000, at Sotheby's, 34–35 New Bond Street, London, contained thirty lots "from the papers of the Senior family." Members of this well-connected family included the influential social reformer and political economist Nassau William Senior (1790–1864). In 1825 he became the initial holder of the Drummond Chair of Political Economy at the University of Oxford. He advised various governments and was influential in drawing up the legislation, which became the foundation for the 1834 Poor Law. His son Nassau John Senior (1822–91) was unsuccessfully proposed in 1871 by George Eliot and others to be the chief secretary of the Education Board. In 1848 he married Jane, the sister of Thomas Hughes (1822–96), the novelist, Christian socialist, and author of among other works, *Tom Brown's Schooldays* (1857). Jane ("Jeanie") Elizabeth (1828–77), like her brother, was deeply committed to philanthropy. A social worker and workhouse visitor, in 1874 she was appointed the first woman Poor Law Inspector. Her son was Walter Nassau Senior (1850–1933).

Lot 48 of the Senior family papers sold at the Sotheby's sale, consisted, to use the words of Sotheby's Sale Catalogue, of a "Fine series of twenty-six autograph letters signed ('M E Lewes'), nearly all to Jane Senior ('Dear Friend'), one to her son Walter, together with two autograph letters signed by G. H. Lewes" (40). Four of the George Eliot letters are included in Gordon S. Haight's edition of *The George Eliot Letters* (9 vols. New Haven and London: Yale University Press, 1955–1978: hereafter referred to as *Letters,* followed by volume and page number). The texts of these four letters published in Haight's edition are based on copies rather than the original holograph manuscript (see *Letters,* 4:365; 5:82–83, 285–86, 372–73). The remaining twenty-two letters, and the two letters written by George Henry Lewes, are unpublished until now.

Controversy surrounded the auction of the letters. Estimated by Sotheby's to fetch a hammer price between £15,000 and £20,000, they were purchased in the rooms at the lower end of the estimate. Quaritch, the well-known old-established London book dealers, paid nearly £18,000 (auctioneers' commission included) on behalf of an unknown purchaser. In fact, Quaritch was acting for the Beinecke Library at Yale University, which has the most extensive archival collection of George Eliot and George Henry Lewes letters and notebooks known to exist. John Ezard reported in the *Manchester Guardian* 27 March 2001, that the Arts Minister in the Labour Government, Alan Howarth, placed a temporary bar on the letters leaving the United Kingdom. A British buyer had until 26 July 2001, to match the sum paid on behalf of the Beinecke Library. Otherwise the letters, which according to Ezard's report, Howarth believed "expressed views central to [George Eliot's] work and were of extensive literary significance," would leave the country. Howarth's Department said that the letters' "rich pattern of language, theme and tone reveals the development of a significant relationship over a sustained period of time."

The British Library managed to raise the necessary sum of money in time. The letters are now in the Manuscript Department of the British Library where they are Add. Mss. 75298. Jonathan G. Ouvry, the great-great-grandson of G. H. Lewes, and holder of the copyright on all unpublished George Eliot and George Henry Lewes materials, has generously allowed publication of these hitherto unpublished letters. Dr. Sally Brown, the curator responsible for them, and the staff at the British Library, has been most helpful in granting access to restricted materials and supplying photocopies of them. Thanks are also due to Professor Donald Hawes, who took the time and trouble from his well-deserved retirement, to thoroughly check and recheck my transcriptions of the letters. Sybil Oldfield who is writing a biography of Jane Senior has also supplied me with valuable information.

Reproduced here are the twenty-two unpublished George Eliot letters and two unpublished George Henry Lewes letters. The copies of the four letters appearing in Gordon S. Haight's edition are also reproduced. Their texts are based on fresh readings of the originals revealing differences in substantives and literals between the Haight text, based on copies of the letters rather than on the originals, and my transcription from the original letters. The letters are presented in the order in which they were written. The two George Henry Lewes letters are undated. They follow the sequence of the George Eliot letters and are arranged in the order in which the editor believes they were written. All the texts given here are transcribed directly from the signed holograph originals. They have been transcribed literally for the sake of fidelity to the originals and in the interest of retaining their flavor as special historical and cultural documents. Some minor regularization has been made. I indicate below exactly which editorial procedures have been followed.

1. Ampersands, contractions, abbreviation, and spelling (for instance, cant for can't), are retained. Uncertain readings, textured cruxes, and canceled material that is still legible and all other editorial insertions appear in square brackets. Word spacing and line division are not reproduced, and to conserve space, line divisions in addresses, headings, and complimentary closes are indicated by a vertical rule (|).

2. Paragraphs are sometimes not clearly indicated in the letters, but a change of subject is indicated by a somewhat larger space than usual between sentences or by a fresh line, not indented. In both of these cases, a new paragraph is started in the transcription.

3. Eliot and Lewes's signatures are reproduced in their various forms. It has not been practical, however, to reproduce their inconsistent underlining of their names. They extensively underlined words or parts of words, including their names, sometimes using a single line or double or treble underlining. All of these underlinings, including their practice of underlining only certain letters for emphasis, are represented by italics.

4. Eliot and Lewes often use both single and double quotation marks inconsistently within the same letter. Here, double quotation marks are used throughout, and punctuation at the conclusion of quotations follows current conventions.

5. Return addresses at the top of each letter are taken from the letter itself. Complimentary closes are brought to the left margin; names of recipients, when written in, appear after the signatures. Printed or embossed headed stationery is represented by bold type.

6. Less familiar foreign phrases are translated, in square brackets, within the texts of letters.

7. In order to avoid lengthy extensive footnote documentation, explanatory notes introduce each letter. The explanatory notes briefly identify references, whether these be personal, historical, or contextual. I have tried to identify every person or title mentioned, usually at the first occurrence. George Henry Lewes's (GHL) unpublished Diary now at the Beinecke Library, Yale University and *The Journals of George Eliot* (GE), edited by Margaret Harris and Judith Johnston (Cambridge: Cambridge University Press, 1998—referred to as Harris followed by the page number), and *The Letters*

of George Henry Lewes (2 vols.) with *The Letters of George Henry Lewes Volume III with New George Eliot Letters*, edited by William Baker (Victoria, B.C.: University of Victoria, English Literary Studies, 1995, 1999—referred to as Baker, followed by the volume and page number), have been frequently cited in order to provide the relevant context for the letter.

8. Information concerning postmarks and watermarks have been excluded.

9. For the sake of convenience, the letters are numerically numbered in chronological order.

❧

1. GHL's Journal for 11 May 1867 doesn't record the names of either Jane Senior or her husband at the evening party held at The Priory.

The Priory, | 21, North Bank, | Regents Park. | April 30.67

My dear Mrs Senior

Mr Lewes & I both regret that our absence from home yesterday deprived us of the pleasure we should have had in seeing you and making the acquaintance of Mr Senior.

We have devised a plan as a dédommagement [compensation] to ourselves, but I fear it is a rather unreasonable one. It is to ask no less than that you & Mr Senior would come to us on the evening of Saturday the 11ᵗʰ., when we shall see a few other friends whom we hope it will be agreeable to you to meet. It seems a larger expectation that you should come so far in the evening, but if you will kindly take that trouble you will give us much pleasure.

Mr. Lewes unites with me in kind regards.

Always, dear Mʳˢ Senior| Yours sincerely| ME Lewes

❧

2. Published with substantive and literal variants in *Letters*, 4:365. Dated by Haight [22 May 1867]. GHL notes in his Journal, 21 May 1867: "Polly & I took a cab to the Br[itish] Museum where Deutsch [Emanuel Deutsch, 1829–73, orientalist and scholar] showed us the Blacas jewels and other memorable additions recently made—especially the grand Asclepius." Haight, in a note to his text of the letter, also cites Oscar Browning referring in his *Life of George Eliot* (London: Warwick Scott, 1890) to a "cast of the

Melian Asclepius—a present, I think from Mr. Deutsch," standing in front of her writing table (90: *Letters*, 4:365, n. 3)

The Priory, | 21, North Bank, | Regents Park. | Wednesday [May 67]

*My dear M*rs *Senior*
You are a good angel for taking trouble to help me in millinery, wh. is a crux to me.
The angels fold their great wings to enter through very small door-places & help the old women & little children. And sometimes they spare a little attention for me.
I am very full of wings—I mean my mind is full of them for we went to the Brit. Museum yesterday & saw all sorts of winged creatures that were seen perhaps by Ezekiel.
I shall expect you on Monday and be in at 4.

Always yours truly | M.E. Lewes

❧

3. GE wrote to her friend Mrs. Charles Bray, 13 June 1869: "We returned from Italy six weeks ago, [5 May] but since then our time and feelings have been absorbed by our poor Thornie, who arrived three days afterwards" (*Letters*, 5:44). "Thornie," GHL's son Thornton Arnott Lewes (1844–69), suffered greatly on his return from Natal. GHL noted in his Diary, Tuesday, 22 June 1869: "Thornie restless in pain last night. Languid all day. Passed a quantity of mucous & bile. Empson [the doctor] came to see him. Also Charles & Gertrude [Thornie's brother and his wife] spent the evening with him. 'Problems' [GHL's book]. Walk with Polly [i.e., 'GE'] in Park: Amelia [housemaid] going to-day; still very feeble."

The Priory, | 21, North Bank, | Regents Park. | June 22.69

*My dear M*rs *Senior*
*Since we saw your bright face troubles have accumulated on us. Our boy has had more frequent attacks of pain. M*r *Lewes & I have been ailing, & now our precious faithful housemaid is ill.*
Remembering your kind promise to come again, I am uneasy that you should manage to spend some of your valuable time in vain for our sakes. Thornie has not listened to any music for the last weeks & we feel so worn in body & spirit that we cannot enjoy even

the sight of a friend. Doubtless better moments will come. Even warmer weather would make a great difference to me. And I will let you know when we can delight as usual in any visit that you can spare us.

With best regards to Mr Senior,

Always yours sincerely | M.E. Lewes

❧

4. GHL noted in his Diary, Wednesday, 7 July 1869: "Walk in Park & sat all the afternoon with Thornie who was fidgety & hysterical. . . . Paget came. Reported no change." James Paget (1814–99), GHL's close friend, doctor, and surgeon. Knighted in 1877, he became sergeant-surgeon to Queen Victoria. He attended Thornie throughout his fatal illness.

The Priory, | 21, North Bank, | Regents Park. | July 7.69

Dear Friend
Yes! we are in better spirits. The boy suffers less & Paget is hopeful. It is good to know that your tender heart is beating in the world. I hope you are going to some pretty place for rest & health.

Always yours affectionately | ME Lewes

Mr Lewes is better than he was. Iam so so

❧

5. There is no record in GHL's Diary for July 1869 of a visit from Mrs. Senior. The date "July 69" is written in an unidentified hand on the letter.

The Priory, | 21, North Bank, | Regents Park. | Wednesday | [July 69]

My dear Friend
Grateful thanks! Things are a little better with our poor lad just now, but we rejoice in any improvement with inward trembling lest it should only be the introduction to a new relapse, as it has always been hitherto. Come on Saturday, pray, & to luncheon at 1/2 past 1 if you can. Of course if 3 is the time that suits you best, I have no reason for disturbing your arrangement.

We have no engagement from home, except for our daily walk.
We shall be cheered by the sight of you

Ever yours affectionately | ME Lewes

❧

6. GE wrote to Mrs. Senior on 4 October 1869. The text, based
on the original, then in the possession of "Mrs. Sherburne Prescott"
is found in *Letters*, 5:57–58. Thornie died 19 October 1869. The
date "Oct 69" is written in an unidentified hand on the letter. GE
notes in her Diary, 19 August 1869: "Since I wrote last I have been
constantly ailing. Poor Thornie has nearly recovered the use of his
limbs but looks more wasted. Yesterday, Charlotte left us on account of ill health, and a new nurse took her place" (Harris, 137).
GE doesn't note whether the replacement proved satisfactory or not
(see *Letter* 7). GHL noted in his Diary 17 August 1869: "engaged
Beale, as nurse [who] came" the next day. On 25 August 1869
GHL wrote in his Diary "Mrs Senior sent papers & flowers to
Thornie."

The Priory, | 21, North Bank, | Regents Park. | Monday 69 | [Oct 69]

My dear Friend
I am unspeakably grateful to you for your thought & effort on
our behalf. At present I am expecting to see a woman who is com-
ing from Bath. She promises to be all we could wish, having lived
for 24 years in the family of the friend who recommends her to
me, & having lately nursed her mistress through her last illness. As
soon as I know whether she will come to us, or not, I will write to
you.
*M*ʳ *Lewes has one serious objection to poor Keefe, namely her*
inability to read & write. He thinks this could hardly be overcome,
because of the morphia, &c which she will have to administer.
What you say about her lot engages my interest in her strongly.
I like to think of your going to Oxford & seeing your son settled
in these delicious October days.
Pity my poor husband, who is this morning lingering in bed with
the fourth day's headache!
Pray excuse my sending a mere message last night. I could not
manage to write.

Ever yours affectionately | ME Lewes

❧

7. GHL wrote in his Diary, Tuesday, 19 October 1869, that Thornie "Died at 7 this evening." GE, in her Diary, put the time "at half past six o'clock" (Harris, 139).

The Priory, | **21, North Bank,** | **Regents Park.** | Tuesday Oct. 19 | [69]

Dear Friend
 I have been a dumb & apparently insensible creature towards you. For the last week I have been crushed by headaches—both Mr Lewes's & my own—all the while our boy has been getting worse. We have been losing all hope that he can revive. He seems now to be sinking fast both in strength & consciousness, & life at present seems only suffering. The one comfort is that the suffering is not acute, but is a vague varying uneasiness.
 Bless you for all the tender feeling you have shown both for him & for us.

Ever your grateful & affectionate | *ME Lewes*

Our old nurse is still with us. The new one is engaged to come to-day week. But we are thankful that no change has been forced on us just now.

❧

8. GE and GHL left for Park Farm Limpsfield Surrey on 23 October 1869. They returned home to the Priory on Saturday, 13 November 1869 from Park Farm "where the profound peace enabled us to transmute our sorrow into a calmness which leaves only a beautiful image of the dear boy" (GHL, Diary).

The Priory, | **21, North Bank,** | **Regents Park.** | Oct. 20.69

My dear Friend
 Our boy is dead. He died last night, quite peacefully. The bitterness is past for him, but not for me.
 We shall go away into solitude on Saturday.

Ever yours affectionately | *ME Lewes*

*

9. Written on black-edged mourning paper.

21 North Bank | Dec. 4.69

My dear Friend
It would be unreasonable to think of seeing the best of creatures
from such far-off countries [sic] as yours while these dark days
last. But we like you to know that we are at home now, & that when-
ever circumstances will let you find your way to us, you will be
warmly welcomed.

Always yours affectionately | ME Lewes

*

10. Written on black-edged mourning paper. GE wrote to her
friend Emily Davies (1830–1921), the women's educational advocate, 7 December 1869: "My friend Mrs. Nassau Senior . . . is anxious to learn about the College" at Hitchin Hertforshire, which
became Girton College Cambridge. GE told Emily Davies "I have
a high esteem for Mrs Senior. She is a woman who tries to put her
beliefs into action, and after having been prejudiced by others
against the College, she is anxious to found her judgment on fuller
knowledge" (*Letters*, 8:469).

21 North Bank | Dec. 10.69

My dear Friend
Supposing that you can maintain any desire or belief in the midst
of this fog, or that the fog may be rather less Cimmerian at Laven-
der Hill, you will be wondering that I have not answered your re-
quest about the College at Hitchin.
I wrote to Miss Davies on the subject, conjecturing that at Christ-
mas the students would be dispersed to their various homes, & en-
quiring whether any lady, would still be there to receive you & give
you information. Last night I had a note from Miss Davies in which
she says, "My friend Mrs. Austin will be here during the Xmas va-
cation, & will be very glad to receive Mrs *Senior & to show her as*
much of the College as will be left when the spirit is absent."
So, at whatever time you may go, you may be certain that the
superintending ladies there will be prepared to receive you.

Always yours affectionately | ME Lewes

&

11. Written on black-edged mourning paper. No Jane Senior visit is noted in GHL's Diary for Tuesday, 8 February 1870. The exact nature of Jane Senior's "anxieties" are unclear.

21 North Bank | Feb. 4.70

Dear Friend
    We shall rejoice to see you on Tuesday, but when you do not fulfil an expressed intention, be sure that I shall never impute it to slackness of conscience.
    I could not help crying over your letter, & the consciousness that we can do nothing to relieve you of your anxieties.

Always yours affectionately | ME Lewes

&

12. Published with substantive and literal variants in *Letters*, 5:82–83. Written on black-edged mourning paper. Jane Senior is among those names included by GHL in his Diary, Saturday, 5 March 1870, whom he and GE presumedly met. He also notes "Went into town. Concert." On Tuesday, 15 March 1870 he and GE left for Brussels and then Cologne and Berlin. They returned home on 6 May 1870. The paragraph beginning "the snow" and concluding with "state of things" has a single vertical ink erasure line through it.

The Priory, | 21 North Bank | Regents Park | March 10.70

Dear Friend
    Bless you first of all for being a good woman, and next for being good to me.
    The sachet came to me quite safely, smelling like the garden of Eden in its most desirable spots where the violets grew.
    So you will be hovering about me like an invisible angel with violet scented wings. Very delicate scents make me feel happy, but I find it too troublesome to get them for myself. So such a present as this is really a greater addition to my pleasure than it could be to most people's.

Keep a little love for me till we come back, for I shall think of you as one of the friends who make an English home dear, and enter into my life quite out of proportion to the number of times that I see them. One lives by faith in human goodness—the only guarantee that there can be any other sort of goodness in the universe.

See how diffusive your one little life may be. I say that apropos of your longing for a wider existence.

The snow astonished us this morning, but Mr Lewes thinks that snow with a quiet wind is more favorable for our voyaging than the former state of things.

Pray offer our kind regards to Mr Senior, and think of me often as

Yours always affectionately | M E Lewes

13. GHL wrote in his Diary, Friday, 10 June 1870: "Tired & stayed in all the afternoon unable to do anything. News of the death of Charles Dickens." The following day GHL wrote "Went to see Dr Reynolds [1828–96: leading authority on nervous diseases] who counsels sea side & rest." On Wednesday, 15 June GHL and GE left for Cromer via Norwich. They returned home Monday, 1 August after having spent time at Whitby and the Yorkshire coast including Harrogate. No record of a Jane Senior visit on either Monday, 13 June or Tuesday, 14 June is found in GHL's Diary.

The Priory, | 21, North Bank, | Regents Park. | June 13.1870

My dear Friend

Alas, we are driven from home again! Dr Reynolds tells Mr Lewes that he must go to a more bracing air than this of the London oven. So on Wednesday or Thursday morning we are to set off for Cromer. Afterwards we shall probably go on to Whitby. I am tired of a migratory life, but I can really wish for nothing else than to do what will best favour the recovery of my dear husband's strength.

It is not that he is ill, but he finds himself quite exhausted after an hour or two of reading & writing. At 1/2 past 11 in the morning, he can work no longer, & in London there is no healthy kind of exercise & amusement to fill up the remaining hours. So unless you happen to come in today or tomorrow, we shall not see your sweet face giving us a parting benediction.

I would willingly have known more details about you before going away.
With best regards to Mr Senior, I am always dear Friend

Yours affectionately | ME Lewes

❧

14. The Franco-Prussian War rumbled on during the autumn of 1870. GHL suffered from intermittent severe headaches and lumbago. GE, on 28 September, GHL found "in bed, abcess in her gum! Strasburg surrended." GE was writing *Middlemarch*. GHL Diary for November doesn't record a visit by Jane Senior. GE wrote in her Journal, 27 October 1870, that since returning from a country visit she has "been continually suffering from headache and depression, with almost total despair of furture work" (*Letters*, 5:120). She wrote to her friend [Mrs. Ernst Leopold Benzon] 21 October [1870] "Pray come & see me! All human goodness & love have seemed more precious to me since this most hideous of wars began" (Baker, 3:60). The Franco-Prussian War began on 15 July, 1870.

The Priory, | 21, North Bank, | Regents Park. | Nov. 12.70

Dear Friend
I have been hindered from writing to you before by ailing health & spirits. But I have all the while been wanting to see you. Can you find time to get to our corner of the universe? Your sweet face would be a welcome bit of harmony with one's struggling hope & trust in these bad times.

Always | Yours affectionately | ME Lewes

❧

15. On 2 January 1871, GE wrote to Emily Davis, "If you have not made up your mind." As Haight notes, her lobbying was unsuccessful: "the appointment went to George Hector Croad" (*Letters*, 9:5). Mme. Du Quairo "lived at 14 Wilton St., Grosvenor Place." She attended a dinner at Lord Charlemont's, also attended by GE and GHL on 20 April 1877 (*Letters*, 6:363, and n. 5). The Congreves, Richard (1818–99) and Maria (d. 1915), positivists and close friends of GE since 1859. There is no evidence I have come across that they attended Lord Charlemont's dinner. GE's letter is written on black-edged mourning paper.

21 North Bank | Jan.2.71

Dear Friend

A more blessed New Year to the world in general & to you in particular!

That would be a glorious post for your husband—and we will not neglect our small possibilities. I write this scrap to say so, with my love inclosed. The envelope shall be dispatched to Mme du Quairo with the Congreve's address which, by the way, is 17 Mecklenburgh Square, W.C.

In haste | Ever your affectionate | M E Lewes

16. GE and GHL were at Shottermill, Hampshire, from 2 May until 1 September 1871 while alterations to their London home at the Priory, St. John's Wood, were made. Jane Senior is listed among the guests they met at a party on Saturday, 11 February 1871, and again on Wednesday 29 March 1871, 5 April 1871 (GHL Diary).

The Priory, | 21, North Bank, | Regents Park. | April 29.71

Dear Friend

Alas, we must go away without seeing you! We are to start early on Tuesday, to make the house vacant at once for builders & bath-fitters & painters. I wish we could have had a parting-meeting, to impress ourselves on your memory for the four or five months in which we shall have sunk below your horizon. But you have the art of making room in your thought & affection, & pray use the art on our behalf.

If it were possible that I could do anything for you in my exile, a letter with the usual address would be forwarded to me. I am just emerging from a cruel headache, & any easy use of my brain seems to belong to a pre-existent state which I remember hopelessly.

Ever yours with love | M E Lewes

17. On 1 December 1871 the first book of *Middlemarch* was published by *Blackwood's*. GE noted in her Diary 20 December 1871 "My health has become very troublesome during the last three weeks, and I can get on but tardily. Even now, I am only at p. 227 of my fourth Part. But I have been also retarded by construction which, once done, serves as good wheels to progress" (Harris, 142). GHL noted in his Diary, Thursday, 14 December 1871: "Polly read Wilke Collins's story *Miss or Mrs?* aloud." This novella, subtitled "A Christmas Story in Twelve Scenes," appeared in the Christmas number of *The Graphic*. It's theme is that "of a secret marriage to a minor and the danger of a charge of abduction" (A. Gasson, *Wilkie Collins: An Illustrated Guide*" [Oxford: Oxford University Press, 1998], 105).

The Priory, | 21, North Bank, | Regents Park. | Dec.14.71

Dear Friend
    I wish your letter had brought me better news of you. You had been missing from my life a long while, but I had faith that you would make me some sign when you could. I always bear in mind how many strings are pulling you.
    We came from the country at the beginning of September. I had not been well all the four months of our stay there, so it hardly seemed a sudden affair that about ten days after our return I was taken ill with severe gastric irritation which laid me rather low for two months.
    I am now much the same sort of bodily specimen as usual. George was brilliant until my illness made a bad time for him—he being nurse & comforter in general, as well as secretary & doer of all the anxiety. However, he is not worse than usual at present, though the foggy days are not friendly.
    Our two old servants have left us! Think of that. But we have three new ones who go on perfectly.
    You will let us know more of you by & by, I hope, & lay a little plan to come & see us conveniently? +

Always yours affectionately | M E Lewes

+ I mean for your convenience—when you are obliged to come to town & will make our house a place of rest.

18. GE writes in her Diary "1872. It is now the last day but one of January. I have finished the Fourth Part. i.e. the 2nd volume of Middlemarch. The First Part published on Dec 1. has been excellently well received, and the second Part will be published the day after tomorrow" (Harris, 142). On Tuesday, 20 February GHL's Diary notes: "Mrs Nassau Senior to lunch. She [sang] & accompanied us into town." On Wednesday, 20 March GHL notes "We met Mrs Senior by appointment & took her to Burne Jones to see his pictures."

The Priory, | 21, North Bank, | Regents Park. | Feb.21.72

Dear Friend
You left a wee wee pocket handkerchief behind yesterday, which I will keep for you until we meet again according to agreement.
One often hears one's own mistakes long after they have been uttered. When we were upstairs I told you that "Miss Brooke" was written at the end of "last year," forgetting that we are now (alas!) in the second month of 1872. Of course I meant the end of 1870.
I hate mis-statements so I am fidgeting until I have corrected this.

Always yours | M E Lewes

❧

19. Published with substantive and literal variants in *Letters*, 5:285–86. GE and GHL stayed in Redhill from 23 May until 28 August 1873. GE was writing *Middlemarch*. Jane Senior, before her marriage, was a Hughes. Her brother, Thomas Hughes (1822–96) wrote *Tom Brown's Schooldays* (1857). Another brother, George Edward Hughes (1821), died on 2 May 1872. In the holograph letter there is a horizontal ink line across the letter separating the second paragraph from the third and a single diagonal ink line "slashed" through the last final seven words of the fourth paragraph and all of the fifth paragraph. The closure following "We want to be absolutely solitary here" is separated from the rest of the letter by a horizontal ink line across the text. Gertrude Lewes gave birth to a daughter, Blanche Southwood Lewes on 18 July 1872. She died in 1964.

Elversley, | Park Road | RedHill | July 1.72.

My dear Friend,
You have very often been in my mind, because, you know, I count you among those who will always be dear to me, but of course I

have been in blank ignorance about all that has been happening to you since we had our few hours together.

You are paying part of the great price for the blessing of being able to love those near to you. It is of no use to offer words under such a trial. Comfort will gradually come in your activity for others, which never leaves you long in the power of your particular lot. Some day I shall ask you to tell me all about your family—I mean the family of Hughes—for I dont half know what I should like to know about it.

We are most comfortably settled in perfect peace, with two of our own servants to take care of us, & the loveliest wooded undulating country around us. Our house is not in the least elegant, but it is convenient enough, stands in a quiet spot quite away from carts & carriages, & has a large garden bounded by meadows.

I am marvellously renovated by the perfect rest from little outward excitements, & am really getting strong. We have taken our house to the end of August, & after that we shall probably go abroad for a month or so.

*M*ʳ *Lewes has just come in from an excursion to Weybridge & has been listening to your letter. He looks very bright, & I hope will now go on well, but hitherto, since we have been down here, he has been teazed with singing in the ears & languor. He sends his brotherly love, which I am sure you will not reject.*

I am thinking anxiously now of our dear Gertrude, who is going to have her baby this month. She has been going on beautifully, & I trust the poor thing will at last have her maternal heart soothed by a living child.

Pray dont tell anybody our address. We want to be absolutely solitary here.

*With best regards to M*ʳ *Senior,*

Always, dear friend | yours affectionately | M E Lewes.

❧

20. Published with substantive and literal variants in *Letters,* 5:372–73. Jane Senior "was appointed 18 January temporary inspector of workhouses and pauper schools—the first woman to hold such a position" (*Letters,* 5:372, n. 2). Gertrude's sister, Octavia Hill (1838–1912), social reformer "although . . . not a hard-liner on temperance . . . knew about the perils of drink." Gillian Darley, adds in her book *Octavia Hill* (London: Constable, 1990), that

"When, in the early 1870s, the public house next to the Sterling sisters' houses [for women] at Walmer Place, the Walmer Castle, had gone up for sale she had tried, and failed, to buy it. She then attempted to prevent it being re-licensed, attracting a great deal of opprobrium in the process. Her justification for doing so was the fact that there were thirty-two other public houses within a 300-yard radius" (208). Gertrude dined at the Priory, Saturday, 25 January 1873 (GHL, Diary).

The Priory, | 21, North Bank, | Regents Park. | Jan. 24.73

Dear Friend
We had already been told something, though inaccurately, of the good news, before your letter came; and we had felt it as a new year's gift to us. Our joy is without misgiving, we feel sure that your work will be done well. May all blessings attend you in it, over & above the affectionate wishes of your friends—wishes which you will carry with you like a host of encouraging guardian spirits.
The influence of one woman's life on the lot of other women is getting greater & greater with the quickening spread of all influences. One likes to think, though, that two thousand years ago Euripides made Iphigenia count it a reason for facing her sacrifice bravely that thereby she might help to save Greek women (from a wrong like Helen's) in the time to come.
There is no knife at your throat, happily. You have only got to be a good faithful woman such as you have always been, & then the very thought of you will help to mend things. Take it as a sign of that, when I tell you that you have entered into my more cheerful beliefs, & made them stronger because of the glimpses I have had of your character & life.
I don't wonder at your not being able to come just now, but you know that we are always glad when you can manage to get to us.
Mr Lewes is better than usual, but I have been tormented with inflamed throat & gums ever since Christmas, & this very morning I have been to have two teeth out!
We are much interested just now in Octavia's new work of buying a public-house to have it under good control. I daresay you know all about it.
Please offer our best regards to Mr Senior, & believe me, dear friend,

Yours with sincere affection | *M E Lewes*

❧

21. GE finished *Middlemarch* 2 October 1872 (*Letters*, 5:313). By 5 November 1873 she is "slowly simmering towards another big book" (*Daniel Deronda*; *Letters*, 5:454). From 5 September to October 1873, she and GHL stay at Blackbrook, near Bickley in Kent. Her letter is written on stationary headed with her London Priory address. She has crossed out this printed address, replacing it in hand with her Kent address. She and GHL from 24 June to 23 August were in France and Germany. She wrote to her friend François D'Albert-Durade, from Homburg on 9 August 1873: "my dear husband has of late been the victim of chills which have attacked his throat and left ear—the latter very severly so as to cause a temporary deafness" (*Letters*, 6:427). GHL went on Saturday, 23 August 1873 to James Hinton (1822–75) "the aurist, who has relieved at once both the inconvenience & the anxiety. The cause was simply an accumulation of hard wax" (Baker, 3:71; GE to Lucy Caroline Smith [23 August 1873]). GHL's Diary does not record a visit from Jane Senior to Blackbrook during their stay. The final sentence of the fifth paragraph and opening two sentences of the sixth up to the words "risen to" have a diagonal single line erasure through them.

Blackbrook | Bickley | Kent. | Sep. 23.73

Dear Friend
*I felt it long, long indeed since any word had passed between us, & in spite of my good reasons in trusting in your affectionate memory, I was diffident about writing to you without other excuse than my anxiety. M*ʳ *Lewes has urged me to write after hearing from M*ʳ *Hughes that your health had been suffering from the strain of work, but I was not sure that a letter seeming to ask for news would not be less friendly than silence. Hardly any one in our choice list of beloved "sisters" has been oftener spoken of between us than you, & I feel as if I had recovered something good this morning now that I have had a letter from you.*
O dear! I can only grown over your bodily affliction. It is no use to wish that it had befallen an idle woman, or, in general, to allow oneself wishes about what cannot be altered. I will rather dwell on the fact that you are getting better & are so good & dear as to want to come to see us in about a fortnight.
This place is about equally near the Chiselhurst & Bickley Stations, i.e. about 10 minutes or less by carriage from each. If you

could fix a time of arrival at either of these stations we would meet you & bring you here in triumph.

We are to remain here until the end of October, & shall then go up to town—though an unusually fine beginning of November might tempt us to linger here.

Our summer was spent partly in the Vosges, a lovely region, but we were driven thence & checked in our enjoyment by an ugly attack of deafness & pain in one ear which Mr Lewes had felt something of before we quitted London, & which grew so much worse after three weeks at Plombières that we were dreading a permanent privation. This dread sent us on to Frankfurt to consult a doctor, who, however, gave an illusory explanation of a hopeful kind which made us content to go on to Hamburg, a place which had simply the virtue of nearness by comparison with any other "Bad." The poor ear got no better, & as soon as we reached London George went to Hinton, who found out the secret & relieved him forthwith. The cause of the deafness & pain was an accumulation of hard wax.

Conceive our joy! Still, he is not quite flourishing, & is fallen from the good estate which for nearly two years he had risen to, above the long previous depression from dyspeptic headaches. But we will tell you all our gossip when you come to see us—that is, after you have told us all your interesting experiences in your work.

I hope Mr Senior & your "boy" are well. Commend us to them & believe me, dear Friend

Your faithfully affectionate | ME Lewes

22. As part of her functions as a Government Inspector, Jane Senior wrote a signed report "Education of Girls in Pauper Schools" published in *Parliamentary Reports: Education*, 25 (1874), 22: 311–94. GE refers to this in a letter to Jane Senior dated [May 1874], now at the Parrish Collection, Princeton (*Letters*, 6:46). GHL notes in his Diary, Monday, 24 November 1873, "Mrs Nassau Senior spent the evening with us." Richard Liebreich (1830–1917), the ophthalmic surgeon, visited GE and GHL at the Priory, on Sunday, 1 June 1873. Both, GE and GHL consulted him (*Letters*, 5:451, and n. 9).

The Priory, | 21, North Bank, | Regents Park. | Nov. 25.73

Dear Friend
We have both read your Report & think it excellent—such as to confirm our pride in you.

*Mr. Lewes has one suggestion to make—that you should see Lie-
breich & consult him as to the causes of Ophthalmia.*
We return the precious M. S. by registered post.
*You put us in spirits about you by your good looks last night. It
was very sweet of you to come.*

Always yours affectionate | ME Lewes

❧

23. GE writes to Jane Senior's son Walter. On Wednesday, 28
October 1874, GE and GHL went to Wiltshire "probably for details
in *Daniel Deronda*." They returned to the Priory on Saturday 31
October 1874 (*Letters*, 6:86, n. 3). GHL notes in his Diary, Saturday, 7 November 1874: "Drove to Mrs Nassau Senior's & to get
the character of a new servant—Kate."

The Priory, | 21, North Bank, | Regents Park | Oct. 28.74

Dear Mr Senior
*Thank you very much for writing to me. Your letter indeed gave
me pain; but since your dear Mother has been & is suffering, I
would rather have the pain of knowing that than remain in ignorance of what befals her.*
*I write this just before starting on a little expedition which will
keep us away from home till Saturday. So will you kindly say to M^{rs}
Senior that any arrangement about my seeing a possible servant
must not be made before the beginning of next week? But pray add
that she must not do anything about that affair of mine, if it requires
more than a verbal message.*
*I wonder whether it would be an undue disturbance to her if we
were one day to take our afternoon drive your way for the possibility of seeing her.*
*It would not signify so far as our drive was concerned if she sent
us away again without admitting us. I am very much interested in
what you tell me about your change of plan as to residence. I trust
that the repose insured by your Mother will make amends for what
must be the sadness of quitting a long-loved home.*

Yours sincerely | M E Lewes

❧

24. In her letter GE refers to a copy of the letter Jane Senior sent to the editor of the *Times* published under the heading "District Pauper Schools and Boarding Out," Wednesday, 27 January 1875, 7f., signed "Jane E. Senior" addressed from "Lavender Hill. S.W.", and dated "Jan. 26." The letter consists of a vigorous lengthy response to a detailed *Times* editorial published on 26 January 1875, 9d–f. The editorial commented on the attacks by Edward Carleton Tufnell, a former inspector of the London Poor Law Schools, on Jane Senior's report and its proposals for reform. On Thursday, 28 January, 11f., Tufnell replied. Francis Peek, Chairman of the National Society for Promoting the Boarding-out of Pauper Children, defended Jane Senior against Tufnell's attacks in a letter published also on 28 January, 11f–g. Jane Senior responded in a letter dated "Jan. 29," and published 30 January 1875, 7j.

Gladstone announced his intention to resign as Liberal Party leader, as reported in the *Times*, 22 January 1875, 9f. The newspaper on 26 January 1875, 9a–c, carried a lengthy editorial on the struggle for the party succession. The leading contender was John Bright, who then threw in his hand. The successor to Gladstone was Lord Hartington (1833–1908), who became leader of the Liberal party in February 1875.

In a letter to her friend Mme. Eugène Bodichon dated 16 July 1874, GE asks "do you know how our dear Mrs Senior is tormented by the officials about her capital Report?" (*Letters*, 6:70). Gertrude Hill (1837–1923), the wife of GHL's son, Charles Lee, was associated with her sister Octavia Hill in social problems. Charles Lee Lewes's "The Education of the Children of State," *Edinburgh Review*, 142 (July 1875), 89–110, defends Jane Senior's report against Tufnell's attacks (see *Letters*, 6:157, n. 2).

The Priory, | 21, North Bank, | Regents Park. | Jan. 26.75

My dear Friend

I must indulge myself by telling you that we have been delighting today in your admirable letter to the "Times", which is as strong & temperate as it could well be. After the vexation of seeing the "Times" article, which was of course written to order, your letter came as the most welcome news that the paper could bring us— much better than the choice of the Liberal Leader. I wish I could take it as a proof that you are stronger, but I have been discouraged by hearing through Kate's sister that you were, about a fortnight ago, as entirely laid up as ever.

Do not for one moment imagine that this note is meant for more

than a wafted kiss which is its own satisfaction & asks no notice.
Some day I shall meet with a friend who has authentic news of you
to give me.

From Madame Bodichon & from Gertrude I have had hints of the
work going on which your labours set on foot. That is something
cheerful to bear in mind when your dear pale face, as I saw it last,
comes back to me with vividness.

Mr Lewes asks you to remember him, & I dare say you have
plenty of time for memories in the long hours when you are obliged
to rest from more taxing thought.

Believe me, dear Friend, | Yours with deep sympathy | M E Lewes

❧

25. GE and GHL were at "The Elms," Rickmansworth, from 17
June until 23 September1875. GE worked on *Daniel Deronda*,
GHL on proofs of his revised *Life of Goethe*, his *Problems of Life
and Mind* and other projects. They settled on the house on Saturday, 29 May 1875—the day GE wrote to Jane Senior. In a later
letter to Jane Senior dated 12 July 1876 GE tells her friend that they
saw a house owned by "Mrs Barrington . . . but found that it had
not comforts enough for us old people" (*Letters*, 6:270).

Mrs. Senior wrote to GE 30 June 1876 that she "left Elm House
for a cheaper house, 4 Lindsey Houses, Old Chelsea" (*Letters*,
6:269, n. 7). She died 24 March 1877. GE grieved for "the loss of
a . . . valued friend—Mrs Nassau Senior, that fair, bright useful
woman" (*Letters*, 6:359).

GE wrote to her friend Mrs. Elma Stuart, 24 March 1875: "M^r
Lewes is both glad and sorry at once that he has to prepare anew
edition of his *Life of Goethe*." Haight notes "George Smith wrote
GHL 23 March 1875 that it was running out of print and proposed
a 3d edition of 200 copies. GHL revised the text 8–17 April, wrote
notes for it in May. The first proofs arrived 24 June and the last
were finished 11 October" (*Letters*, 6:133–34, n. 5).

GE and GHL met Tomasso Salvini at Mrs. Benzon's on 23 May
1876. GE describes him as "a genuinely great actor." She and GHL
saw his "Othello twice," 7 and 19 April, and his Hamlet, 31 May
and 14 June 1875 (*Letters*, 6:147; 9:175, n. 9 and Baker, 3:94, n.
6). GHL's "First Impressions of Salvini. 1875," which his Diary
records as "began an art. On Salvini," Saturday, 29 May 1875, was
appended to his *On Actors and the Art of Acting* reprinted by Smith
Elder and published 3 July 1875.

The Priory, | 21, North Bank, | Regents Park. | May.29.75

Dear Friend
   The news of your friend's very promising house came just a little too late. We have decided on a place at Rickmansworth, which will have the advantage of making us acquainted with a bit of the country less familiar than Surrey, where we have been for three successive summers. I am very glad that you had this little errand of service to Mrs. Barrington & to us, because in this way I have gained more definite news about you than I have been able to get for a long while. That you should be in the same room with a piano again is one good sign, & the prospect of your going to the Isle of Wight for a peaceful change is something still better. The nearness of the railway station is a cruel condition of your life just now. Even when there are not extra trains, the chronic screeches & gratings must be hard to bear. In some states the sudden opening of a door is enough to send a shock of misery through one's system.
   We are delighted to hear that you think well of Charlie's article. He told me after he had read it to you that your approbation would console him if the article were not accepted, & that modesty of hope made his success the sweeter.
   I am better. The Doctors decided that my pains meant nothing important & I have felt rather ashamed of myself for making a fuss about them. But I am in rather a spiritless condition, & long for the country, to which haven we shall not get till the 16th.
   I quite agree with you in your feeling about Goethe. His domestic history is piteous. A new edition of the Life is wanted—mean the longer work—& Mr Lewes has just finished preparing it. He is on the whole flourishing, but has an occasional long headache to keep up his sense of identity.
   I dare say you have had many friends talking to you about Salvini. Pray believe those who admire him—believe, that is, in their judgment. His Othello has given me a greater thrill than I ever had from acting, even from Rachel's. But I have no hope that he will produce an equal effect in Hamlet, which we shall see him in on Monday.
   I return Mrs. Barrington's letter, which may be useful in some other direction. Her brief hints of description are more attractive than any advertisement could be. They make me feel that the house belongs to nice people, & that their furniture would soothe one's soul. Instead of exasperating it, as that of hired houses is apt to do.
   For us, if we had not already fixed ourselves, the place would

apparently have had but one drawback—that of being a little too near town for our unsociable summer habits.

Much longing that you may have blessings unperturbed by bodily suffering, dear friend, is the feeling with which you are often thought of by

Your affectionate | M E Lewes

❧

26. Written on black-edged mourning paper to Jane Senior's son Walter.

The Priory, | 21, North Bank, | Regents Park. | Mar.4.79

Dear Mr Senior
I enclose a cheque as my subscription to the Assocⁿ for placing Orphans, established in memory of your beloved Mother.

Yours sincerely | M E Lewes | W. N. Senior Esq

❧

27. GHL noted in his Journal, 4 February 1864 "This is our new pet, a lovely bull terrier, a present from Williams [Samuel D. Williams, Jr.—see *Letters*, 4:17, n. 3] who is fast becoming the pet and tyrant of our household"—Ben (*Letters*, 4:150, n. 9). Ben died early in 1871 (*Letters*, 9:15). Nassau William Senior died on 4 June 1864. According to Sybil Oldfield, around that time Jane, her husband, and family probably moved to Lavender Hill, Wandsworth. The eldest adopted daughter was Emily Hughes who was born December 1863. Given that the first letter to Jane Senior that we are aware of is dated April 1867 and rather formal, GHL's letter was probably written between April 1867 and early 1871.

The Priory, | 21, North Bank, | Regents Park. | Tuesday [nd]

My dear Mrs Senior
Will you please hand the book which accompanies this to your oldest daughter with the following veracious history:
Once upon a time, a great many years hence, there lived in the Wood of St. John, at a dismal Priory, a small Wise Man with a large wise Bull Dog.

The Bull Dog, who had a black patch on the left eye, & was consequently named Ben, often murdered fleas, but never the Queen's English.

He was a Prince in disguise. A wicked magician having transformed him into a Dog. That is why he barked at the Moon, & lived with the small wise Man, who was so wise that nobody knew how much he knew, you know! He knew which side his bread was buttered: & always ate dry toast. He knew what little girls were made of—"much that was naughty & little of nice."

And he knew

That three Sprigs of Lavender flourished at Wandsworth "in human form"!

So he one day said to his Bull Dog, O Ben what shall we do to have a sniff of those Sprigs of Lavender? Ben looked very wise & turned the conversation.

But the small Wise Man, because he was bald, and generally acquainted with the stars, was not thus to be put off. So he said: "O Ben! suppose I send a fairy gift to Wandsworth, it may bring a pleasant smile into the face of the Sprig, & when we meet she will embrace me."

Hereupon Ben, who was deeply enamoured of Sprig the elder, gave a jealous growl, and ate up a kitten—for he was particular about his food, and liked it "tasty."

However it so happened that the gift was sent. The Sprig's lovely face was lighted up with pleasure; the light caught the tinder [sic] part of Ben's heart

([N] B. Ben is an Irish Bull)

and this, flaming amid the fireworks of his feelings, there was a general squish, fizz, suck, bang, sssssss! In fact Ben blew up— nothing remained but a cloud of smoke, which cleared off, & revealed the young Prince in a human form, who straightaway led Sprig to the halter & hanged her—

No, this was what the wicked magician wanted, but the small Wise Man stepped in, &

Ben-Prince led her to the Altar & married her.

They lived happily together ever after and had many puppies all with patches on their eyes so that people knew them to be Princes. Why I don't know.

This, my dear Mrs Senior, is the history recorded in the most ancient Hibernian M.S. in the possession of

Yours faithfully | G.H. Lewes

I reopen this on receipt of your kind letter to say how pleasant it is that you should be thinking of the Priory at the time the Priory was thinking of you. The Princess will answer.

❧

28. Written on black-edged mourning paper. GE noted in her Journal, 10 December 1870: "George's Mother died this morning, quite peacefully as she sat in her chair" (*Letters*, 5:125).

Tuesday

Dear Mrs Senior
It will not do to waste influence by needless application, so we hold our hands until you or Mr Senior have found out whether there is a situation vacant, & one that would be acceptable. I cannot undertake to do this being just now overwhelmed with business affairs consequent on my mother's death, otherwise I would enquire,

Polly sends her love | Ever yours truly | G.H. Lewes

"Taking Off" the Neighbors:
Margaret Oliphant's Parody of *Romola*

ELIZABETH WINSTON

At the end of chapter 4 in *MISS MARJORIBANKS*, MARGARET Oliphant describes her heroine's walk through the neighborhood to confirm the social preeminence of her family's address. Satisfied with what she sees, Lucilla takes an alternate way home through Grove Street, where she is surprised to hear the rich contralto of Barbara Lake, older daughter in a family of unconventional artists. In an instant, Lucilla realizes that this voice is "precisely adapted to supplement without supplanting her own high-pitched and much cultivated organ" at the Thursday evenings she intends to establish for the pleasure and unification of Carlingford society. She deftly maneuvers the proud, affronted Miss Lake into singing an operatic duet and agreeing to sing at the Marjoribanks house. "Lucilla," remarks the narrator, "had already foreseen that to amuse her guests entirely in her own person, would be at once impracticable and 'bad style.'" Despite her pride in her own voice, the narrator continues, Lucilla is willing to forego "the sweetness of individual success . . . for the enhanced and magnificent effect which she felt could be produced by the combination of the two voices" (59–60).

This incident in Grove Street is an emblem of Oliphant's decision to write what Mikhail Bakhtin has called "double-voiced discourse,"[1] her plan to amuse herself and her readers by—among other strategies—parodying an older female voice in the sacred grove of literature. That Miss Lake when first seen at the Marjoribanks gathering is identified by most of Lucilla's guests as "an Italian whom Lucilla had picked up somewhere in her travels" (107–8) makes the literary joke that much more delicious.

Like the caricaturist Mrs. Woodburn, another Carlingford resident, Margaret Oliphant enjoyed "taking off" the neighbors. For Oliphant, it was a delight—and as Lucilla Marjoribanks would have asserted, a public duty—to entertain her readers. Oliphant achieves this goal in her fourth *Chronicles of Carlingford* novel by incorporating into her narrative "parodic stylizations," playing many languages and their embedded worldviews off against each other (Bakhtin, *Dialogic Imagination,* 302, 311). She parodies the languages of the sentimental novel and the epic; the professional language of the historian, the clergy, and the political candidate; the language of the older generation to the younger, and of one social class to another.

In *Miss Marjoribanks*, Oliphant also parodies the narrative form and themes of several fictional genres, among them the *Künstlerroman*, the novel of manners (especially Austen's *Emma*), and the historical novel's focus on the biographies of great men or a society in conflict. Although *Emma* may be the dominant intertext for *Miss Marjoribanks*,[2] when Oliphant's narrative diverges from Austen, I propose that Oliphant is parodying a contemporary rival for the public's attention: George Eliot. In particular, Oliphant mocks the structure, learned style, and tragic mode of *Romola*, Eliot's historical novel and female *Bildungsroman* set in late-fifteenth-century Florence and serially published in 1862–63.

Yet Oliphant does not simply subject Eliot's narrative to comic ridicule. Instead, Oliphant's parodic response exemplifies the more inclusive understanding of parody described by Margaret Rose in her historical survey and analysis of the form, *Parody: Ancient, Modern, and Post-Modern*. As Rose's review of scholarly commentary on the term reminds readers, the word *parody* itself expresses a duality, an ambiguity, since *para* sometimes means "beside" and at other times means "opposite," as we can see in words like *parallel* and *paradox*. For Rose, theories and uses of parody based on this broader interpretation of the term are truer to the word's original meaning as "both a song sung 'against' or 'in opposition' to another and a song sung 'beside' or near to another . . ." (46). In *Miss Marjoribanks*, Margaret Oliphant dramatizes both critical and sympathetic voices in her complex response to Eliot's Italian novel.

Oliphant's familiarity with *Romola* is easily documented. That she had read at least book 1 of the novel by early 1863 is clear from her request to review a new translation of Villari's *Savonarola and His Times*. Responding to her publishers' fear that the review might detract from *Romola*, then appearing in *Cornhill Magazine*, Oliphant asserts that George Eliot's Savonarola "so far has only been brought in as the inevitable priest in a medieval novel" (*Autobiography and Letters,* 190). The comment suggests that she had read only through the October 1862 installment, in which Savonarola figures as the shadowy presence at the deathbed of Romola's brother, Dino.

In her completed review of Villari's book, published in *Black-wood's* in June 1863, Oliphant refers several times to Eliot's novel, twice to events from the part for April 1863, well into book 3—suggesting that she, like many Victorians, was now reading *Romola* as soon as each part appeared.

Eighteen months after Oliphant completed "Savonarola," when she began writing the history of Lucilla Marjoribanks (serialized February 1865–May 1866), she opened with the death of Lucilla's mother. Like the marriage of Emma Woodhouse's governess, this event fits the pattern discerned by Marianne Hirsch: the daughter's narrative is initiated by the mother's absence (57).[3] Yet there is an important difference in the status of the two fictional daughters in question: Emma is already the reigning mistress of Hartfield. Her mother-surrogate's departure to marry Mr. Weston represents no challenge to Emma's position as first lady of Highbury. Lucilla, in contrast, is away at school when her mother dies, and although "already an important personage at Mount Pleasant" (26), she is considered too young to stop her formal schooling.

Oliphant treats the death of Mrs. Marjoribanks as precipitating not only a social crisis but also a political one: will the traditional forces of Dr. Marjoribanks and his housekeeper Nancy hold sway or will a new form of government be established? In this way the opening of *Miss Marjoribanks* resembles not *Emma* so much as *Romola*, which opens with the death of Lorenzo de' Medici. As Andrew Sanders has written, *Romola* portrays "a society which is seeking new directions" (29). By comparison, the people of Carlingford may not be actively seeking a leader—and certainly not a young woman to rule—but Miss Marjoribanks is determined to lead them for their own good.

Oliphant's parody of the historical novel and *Romola* begins with her title. Like Walter Scott's first novel in this genre, *Waverley* (1814), Eliot's historical novel bears the name of its protagonist. *Romola*, as Eliot confirmed in a letter to Alexander Main (3 August 1871, *Letters*, 5:174), is the Italian feminine equivalent of Romulus—the name of the mythical founder of Rome. In Felicia Bonaparte's view, Eliot portrays Romola as an epic hero whose journey from the pagan classical worlds of her scholarly father and Greek husband through the Christian world of Savonarola to the secular humanistic world of the epilogue recapitulates the history of Western civilization (20–21; 232–38). Oliphant's female protagonist also has a Roman sounding first name, *Lucilla*;[4] but Oliphant chooses to call her novel *Miss Marjoribanks*, which, by its courteous title, stresses Lucilla's social position as the unmarried only daughter of Carlingford's "favourite doctor" (29).[5] As the language describing Lucilla makes clear, however, Miss Marjoribanks means to play heroic protagonist in the epic narrative of the life of her small town. Following in the comic tradition of Fielding, Oliphant calls *Miss Marjoribanks* a history and the narrator an historian or biographer. When, at the beginning of chapter 3, the narrator pauses to explain to readers what pre-Lucillan life in Carlingford was like, Oliphant seems to be spoofing the Victorian analogical method of historical writing. Lucilla is termed a "revolutionary," and social conditions prior to her Thursday evenings are compared to those of the prehistoric age. That comment parodically echoes Macaulay in his *History of England*, when he declares that for the changes occurring between 1685 and the time of his writing in 1848, "the history of the old world furnishes no parallel" (quoted in Culler, 20). The implication is that Miss Marjoribanks is about to effect change as sweeping as the industrial revolution, bringing organization and central control to Carlingford society.

The titular heroine of this "history" is initially described in a way that parodies Eliot's idealized description of Romola from book 1, chapter 5. Readers first see Romola in her father's domain, surrounded by his books and antiquities, reading patiently to the blind scholar from a Latin text. The narrator describes her as "a tall maiden of seventeen or eighteen," with long "reddish gold" hair which is pulled back "above her small ears," then ripples forward making "a natural veil for her neck" (93). Romola walks, we are told, "with a queenly step . . . the simple action of her tall, finely wrought frame" (95). Awaiting the entrance of Tito and Nello, Romola stands "at her full height, in quiet majestic self-possession." Throughout the description, the narrator stresses Romola's nobility, as well as her long-suffering, tender sympathy for the proud but bitter father who depreciates her "feminine mind" and longs for "the sharp edge of a young [masculine] mind" to help him in his research (98).

The description of Miss Marjoribanks, in contrast, is striking for its affectionate irony, lack of idealism, and difference from the other nonidealized descriptions of heroines like Jane Eyre, who are small and dark. Lucilla is first presented to us on the journey home from school, lying "back in the corner of the railway carriage, with her veil down," rehearsing the meeting with her recently widowed father and perfecting her plans of daughterly devotion:

> Miss Marjoribanks sketched to herself . . . how she would wind herself
> up to the duty of presiding at her papa's dinner-parties, and charming

everybody by her good humour, and brightness, and devotion to his comfort; and how, when it was all over, she would withdraw and cry her eyes out in her own room, and be found in the morning languid and worn-out, but always heroical, ready to go downstairs and assist at dear papa's breakfast, and keep up her smiles for him till he had gone out to his patients. (26)

The picture is "a very pretty one," admits the narrator, and understandable, given Lucilla's age (she is only fifteen) and her extensive knowledge of bereaved young ladies in novels. Unfortunately, the narrator points out, she lacks "the kind of figure for this *mise en scène*."

For Miss Marjoribanks is "'a large girl' . . . not . . . a tall girl—which conveys an altogether different idea—but she was large in all particulars," large features, hands, and feet. Her hair, "if it could but have been cleared a little in its tint, would have been golden, though at present it was nothing more than tawny, and curly to exasperation" (27). Said curls "did not, however, float or wave, or do any of the graceful things which curls ought to do." (We can safely assume that they did not "ripple" like Romola de' Bardi's bright tresses.) The crowning frustration was that Lucilla's hair never grew long, only thick, ponderous, unmanageable. Jane Austen does not describe Emma's hair or size, so that readers of Oliphant's novel, prepared by the subject and tone of Oliphant's narrative for parallels to *Emma*, find the picture of Lucilla Marjoribanks that much more marked.

In structure, Eliot's and Oliphant's novels initially resemble each other, both opening with a death and a motherless adolescent daughter who is firmly under her father's control. From this pattern, however, Oliphant soon diverges, showing her female protagonist's swift but artful assumption of power. In *Romola* Eliot had crossed the novel of development with the historical novel, connecting the narrative of Romola de' Bardi with the narrative of Girolamo Savonarola through their common struggle to reconcile duty and desire: Romola in her domestic roles as a daughter and wife, Savonarola in his public roles as a Dominican monk subject to the Borgian Pope and a political leader committed to Church reform. Oliphant fuses the two narratives and the two protagonists into a single narrative of a young woman who like Romola faces patriarchal restrictions on women's action but who confidently assumes the public role of social reformer. Lucilla experiences no conflict at all between her chosen duty to be a comfort to her widowed father and her desire to bring Carlingford society—including Dr. Marjoribanks—into line.

Lucilla sees herself and her duty in heroic, even Biblical terms: "She felt like a young king," we are told, and viewed the family drawing room as "a waste and howling wilderness" in need of reforming before it may serve as the "inner court and centre of her kingdom" (48). Thus choosing a new color scheme for this room to suit her complexion is a matter of crucial significance, as is finding a contralto to sing at her evenings who will complement her own voice. As readers we may initially align ourselves with Dr. Marjoribanks, interpreting his daughter's actions as clever performances to accomplish her goals. But the narrator repeatedly asserts Lucilla's perfect sincerity, shows the inaccuracy of the doctor's admittedly plausible interpretations,[6] and occasionally even affirms the appropriateness of the heroic language in which Miss Marjoribanks understands her life. After all, though some of her "principles" may seem silly ("It is one of my principles always to flirt in the middle of the company" [119]), Lucilla does manage, by adhering to these ideals, to bring proud, timid lovers together, prevent a quarrel from irrevocably damaging social relations, and preserve domestic harmony for women unable to act as fearlessly as she. As monarch of her world, Lucilla acts with beneficent results.

If one compares the three-volume structure of Eliot's novel with Oliphant's, the younger writer's parodic revision emerges distinctly. Book 1 of *Romola* ends with the betrothal of Romola and Tito, and their encounter with the procession of chanting figures dressed like corpses, a reminder to Romola of her brother's deathbed vision in which she married "the Great Tempter." In volume 1 of *Miss Marjoribanks*, Lucilla rejects a marriage proposal from her cousin Tom, and then dreams "that she stood at the altar by the side of the member for Carlingford, and that Mr. Bury, with inflexible cruelty, insisted upon marrying her to Tom Marjoribanks instead . . ." (83). The volume ends with Lucilla's discovery that an imposter has been unwittingly admitted into Carlingford's best society.

In book 2 of Eliot's novel, Romola discovers her husband's infidelity, leaves him and Florence to seek a new life, but is called back to her civic duty by Savonarola. Eliot describes Romola as an Ariadne who "was going to thread life by a fresh clue"—Christian renunciation (440). Volume 2 of *Miss Marjoribanks* finds Lucilla disappointed by two men, Mr. Cavendish and Archdeacon Beverley, whom she had expected to ask for her hand in marriage but who have instead fallen in love with other women. She rebounds by successfully executing a plan to manage the two men for their own good and to bring about a marriage that will resolve her protégée

Mrs. Mortimer's romantic difficulties. The narrator describes Lucilla's having devised this plan "the moment she had laid hold of the
clue which guided or seemed to guide her through the labyrinth"—an intuition about the resiliency of first love.

In the final volumes of both novels, each female protagonist is
still in her place: Romola serves the poor of Florence, pleads unsuccessfully for her godfather's life, leaves the city a second time,
tends the sick in a plague-ridden village, then returns to care for her
dead husband's other "wife" and two children. Though she has not
become a scholar herself like the learned Cassandra Fedele, Romola
is guiding her stepson in the interpretation of difficult texts that
honor the noble life. For her part, Lucilla, now twenty-nine and still
unmarried, continues to lead Carlingford society, helps to elect Mr.
Ashburton (instead of Mr. Cavendish) as the Member for Carlingford, recovers from her father's sudden death and the loss of the
family fortune, and recognizes that what she had originally called a
nightmare—marrying her cousin—is in fact a dream come true, as
long as Tom buys their great grandfather's estate in the village of
Marchbank, so that she can reform "the moral wilderness" (496)
and perhaps get her man elected as Member for the County.

One sees by the status of their female protagonists at novel's end
that Eliot and Oliphant are challenging the generic conventions, respectively, of historical romances like G. P. R. James's *Leonara
d'Orco* (1858) and female *Bildungsromane* like *Emma* (1816). Romola does not, at last, unite with a husband both brave and faithful,
like the Italian cavalier Lorenzo Visconti, who wins Leonara d'Orco's heart.[7] Lucilla Marjoribanks is not given the marital choice that
Emma receives—that of the most respected gentleman in her circle,
a mentor who has promoted her moral education with loving reserve. Lucilla marries her good-hearted blundering cousin, taking
him as her new project, and thereby showing that she has changed
little since leaving Mount Pleasant Academy for Carlingford.[8] In
their rejection of traditional romantic resolutions, Eliot and Oliphant are sympathetically aligned, their voices harmonious rather
than opposed.

What most distinguishes *Romola* from *Miss Marjoribanks* is the
relationship established between narrator and female protagonist.
Though occasionally distancing Romola by acknowledging her
"girlish . . . ignorance concerning the world outside her father's
books" (104), Eliot's narrator, nevertheless, consistently presents
this character without condescension, and with admiration for Romola's struggle with competing moral claims. The narrator of *Miss
Marjoribanks*, in contrast, clearly admires Lucilla for her qualities

as a leader—her self-confidence, foresight, decisive action; she admires as well Lucilla's gift for transforming the constrictive traditional demands for feminine self-sacrifice and domesticity to achieve her own purposes. But at the same time the narrator mocks Lucilla's egoism and her unshakable belief in the supreme importance of her "mission."

These divergent responses, occurring at times within the same passage, exemplify Bakhtin's description of comic style, a special form of that heteroglossia which for Bakhtin constitutes the novel.[9] Oliphant creates her comic narrative through "a continual shifting of the distance between author and language": in this case, the distance between the older, retrospective narrator's discourse and Lucilla's speech and beliefs, as well as the gap between the narrator and the "common language" and viewpoint of Carlingford society (Bakhtin, *Dialogic Imagination,* 302).

Nowhere is this shifting distance more noticeable than in the dialogue Oliphant creates between narrator Lucilla and Carlingford society on the subject of religion. Lucilla professes strictly orthodox religious views. She also accepts society's double standard regarding religious skepticism, and is thus alarmed that the joking remarks of two male guests at luncheon might cause the Rector's sister to doubt Lucilla's principles: "for people can stand a man being sceptical, you know," Miss Marjoribanks justly observed, "but everybody knows how unbecoming it is in a woman—and me who have such a respect for religion!" (83).

Yet though she considers it one of her "principles never to laugh about anything that has to do with religion" (78), she does not hesitate to use her theatrical skills to vanquish the Rector when he tries to interfere with her plans for ruling alone in her father's house. And, she interprets her successes in organizing Carlingford society as signs of Providential approval: Mrs. Woodburn's brilliant caricature of Archdeacon Beverley which so entertained everyone at an especially difficult Thursday evening is dubbed a "reward" for Lucilla's virtue (174). As the narrator comments early in the novel,

> Miss Marjoribanks was of the numerous class of religionists who keep up civilities with heaven, and pay all the proper attentions, and show their respect for the divine government in a manner befitting persons who know the value of their own approbation. (39)

The narrator is both delighted by Lucilla's triumphs and amused by her oft asserted regard for Providence which is, in reality, regard for self.

"But," writes Oliphant in "Two Cities—Two Books," her July 1874 critique of George Eliot's novel, "there is no tender amusement in the author's tone" toward "her beautiful Romola . . . but a gravity which precludes all possibility of humour . . ." (78). For Oliphant, Romola is a figure too lofty and noble, proudly contemptuous of Christianity, and "never misconstrued or unappreciated as, alas! real greatness often is" (78)—a truth Miss Marjoribanks resigns herself to accepting (93). Oliphant also pronounces as "a failure in art" Romola's response to her husband Tito's betrayal: instead of reacting as ordinary women do when disappointed in love—struggling painfully to revive the relationship—Romola "is able to drop [Tito] like a stone" (79). "Her love is more like the love of man than of woman," declares Oliphant.

Whereas Oliphant criticizes Romola de' Bardi's unremitting moral grandeur, she warmly defends Tito Melema, affectionately parodying him in *Miss Marjoribanks* as Mr. Cavendish. Cavendish is a social imposter, the man who is discovered to have been not "one of the Cavendishes" but plain Mr. Kavan, "a son of a trainer" (169). Kavan had acted as a son to the widowed Mrs. Mortimer's uncle and had inherited the uncle's money instead of Mrs. Mortimer. The scene at one of Lucilla's evenings (chapter 16) in which the Archdeacon's entrance evokes in Cavendish "a look of dead stupefied terror" recalls the scene in chapter 22 of *Romola* in which Tito is struck with terror by the sight of his adoptive father, Baldassarre. Oliphant's treatment of her "imposter" through Lucilla's tolerant rescue of Cavendish from the avenging Archdeacon contrasts sharply with Eliot's treatment of Tito. Of course, Cavendish has done nothing really criminal: "he was an adventurer, but he was not a base one" (285); and he had been very useful to Lucilla as a man who could flirt. Thus, at the dinner which Lucilla organizes to provoke the confrontation between the Archdeacon and Cavendish, she prevents Mr. Beverley from denouncing Cavendish publicly by implying that Cavendish is a "very particular friend" of hers. At the supper in the Rucellai gardens, Tito must rely on his own resources to defend himself against the charge of treachery.

Reading Cavendish as a parodic version of Tito might seem fanciful, but Oliphant's own discussion of Tito in "Two Cities—Two Books" lends weight to the claim. Oliphant strongly criticizes George Eliot for what Oliphant calls her "cruel," "vindictive" treatment of Tito, for showing no pity to "the beautiful, bright, young adventurer," using the same word, *adventurer*, to describe Tito that Lucilla and the narrator use to describe Mr. Cavendish.

Elsewhere I have argued that in *Miss Marjoribanks*, Oliphant explores her ambivalent attitudes toward the artist's life through the characters of Rose Lake and Lucilla Marjoribanks. I contend that by excising much of Rose's story as she revised for the novel's volume edition, Oliphant concentrated readers' attention on Lucilla, thereby affirming the pragmatic, resourceful writer in herself rather than the passionate, idealistic artist.[10] I now see Oliphant's self-parody as extending to include Mrs. Woodburn and her brother, Mr. Cavendish, and functioning as disguised self-defense. When the narrator puts down the caricaturist, Mrs. Woodburn, calling her superficially clever in her effects, with "very little real knowledge of character" (325), Oliphant is parrying criticism from literary reviews of her work.[11]

Oliphant's defense of Tito Melema and her critique of Romola strike me as similarly self-protective acts. Both Tito and Lucilla are triple agents. To gain wealth and influence, Tito spies for three fiercely opposed Florentine political parties: the Mediceans, Savonarola's popular party, and the aristocratic Arrabbiati (556). Lucilla also dares a triple game, deftly playing three different people off against each other—the Archdeacon, Mrs. Mortimer, and Mr. Cavendish—to keep the peace and save her grand social design. Like Tito, Lucilla and her creator regularly use their talents to please their constituents, while at the same time pleasing themselves. No wonder Oliphant seems personally affronted by Eliot's inexorable judgment of the amiable, crowd-pleasing Tito and by her elevation of Madonna Romola beyond the moral reach of ordinary readers.

As we have seen in the authors' contrasting uses of the Ariadne myth, one way that Oliphant deflates Eliot's high-toned treatment of Romola is by parodying the earlier novel's learned style. Tito's wedding gift of a miniature tabernacle, decorated with scenes of Ariadne and Bacchus, becomes, in *Miss Marjoribanks*, housekeeper Nancy's gift of a special dessert to console Lucilla when, instead of proposing marriage, Mr. Cavendish defects to Barbara Lake: "The faithless could not be brought back again; but Ariadne might at least have any little thing she could fancy for dinner . . ." (144). The somber explanation for Tito's moral decline as illustrating "that inexorable law of human souls, that we prepare ourselves for sudden deeds by the reiterated choice of good or evil which gradually determines character" (287) is reduced to eight words by Dr. Marjoribanks: "a man is what his habits make him" (32). Tito's visit to the gentle, nonjudging Tessa after a political plot goes awry parallels Mr. Cavendish's return, two nights before losing the parliamentary election, to the Lake house in Grove Street, drawn there by Barbara's "magnificent gush of song" (442). Like Tito, Cavendish is following a habit of long standing: seeking the company of a woman in whose eyes "he was still a great man" (444).

How does Oliphant's parodic duet with Eliot transform the repertoire of nineteenth-century English novels? By sometimes affirming Lucilla's assumption of the moral high ground, while at other times exposing the ego-serving dimension of feminine renunciation, Oliphant creates in the words of Q. D. Leavis, "a triumphant intermediary between [Austen's] Emma and Dorothea" (vii), probably influencing George Eliot's "attempt at ironical treatment" of Miss Brooke and her last heroine, Gwendolen Harleth (12).

Joseph Wiesenfarth has demonstrated the value of reading *Middlemarch* as George Eliot's rewriting of "the expectations story," her transformation of Dickens's *Great Expectations* "by reducing the mythic and the Gothic elements to everyday reality" (109–10). One implication of my study is that *Miss Marjoribanks* may have contributed to Eliot's reimagining of the *Bildungsroman*. In her parody of *Romola*, Oliphant had already reduced "the mythic . . . to everyday reality," had already rehabilitated the man described by respectable people as "an adventurer." Though Mr. Cavendish is clearly not, as Wiesenfarth defines Will Ladislaw, an Arnoldian "alien . . . the thinking man who provides the only hope for the future of England" (111), Cavendish, too, renounces money to marry for love. He is an intermediary between Tito and Will, ending up neither murdered by his Nemesis, the Archdeacon, nor working for Reform in Parliament, but marrying the poor artist, Barbara Lake, Lucilla's reluctant singing partner and sometime rival. Lucilla's fate differs significantly from Dorothea Ladislaw's: As *Mrs. Marjoribanks*, she continues to gratify her desire for social preeminence in a new location. Oliphant thus constructs a self-assertive character unlike the Dorotheas who live "a hidden life" (*Middlemarch*, 838). As has often been noted, Eliot was better at showing "how people subject the self than how they fulfill the self."[12] In *Miss Marjoribanks*, Oliphant creates a heroine who dares to please herself, confidently stretching the limits of her patriarchal world.

Oliphant's official response to *Romola* appeared in the "Two Cities—Two Books" review of 1874.[13] I believe that she gave a more immediate response in the pages of *Miss Marjoribanks*. Instead of Tito, the political agent who has two wives, she offers Mr. Cavendish, the flirt who courts two women. Instead of Savonarola's tragic struggle between obedience and resistance to a corrupt Pope, she shows Mr. Cavendish "torn asunder . . . by inclination and interest" (200): should he marry the seductive drawing-master's daughter or Miss Marjoribanks? Instead of Savonarola's prophetic visions of Charles VIII coming to purify the Church, she presents Lucilla's "special Intimation" of the man who should be Member for Carlingford (368). Finally, instead of the idealized Romola, who is tragically disappointed in marriage, there is sensible Lucilla Marjoribanks, who—after repeatedly expecting marriage proposals that never occur—weds her cousin Tom. In so doing she keeps her family name and her opportunities for enlightened management intact. It was an outcome her creator knew firsthand.

NOTES

1. Bakhtin's discussion of parody as "Vari-directional double-voiced discourse" comes in his *Problems of Dostoevsky's Poetics* (199, 203). See also Rose (126ff).

2. Many literary scholars have noted parallels between *Emma* and *Miss Marjoribanks*, among them Vineta and Robert A. Colby, *The Equivocal Virtue: Mrs. Oliphant and the Victorian Literary Marketplace* (New York: Archon Books, 1966), 65 and Q. D. Leavis (see my discussion at the end of this essay).

3. "It is the mother's absence," says Hirsch, "which creates the space in which the heroine's plot and her activity of plotting can evolve."

4. Vineta and Robert A. Colby have suggested that Oliphant may have named Miss Marjoribanks "Lucilla" after the heroine in Hannah More's *Coelebs in Search of a Wife* (1810). If Oliphant did, it was a parodic naming, since Oliphant's Lucilla is both physically and temperamentally the opposite of More's modest, delicate Lucilla Stanley. See Colby (255, n. 26).

5. Elisabeth Jay points out that "this novel alone out of all Mrs. Oliphant's titles proudly proclaims the heroine a spinster." See *MRS. OLIPHANT: A Fiction to Herself* (Oxford: Clarendon Press, 1995), 105.

6. For instance, when Dr. Marjoribanks discovers his daughter pacing the drawing room after dinner, he assumes that she's affecting a tragic pose: "What were you doing, Lucilla? . . . rehearsing Lady Macbeth, I suppose." The narrator has already explained that Lucilla is "pacing, not in the sentimental sense of making a little promenade up and down, but in the homely practical signification, with a view of measuring, that she might form an idea how much carpet was required" for the room's renovation. Yet a basis for the doctor's reaction is also acknowledged: Lucilla's "long step giving rather a tragedy-queen effect to her handsome but substantial person and long, sweeping dress." Thus Oliphant distinguishes her heroine from posturing characters like Austen's Miss Bingley (*Pride and Prejudice*, chapter 11) while also showing that a "queenly" carriage may express not only a noble spirit like Romola's, but a practical one as well.

7. In his silent film adaptation of Eliot's novel, Henry King supplies the widowed Romola with a second, this time noble, husband in the artist Carlo Bucellini, a character created by the conflation of two characters from the novel: Piero di Cosimo and Romola's uncle Bernardo. See Kevin W. Sweeney and Elizabeth Winston, "Redirecting Melodrama: Gish, Henry King, and *Romola*," *Literature/Film Quarterly* 23 (1995): 137–45.

8. For Linda Peterson, in *Miss Marjoribanks* Oliphant "undercut[s] both the central assumption of the traditional female *bildungsroman* (that moral growth re-

sults from romantic or emotional trials) and the philosophy of the heroine whom Oliphant offers in contrast (that young women do best avoiding such trials)." See "The Female *Bildungsroman*: Tradition and Revision in Oliphant's Fiction," in *Margaret Oliphant: Critical Essays on a Gentle Subversive*, ed. D. J. Trela (London: Susquehanna University Press, 1995), 70.

9. See *The Dialogic Imagination* (263, 300, 324). Perhaps one way to understand the relation of double-voiced parodic discourse within a many-voiced comic novel like *Miss Marjoribanks* is to recall another early meaning of *parodos*: "the side entrance of the ancient theatre through which the chorus of the drama first entered, or their first song" (Rose, 7). This *chorus* of voices sometimes supported and at other times opposed the actions of the principal characters in the drama.

10. See Winston, "Revising *Miss Marjoribanks*," *Nineteenth Century Studies* 9 (1995): 85–97.

11. See, for example, *The Nonconformist*, 25 February 1863, 157. Margarete Rubik cites this review in her discussion of contemporary criticism of Oliphant's fiction in *The Novels of Mrs. Oliphant: A Subversive View of Traditional Themes* (New York: Peter Lang, 1994), 227. The reviewer for *The Spectator* (26 May 1866) also links Oliphant to Mrs. Woodburn, but where I see a deft example of self-parody, this reviewer finds shared superficiality: like her character, "the authoress of the *Chronicles of Carlingford* . . . catches the accent and mannerism of a school or an individual" but "seldom gets to the human nature beneath the characteristic turns of feature which she touches so skillfully" (579).

12. The words are Jerome Beaty's in a 1980 National Endowment for the Humanities Summer Seminar on "George Eliot and Other Victorian Novels," at Emory University.

13. An observation by D. J. Trela may account for this delayed response. In "Two Margaret Oliphants Review George Eliot," Trela points out that since Oliphant and Eliot had the same publisher, John Blackwood, Oliphant's articles criticizing Eliot in *Blackwood's* "appeared some time after the publication of the work in question and they were not exclusively devoted to Eliot." See Trela, *George Eliot-George Henry Lewes Studies* (September 1993): 45–49.

In *Romola* Eliot had crossed the novel of development with the historical novel, connecting the narrative of Romola de' Bardi with the narrative of Girolamo Savonarola through their common struggle to reconcile duty and desire: Romola in her domestic roles as a daughter and wife, Savonarola in his public roles as a Dominican monk subject to the Borgian Pope and a political leader committed to Church reform. Through the narrator of *Miss Marjoribanks* and her heroine, Lucilla, Margaret Oliphant voices her complex response, critical and sympathetic, to Eliot's Italian novel.

As readers we may initially align ourselves with Dr. Marjoribanks, interpreting his daughter's actions as clever performances to accomplish her goals. But the narrator repeatedly asserts Lucilla's perfect sincerity, reveals the inaccuracy of the doctor's admittedly plausible interpretations, and occasionally even affirms the appropriateness of the heroic language in which Miss Marjoribanks understands her life. See *Agnes of Sorrento* (1861–62), *Pride and Prejudice* (1813), for other daughter-narrator plots. Asserts Leavis, "Nowhere earlier than the 'Miss Brooke' or Book I of *Middlemarch* does George Eliot adopt an aloof, ironic view of a heroine and invite the reader to see her as amusing . . . ."

The similarities between Lucilla Marjoribanks's marriage and Dorothea Casaubon's union with Will Ladislaw suggest to Leavis that Eliot had "absorbed unconsciously or tried to emulate" the younger author's narrative stance toward her heroine (13). Despite this disappointment with her hair and with her initial attempts to take charge in her father's house, Miss Marjoribanks does succeed in having her mourning dresses made in the long style worn by grown women, and this little victory sustains her during the four years before she returns to Carlingford to begin what the narrator describes as her "glorious reign" (40).

In their criticisms of *Miss Marjoribanks*, reviewers for *The Spectator* (26 May 1866, 579–80), *The Athenaeum* (7 July 1866, 12–13), and *The Nonconformist* (26 May 1866, 565) cite the preceding novels in the series. For this reviewer and those for *The Athenaeum* (7 July 1866, 12–13) and *The Nonconformist* (26 May 1866, 565), this latest novel in the series exhibits the faults of the earlier tales: an absurdly unrealistic portrayal of the clergy.

References

Bakhtin, M. M. *The Dialogic Imagination: Four Essays*. Edited by Michael Holquist. Translated by Caryl Emerson and Michael Holquist. Austin: University of Texas Press, 1981.

———. *Problems of Dostoevsky's Poetics*. 1963. Translated by R. W. Rotsel. Ann Arbor, Mich.: Ardis Press. 1973.

Bonaparte, Felicia. *The Triptych and the Cross: The Central Myths of George Eliot's Poetic Imagination*. New York: New York University Press, 1979.

Culler, A. Dwight. *The Victorian Mirror of History*. New Haven: Yale University Press, 1985.

Eliot, George. *The George Eliot Letters*. Edited by Gordon S. Haight. 9 vols. New Haven: Yale University Press, 1954–1978.

———. *Middlemarch*. 1872. Edited by Rosemary Ashton. Penguin Classics. Reprint, New York: Penguin Books USA, 1994.

———. *Romola*. 1863. Edited by Andrew Sanders. Reprint, Harmondsworth: Penguin, 1980.

Hirsch, Marianne. *The Mother/Daughter Plot: Narrative, Psychoanalysis, Feminism*. Bloomington: Indiana University Press, 1989.

Leavis, Q. D. Introduction. *Miss Marjoribanks*, by Margaret Oliphant. London: Zodiac Press, 1969.

Oliphant, Mrs. Margaret O. W. *The Autobiography and Letters of Mrs. M. O. W. Oliphant*. Edited by Mrs. Harry Coghill. Reprint, [Leicester]: Leicester University Press, 1974.

———. *Miss Marjoribanks*. 1866. Introduced by Penelope Fitzgerald. Reprint, New York: Penguin/Virago, 1988.

Peterson, Linda. "The Female *Bildungsroman*: Tradition and Revision in Oliphant's Fiction." In *Margaret Oliphant: Critical Essay on a Gentle Subversive*, edited by D. J. Trela. Selinsgrove, Pa.: Susquehanna University Press, 1995.

Rose, Margaret A. *Parody: Ancient, Modern, and Post-Modern*. Cambridge: Cambridge University Press, 1993.

Sanders, Andrew. *The Victorian Historical Novel, 1840–1880*. New York: Macmillan, 1979.

Trela, D. J. "Two Margaret Oliphants Review George Eliot." *George Eliot–George Henry Lewes Studies* (September 1993): 37–60.

Wiesenfarth, Joseph J. *Gothic Manners and the Classic English Novel.* Madison: University of Wisconsin Press, 1988.

Winston, Elizabeth. "Revising *Miss Marjoribanks.*" *Nineteenth Century Studies* 9 (1995): 85–97.

"The Honey of Romance":
Oscar Wilde as Poet and Novelist

JAMES G. NELSON

AMONG THE ATTRACTIVE YOUNG MEN OF THE OLD TESTAMENT IS King Saul's son, Jonathan, remembered, perhaps, most for his love for and friendship with David, but also for his transgression of his father's interdict: "Cursed be the man that eateth any food until evening, that I may be avenged on mine enemies." Not having heard Saul's oath, Jonathan, as readers of the Bible may recall, soon after passed through a wood where there was honey on the ground. And in the words of the Old Testament, he "put forth the end of the rod that was in his hand, and dipped it in a honeycomb, and put his hand to his mouth; and his eyes were enlightened." Condemned to die by an unforgiving father, Jonathan, in words which were to have a curious attraction for some later Victorians, replied: "I did but taste a little honey with the end of the rod that was in mine hand, and, lo, I must die."[1]

How symbolic this incident must have been to the romantic poet, William Blake, who surely saw it as yet another biblical embodiment of the struggle between the youthful Orc, the voice of desire and rebellion, and the aged Urizen, the principle of tyranny and obedience unto the Law. Later, it was the metaphoric (and, perhaps, onanistic) implications of Jonathan's words which stirred the imagination of Walter Pater who associated Jonathan's honey and his enlightenment with all and even more than Matthew Arnold's Hellenism encompassed—in particular, the desire for physical beauty, the life of the senses, and the search for sensations.

In his essay on Wincklemann, which in 1873 was published as part of *Studies in the History of the Renaissance*, Pater, in calling attention to the ascetic bent of Christianity, its antagonism to "the artistic life, with its inevitable sensuousness," quoted with consummate effect Jonathan's words: "I did but taste a little honey with the end of the rod that was in mine hand, and, lo! I must die,"[2] thus enshrining David's passionate young companion as one of the

130

saints of aestheticism who had fought the good fight in the cause of beauty.

This act of canonization was not lost upon one of Pater's earliest and most devoted followers, Oscar Wilde, who in the sonnet which he chose to preface his *Poems* of 1881, "Hélas!," associated his life with that of Jonathan's. Bemoaning the fact that he already had "given away" his "ancient wisdom, and austere control" in order to, in true aesthetic fashion, "drift with every passion till my soul / Is a stringed lute on which all winds can play," Wilde climaxed his poem with a paraphrase of Jonathan's poignant words:

> lo! with a little rod
> I did but touch the honey of romance—
> And must I lose a soul's inheritance?[3]

With his predilection for Arnold's "sweetness" and Pater's "honey," Wilde could hardly fail to have read in Jonathan's fateful history his own, given as he was to that sense of doom which readers of his work discern. Indeed, Jonathan's appetite for honey and, consequently, his inevitable clash with the Hebraic spirit embodied in Saul,[4] is the history not only of Wilde but of so many of his central characters. His desire for beauty, his ideal of self-realization through pleasure, his devotion to the life of the senses was to set him at every turn in opposition to the restrictive nature and ascetic bent of the Judaeo-Christian tradition. And although he was to flirt with the Roman Catholic church, pose as the guilt-ridden penitent, and imitate the life of Christ, Wilde genuinely was, like his poetic forebear, John Keats, a pagan, the exponent of an aesthetic creed and philosophic ideal hostile in the extreme to Christianity and the established paternalistic/patriarchal culture of his times.

If we can read his early poems as a reflection, at least in part, of his concerns as a young Oxford undergraduate, Wilde already had experienced the struggle between his pagan desires and his Christian conscience.[5] A trip to Italy in 1875 evidently brought on his first flirtation with Roman Catholicism which resulted in yet a second trip to Rome the following year and an audience with the Pope. Back at Oxford, he hung his walls at Magdalen with, among other things, photographs of the Holy Father and Cardinal Manning. Yet of symbolic significance is a further trip to Italy in 1877 which concluded with an excursion to Greece under the aegis of his old Trinity College, Dublin, professor of classics, John Mahaffy. Perhaps alarmed by Wilde's dalliance with Rome, Mahaffy, who had

trained Wilde to be an excellent Greek scholar, told his pupil that
he intended to make "an honest pagan out of" him.[6]

That Mahaffy's intentions were realized is suggested by the fact
that the "Rosa Mystica" section of *Poems*, which is devoted primarily to Wilde's Italian journeys and his attraction to Roman Catholicism, concludes with "The New Helen," a poem which
intimates the demise of Christianity and celebrates the rebirth of the
worship of beauty in the form of Helen.[7] If Wilde did not intend for
"The New Helen" to serve as his final thought on religious matters—at least for a time—one wonders why he deliberately chose
to conclude the "Rosa Mystica" section with it. For the religion of
suffering which he celebrated in the previous poems is clearly re-
jected in "The New Helen" in favor of a symbolic embodiment of
the preeminence of fleshly beauty and the pleasures of the senses.
If after all of his posturings, the young Wilde had failed to bend the
knee to the Christian God, here he dedicates himself with fervor to
his newly deified Helen, the latest (after Keats's Psyche) Olympian:
"Yet care I not what ruin time may bring," he cries in words which
were to prove prophetic, "if in thy temple thou wilt let me kneel"
(108, ll. 59–60).

A kind of Swinburnean femme fatale, Wilde's Helen has been
hiding out with Aphrodite "in that hollow hill"—presumably that
Venusberg in Bavaria—while her Christian counterpart, Mary,
Queen of Heaven—"Who gat from Love no joyous gladdening, /
But only Love's intolerable pain" (108, ll. 47–48)—has been re-
ceiving the world's obeisance. Now, however, Helen has returned

> . . . our darkness to illume:
> For we, close-caught in the wide nets of Fate,
>   Wearied with waiting for the World's Desire,
>   Aimlessly wandered in the House of gloom,
> Aimlessly sought some slumberous anodyne
>   For wasted lives, for lingering wretchedness,
> Till we beheld thy re-arisen shrine,
>   And the white glory of thy loveliness.
>
> (109, ll. 93–100)

The pagan virtues which Wilde's Helen represents and the enthu-
siasm with which he celebrates them are central to a number of
other early poems in which the bright sensuous landscapes and
idyllic pleasures of Greek paganism are played off against the gray,
ugly, materialistic, puritanical world of the present. In such longer
poems as "The Garden of Eros," "Panthea," and "The Burden of

Itys," Wilde plays upon themes which, though largely unoriginal, clearly are close to his heart. And although his penchant for myth-making and his zest for sensuous paganism remind one inevitably of Keats's early poetry, especially "I Stood Tip-toe" and "Sleep and Poetry," the evident joy and ease with which he writes reminds one that the most convincing portions of his poetry and prose are those in which the pagan element—so often exploited by A.C. Swinburne—is given full expression.

Having dedicated himself to "the Spirit of Beauty" in "The Garden of Eros," and having assured her that there are still "a few" who have "in thy temples found a goodlier feast / Than this starved age can give" (131, ll. 112–13), Wilde in "The Burden of Itys" voices his genuine hope that Beauty somehow can triumph and bring back an age of pagan freedom and joy:

> Sing on! Sing on! Let the dull world grow young,
>   Let elemental things take form again,
> And the old shapes of Beauty walk among
>   The simple garths and open crofts, . . .
>
> (62, ll. 169–72)

And in "Panthea," he enunciates fully (despite the Swinburne-sque garb and Paterian sentiments) the ideas about the life of sensa-tions and the pursuit of pleasure upon which he was, in time, to put his own stamp as they found expression in, among other works, his literary criticism and his novel, *The Picture of Dorian Gray*. As-suming a Rubáiyát-like stance toward life, Wilde forbids his com-panion to trouble herself with "idle questions": "Nay," he goes on to urge, "let us walk from fire unto fire, / From Passionate pain to deadlier delight" (110, ll.1–2); and voicing sentiments Lord Henry Wotton later might have repeated to Dorian Gray—"For, sweet, to feel is better than to know"—the poet declares:

> One pulse of passion—youth's first fiery glow,—
>   Are worth the hoarded proverbs of the sage:
> Vex not thy soul with dead philosophy,
> Have we not lips to kiss with, hearts to love, and eyes to
> see!
>
> (110, ll. 7, 9–12)

Like Lord Henry who in the novel will urge the Paterian philosophy of the moment on Dorian, Wilde in "Panthea" views life essentially as "One fiery-coloured moment: one great love; and lo! we die"

(113, l. 84). So lived, life after death will be an eternal oneness with "all sensuous life" (114, l. 146).

The early poems not only embody in imitative form their author's pagan attitudes, but also provide us with our first acquaintance with the figure or image which is to become the central focus of Wilde's work. For example, this figure is appealingly embodied as the hero in what is supposed to be the poet's favorite poem, the early, rather Keatsian narrative romance entitled "Charmides." Named for the exceedingly beautiful and charming youth in Plato's early dialogue, "Charmides," Wilde's hero has the beauty and the youth but significantly lacks the central quality debated in the dialogue, namely, *sophrosyne*, roughly translated as moderation, self-control over one's physical appetites. A projection in art of Wilde's pagan self, Charmides is a "Grecian lad" of godlike beauty whose type is to blossom into the progressively more fully realized characters of Wilde's later works, above all, Dorian Gray whose handsome features are those of Charmides: "finely curved scarlet lips," "frank blue eyes," "crisp gold hair," and what Lord Henry describes as "all youth's passionate purity."[8]

Summing up within himself all those deeply romantic elements and pagan impulses which ruled the inner life of Wilde, Charmides is narcissistic, daring, a worshiper of beauty, and a passionate seeker of sensual pleasure. A youthful Greek mariner, Charmides, having returned from Sicily with his galley laden with "pulpy figs and wine," sets forth on a daring quest. Making his way at evening to the temple of Athena, he secretes himself within its precincts until all the priests and people have gone. When "through the open roof above the full and brimming moon / Flooded with sheeny waves the marble floor" of the temple, "the venturous lad" left his hiding place and flung wide "the cedar-carven door" which revealed Athena, "an awful image saffron-clad / And armed for battle!" (72, ll. 60–65). With total disregard for the sanctities of such a holy shrine and "ready for death," the audacious lad stood "well content at such a price to see / That calm wide brow, that terrible maidenhood, / The marvel of that pitiless chastity" (73, ll. 91–94). And despite the fact that "the twelve Gods leapt up in marble fear" and "on the frieze the prancing horses neighed" (73, ll. 86, 89), Charmides, his passion for the goddess fully aroused by her lovely form,

> . . . nigher came, and touched her throat, and with
> hands violate
> Undid the cuirass, and the crocus gown,
> And bared the breasts of polished ivory,

Till from the waist the peplos falling down
    Left visible the secret mystery
Which to no lover will Athena show,
The grand cool flanks, the crescent thighs, the
    bossy hills of snow.

(73, ll. 102–8)

Resting his "greedy eyes" on the "burnished image, till mere sight / Half swooned for surfeit of such luxuries," the lad, "his passion's will" unchecked, "flung his arms" about "the towered neck" while "his lips in hungering delight / Fed on her lips" (74, ll. 109–14). In what must be one of the strangest, albeit passionate, trysts in literature, Charmides spends the night with this image of Athena, never drawing "his lips from hers till overhead the lark of warning flew" (74, l. 126).

Needless to say, this act characterizes Charmides as a fearless youth whose curiosity about secret knowledge and whose desire for beauty and erotic pleasure prod him to a deed of daring and defiance as monumental as those of Faust and Prometheus. Like the young mariner in Coleridge's famous "Rime," Charmides sets himself apart from his fellows by his act of sacrilege which at once opens his eyes and seals his doom. Flying in the face of established taboos, he gazes upon "the secret mystery" of Athena, an enlightenment and act of passion for which he pays with his life.

Athena's beauties are not the only center of Charmides' attention, however. All beauty being but a reflection of his own, one is not surprised when, leaving Athena's shrine, Charmides seeks out "a little stream, which well he knew" (74, l. 139) where

... down amid the startled reeds he lay
Panting in breathless sweet affright, and waited for the day.
On the green bank he lay, and let one hand
    Dip in the cool dark eddies listlessly,
And soon the breath of morning came and fanned
    His hot flushed cheeks, or lifted wantonly
The tangled curls from off his forehead, while
He on the running water gazed with strange and secret smile.

(75, ll. 143–50)

Although some shepherds who pass by take Charmides to be either "young Hylas" or "young Dionysos," others, more perceptive, recognize in his beauty as well as in his streamside pose, the classic features of Narcissus, that lovely lad whom Ovid in *Metamorphoses* had made the androgynous son of a nymph and a river-god: "It is

Narcissus," they cry, "his own paramour, / Those are the fond and crimson lips no woman can allure" (75, ll. 167–68).

While the following evening his mariners on shipboard cringe in fear, Charmides, "the over-bold adulterer, / A dear profaner of great mysteries, / An ardent amorous idolater," with ecstatic joy and the cry of "I come" on his lips, plunges into the sea to join the vengeful Athena, who lures "her boy lover" to his death (78, ll. 253–55, 257, 264).

Washed ashore on a Greek isle, Charmides' body is feared by all "save one white girl, who deemed it would not be / So dread a thing to feel a sea-god's arms / Crushing her breasts in amorous tyranny" (80, ll. 343–45). The white girl, especially her salient features— innocent purity allied with sensual passion—reminds one of Byron's Haidee, whose relationship with the young Juan is faintly paralleled here, and prefigures Sibyl Vane, whose fatal love for Dorian Gray, in the novel of that title, also centers in an impossible object.

Bound by an oath to Artemis, the white girl, nevertheless, has little use for what she refers to as her "pallid chastity"; thus overwhelmed by passion and desire for the object of her love, she offends the virgin huntress who, as vengeful as Athena, slays her.

> Sobbing her life out with a bitter cry,
>   On the boy's body fell the Dryad maid,
> Sobbing for incomplete virginity,
>   And raptures unenjoyed, and pleasures dead,
>   And all the pain of things unsatisfied,
> And the bright drops of crimson youth crept down
>   her throbbing side.
>
> (85, ll. 523–28)

Unable to countenance so terrible a waste of beauty and passion, and loath to lose yet one more opportunity to indulge himself in an orgy of sensual rapture, the young Wilde translates Charmides and the white girl to Hades where in death's despite and through the good offices of Venus, they are brought together in an intensely erotic union of "rapturous bliss" (89, l. 633).

The pattern one discerns in "Charmides"—an act of daring, the product of both curiosity and desire, which incurs the wrath of the gods—as well as the type—that is, what I term the Charmides Self—are basic to some of Wilde's most famous works, including *The Picture of Dorian Gray*. Those familiar with the novel will recognize this Wildean type in the book's handsome and daring hero.

But Lord Henry Wotton and Basil Hallward also are projections of this type. In other words, the three central characters of the novel in their own several ways mirror Wilde's pagan self.[9] Briefly stated, Dorian is the Charmides Self as romance hero, the quester seeking adventure in the magical realm of sensations; Basil is the Charmides Self as artist; whereas Lord Henry is the Charmides Self in its ultimate stage: the Charmides Self as philosopher and mentor.

Dorian as Charmides Self can best be seen in terms of the romance tradition, that is, as a young knight who sets out upon a quest in the course of which he has many adventures. Viewing Dorian, thus, in no way violates the nature of Wilde's fiction, which itself can best be understood in terms of narrative romance and what Robert Kiely calls the English romantic novel.[10]

Wilde was contemptuous of the naturalistic novelist of the day—Emile Zola bearing the brunt of his criticism. For instance, in "The Decay of Lying," Vivian, in the course of his dialogue with Cyril, finds Zola's work

> entirely wrong from beginning to end, and wrong not on the ground of morals, but on the ground of art. From any ethical standpoint it is just what it should be. The author is perfectly truthful, and describes things exactly as they happen. . . . But from the standpoint of art, what can be said in favour of the author of *L'Assommoir, Nana,* and *Pot-Bouille?* Nothing. Mr. Ruskin once described the characters in George Eliot's novels as being like the sweepings of a Pentonville omnibus, but M. Zola's characters are much worse. They have their dreary vices, and their drearier virtues. The record of their lives is absolutely without interest. Who cares what happens to them? In literature we require distinction, charm, beauty and imaginative power.[11]

"Imaginative power," that, in Vivian's opinion—as well as in Wilde's—is what was lacking in the naturalistic novel. Speaking of Balzac, Wilde's favorite novelist, as being "a most remarkable combination of the artistic temperament with the scientific spirit," Vivian points out to Cyril that the difference between a Zola novel and a Balzac novel "is the difference between unimaginative realism and imaginative reality."[12] Opposed to the basic principle of the traditional novel, that is, the mimetic principle, Wilde sought in *Dorian Gray* to write fiction which would be the product of "imaginative reality," one which would embody the artist's own subjective impressions of life. As Epifanio San Juan has said, "the function of mirroring reality serves less an imitative than an idealizing purpose" in Wilde's work where "the dimensions of reality reach us only after their passage, in sensory experience, through the peculiarly tuned sensibility of an individual."[13]

This rather Paterian view of art makes Wilde highly susceptible to the strengths and special appeal of romance. And, as we have seen, in his early sonnet, "Hélas!," Wilde, at the outset of his artistic career, connected the quest for beauty with romance. Moreover, Dorian, at the height of his adventures, explicitly links "his search for sensations that would be at once new and delightful" with "that element of strangeness that is so essential to romance" (132). Even after his gruesome experience in Reading Gaol, could Wilde ever have penned a novel in what he viewed as the realistic tradition of his day or have written *Dorian Gray* under the impression that he must not intrude such elements as a Faustian pact with the Devil and the magic of an aging portrait?

If, then, *The Picture of Dorian Gray* is in some important respects more romance than novel, its hero is more knight than knave. Dorian, unlike so many of his contemporaries in the realistic novel of the day, is an aristocrat whose business is not to do so bourgeois a thing as to make money, but, rather, to devote himself to the higher spheres of conduct. Initially the protégé of Lord Henry Wotton's aunt, Lady Agatha, who has called him to good works among the poor in the East End of London, Dorian is, in the opening scene of the novel, about to attend to yet a higher calling, one which comes to him with the impact and the effect of an epiphany.

Having just responded with great emotion to Lord Henry's "strange panegyric on youth, his terrible warning of its brevity" (25), Dorian, "as if awakened from some dream" (24) gazes for the first time on the full-length portrait of himself just completed by his artist friend, Basil Hallward.

> When he saw it he drew back, and his cheeks flushed for a moment with pleasure. A look of joy came into his eyes, as if he had recognized himself for the first time. He stood there motionless and in wonder, dimly conscious that Hallward was speaking to him, but not catching the meaning of his words. The sense of his own beauty came on him like a revelation. He had never felt it before. (24–25)

Like the knights of old struck dumb by the vision of their goal, the Holy Grail, Dorian stands narcissus-like "gazing at the shadow of his own loveliness" (25) with Lord Henry's exhortation ringing in his ears:

> Ah! Realize your youth while you have it. Don't squander the gold of your days, listening to the tedious, trying to improve the hopeless fail-

ure, or giving away your life to the ignorant, the common, and the vulgar. These are the sickly aims, the false ideals, of our age. Live! Live the wonderful life that is in you! Let nothing be lost upon you. Be always searching for new sensations. Be afraid of nothing. . . . A new Hedonism—that is what our century wants. You might be its visible symbol. (22)

Inspired now to become, indeed, that "visible symbol" of a new way of life, Dorian daringly barters his soul away for eternal youth and beauty. Determined to sacrifice all for beauty and the life of the senses, he enlists under the banner of the new Hedonism which Lord Henry has prophesied and sets out to save his world "from that harsh, uncomely puritanism that," as he later views it, "is having, in our own day, its curious revival" (130).[14]

Filled "with a wild desire to know everything about life," (47) Dorian at first tentatively ventures forth into Piccadilly where for days he seeks to satisfy his curiosity by examining the faces he meets there, some fascinating, others fearful. But at length he determines "to go out in search of some adventure," recalling what Lord Henry had said "about the search for beauty being the real secret of life" (48). Consequently, one evening he finds himself wandering "eastward" where soon after he loses his "way in a labyrinth of grimy streets and black, grassless squares" (48).

Having descended into the demonic realm of London's East End, not as Lady Agatha's Christian knight, but as Lord Henry's quester in search of sensational adventures, Dorian, instead of seeking out the poor in the workhouses and hospitals, looks for beauty and pleasure and finds it in what he later describes as "an absurd little theatre, with great flaring gas-jets and gaudy play-bills" (48). "A hideous Jew," which he later characterizes as "such a monster," is the novel's counterpart to the demonic tempters of romance who seek to waylay the hero and divert him from his quest. And that Dorian's Jew, who entices him "with an air of gorgeous servility" (48) into the wretched theater, plays such a role is borne out by the fact that Sibyl Vane, the idyllically beautiful young actress Dorian discovers there, is, in the end, ironically, a temptress who draws our hero into the bourgeois morass of "real life" with its middle-class domesticities and philistine views and virtues.

Sibyl, despite her alluring profession, is a denizen of her demonic surroundings (the Wildean counterpart to the naturalistic novel's realistic settings), and in time, like Cinderella at the ball, she must return to her rags and ashes. Armed as he is with the twin charms of beauty and youth, Sibyl's hold over Dorian is temporary and ultimately serves but to promote his self-realization through the pursuit of beauty.

With the help of Lord Henry's timely disquisition on art and life designed to comfort Dorian on hearing of the actress's suicide, Dorian is able to accept Sibyl as "a wonderful tragic figure sent on to the world's stage to show the supreme reality of love" (105). For Dorian the whole episode has been, as he tells Lord Henry, "a marvelous experience. That is all. I wonder if life has still in store for me anything as marvelous" (103).

Marvelous, indeed, are to be his further adventures as he is led on (in Huysmansesque fashion)[15] to one form of beauty after another—exotic perfumes, strange and bizarre sorts of music, treasure troves of jewels, mysterious sins, and wild sensations—by his seemingly insatiable curiosity and desire for adventure. None, however, is more unexpected and grotesque than Dorian's final interview with Basil Hallward which ends with the murder of the painter. On this particular occasion, Basil has sought out Dorian in order to confront him with the ugly rumors centering about his name which have been circulating for some time throughout society. Desirous of being assured by Dorian that there is no truth in them, Basil presses his friend: "Deny them, Dorian, deny them! Can't you see what I am going through? My God! Don't tell me that you are bad, and corrupt, and shameful" (154). Enraged, Dorian escorts Basil to the attic schoolroom where after unveiling the portrait in all its hideous corruption, he fatally stabs him.

Basil's death at the hands of Dorian is, in a sense, a fitting climax to the relationship between the two men. For Basil's denial of his Charmides Self in Dorian has led not only to their estrangement, but also has effectually put an end to Basil's new artistic mode which, of course, culminated years earlier in his painting of Dorian's portrait. Under the dominance of Dorian's Charmides Self, Basil had developed his art in a new direction. "His personality," he once told Lord Henry,

> has suggested to me an entirely new manner in art, an entirely new mode of style. I see things differently, I think of them differently. I can now recreate life in a way that was hidden from me before. . . . Unconsciously he defines for me the lines of a fresh school, a school that is to have in it all the passion of the romantic spirit, all the perfection of the spirit that is Greek. (10)

That the ultimate expression of this new mode is the picture of Dorian is, of course, agreed by all. Yet Basil's response to his *chef-*

d'oeuvre is ambivalent. On completing it, he announces to the surprise of Lord Henry and Dorian that he intends not to exhibit it before the public, because, as he says, "I am afraid that I have shown in it the secret of my own soul" (5). Continuing, then, with a statement which seems to approve such an expression of the artist's self in his work, Basil explains to Lord Henry: "every portrait that is painted with feeling is a portrait of the artist, not the sitter" (5)—a view, one assumes, which is in keeping with his new artistic mode.

However, as the painter continues to talk, he appears to revert to old principles when he suddenly lashes out against those who "treat art as if it were meant to be a form of autobiography" (11). Making an assertion which is at odds with his earlier statement, Basil declares that "an artist should create beautiful things, but should put nothing of his own life into them. . . . We have lost the abstract sense of beauty. Some day I will show the world what it is; and for *that reason* the world shall never see my portrait of Dorian Gray" (11, emphasis added).

Although Basil's restatement of his reason for hiding the portrait is different in its emphasis from his initial statement, the reader is aware that the painter's resolve to keep the portrait from the prying eye of the public is motivated by personal rather than aesthetic considerations. In other words, Basil recognizes that in his portrait of Dorian, he has revealed his most carefully guarded secret, namely, his Charmides Self.

That what Lord Henry refers to as Basil's rather dull, conventional, intellectual self is but a mask for the Charmides Self is hinted at when, in introducing the reader to Basil, the narrator refers to the painter's "sudden disappearance some years ago," which had, at the time, caused considerable "public excitement, and [had given] rise to so many strange conjectures" (1). Moreover, Basil's initial conversation with Lord Henry about the identity of Dorian Gray reveals some curious facts, not the least of which is the painter's penchant for secrecy and mystery. "When I like people immensely," he explains, "I never tell their names to any one. It is like surrendering a part of them. I have grown to love secrecy." And as he goes on to remark, "when I leave town now I never tell my people where I am going. If I did, I would lose all my pleasure. It is a silly habit, I dare say, but somehow it seems to bring a great deal of romance into one's life" (4). One has the unmistakable feeling that the conventional, socially correct Basil is something of a "Bunburyist," one who, indeed, has something to hide, an aspect of himself which is deeply repressed.

However, as we come to know, this secret self suddenly has sur-

faced in the person of Dorian Gray, an occurrence that, at least initially, has had the effect of a traumatic shock on the artist. In
language highly suggestive of one's encounter with another aspect
of the self, Basil recalls for Lord Henry his first meeting with Dorian at Lady Brandon's "crush":

> I suddenly became conscious that some one was looking at me. I turned
> half-way round, and saw Dorian Gray for the first time. When our eyes
> met, I felt that I was growing pale. A curious sensation of terror came
> over me. I knew that I had come face to face with some one whose mere
> personality was so fascinating that, if I allowed it to do so, it would
> absorb my whole nature, my whole soul, my very art itself. (6)

So repressed has been his Charmides Self until the advent of Dorian in his life, that not even so astute and clever an observer of
character as Lord Henry has fathomed in this outwardly rather dull,
intellectual friend such another self. Having immediately recognized the portrait of Dorian Gray as a type of the Charmides Self—
"Why, my dear Basil, he is a Narcissus" (11)—Lord Henry is quite
surprised when Basil states: "I have put too much of myself into it"
(2–3).

Basil's continued resolve to hide his Charmides Self (even
though this strange cat is now, in a manner of speaking, out of the
bag) is motivated by the artist's realization that not only has the
influence of his Charmides Self been manifested in a new mode of
art, but also in his idolatrous worship of physical beauty centered
in Dorian, and in the painter's narcissistic self-love, projected in
terms of a homosexual passion for Dorian—behavior not to be tol-
erated either by his puritanical conscience or his Hebraic, paternal-
istic society.

Consequently, Basil persuades himself that what he really sees
and worships in Dorian is not the Charmides Self, but an ideal embodiment of beauty and goodness, a quintessential expression of the
highly acceptable Ruskinian philosophy of art. Having convinced
himself that the portrait is, indeed, a mirror image of the sitter's
innocence and purity, Basil announces to Dorian his plan to exhibit
the portrait in Paris. But by this time, the Charmides Self has taken
on the corrupt and demonic expression the puritanical conscience
habitually assigns it. Consequently, Basil could not have persisted
in the folly of perpetuating his illusion if Dorian had allowed him
to view it. As we know, Dorian does refuse his friend's request,
even though he suspects, as well he should, that an intimate link
exists between Basil's secret and his own.

Shunned by Dorian and unable to see his portrait, Basil becomes the hero's chief antagonist as he intensifies his moral crusade against his own and Dorian's Charmides Self which, as it rightly should, infuriates the youth and leads ultimately to the murder. Functioning in the end—to some extent at least—as a Fury harassing Dorian with moralistic preachments and dire warnings of impending doom, Basil is succeeded in his role by Jim Vane, Sibyl's vengeful brother, who after the artist's death, continues doggedly to haunt the hero's quest for sensations. Also an embodiment of Old Testament Law—the Hebraic code of "an eye for an eye"— Jim in his pursuit of Dorian, ironically, falls, himself, victim to a hunter's bullet.

Yet another example of Dorian's "charmed" life, Vane's fortuitous removal from the scene points up the fact that Dorian is, in the end, self-defeated, doomed by the enemy within, his own conscience. As his quest to become the "visible symbol" of a new hedonism draws to its close, Dorian, viewed from outside, appears to have attained his goal. Sinking deeply into old age, Lord Henry views his disciple as a miraculous being, who, having succeeded in his adventures, has returned with the talisman of perpetual youth and beauty with which he will bestow boons on his fellow beings. "Ah, Dorian, how happy you are!" he exclaims.

> What an exquisite life you have had! You have drunk deeply of everything. You have crushed the grapes against your palate. Nothing has been hidden from you. And it has all been to you no more than the sound of music. It has not marred you. You are still the same. (216)

And although Dorian protests he is not the same, Lord Henry persists: "yes, you are the same. I wonder what the rest of your life will be. Don't spoil it by renunciations. At present you are a perfect type" (216).

Having succeeded in making art of his life, Dorian is, in Lord Henry's opinion, what the world needs: "You are the type of what the age is searching for" (217). Expressing his admiration for his pupil in terms especially dear to his own heart, Lord Henry continues: "I am so glad that you have never done anything, never carved a statue, or painted a picture, or produced anything outside yourself. Life has been your art. You have set yourself to music. Your days are your sonnets" (217).

Unfortunately, since Dorian can never grow older, never, in other words, move beyond the youthful stage to the fully matured, passive, philosophical stage of the Charmides Self which his mentor has attained, he, ironically, cannot share Lord Henry's ultimate philosophical point of view, that of a contemplative observer of culture who lives in the light of Pater's memorable aesthetic put forward in his early essay on Wordsworth. Lord Henry has long since learned not only to "treat life in the spirit of art,"[16] but also to cultivate highly refined states of mental activity—Pater's "impassioned contemplation"[17]—as ends in themselves.

Vampirelike, he has lived life intensely but at a distance through Dorian whose active pursuit of experience has been a source of great interest and pleasure to him. For instance, confronted with the fact of Dorian's infatuation with Sibyl, Lord Henry had been able to contemplate the affair without "the slightest pang of annoyance or jealousy." Rather, as the narrator tells us,

> he was pleased by it. It made him [Dorian] a more interesting study. He had been always enthralled by the methods of natural science, but the ordinary subject-matter of that science had seemed to him trivial and of no import. And so he had begun by vivisecting himself, as he had ended by vivisecting others. (56)

Unable to mature into the passive philosophical observer of life, Dorian is overwhelmed at last by *ennui* as his adventures begin to cloy. Above all, he begins to moralize and, worse still, to talk about being good. And although Lord Henry begs him not to spoil it all "by renunciations" (216), his influence with Dorian is at an end. Now at the mercy of his conscience, the protagonist in the final phase of the novel is close to succumbing to the enemy, going so far as to consider his release of the country maid, Hetty, as an act of self-abnegation.[18] Of course, Lord Henry sees this act for what it really is—"I should think the novelty of the emotion must have given you a thrill of real pleasure"—but Dorian persists in his illusion:

> "Harry, you are horrible! You mustn't say these dreadful things. Hetty's heart is not broken. Of course she cried, and all that. But there is no disgrace upon her. She can live, like Perdita, in her garden of mint and marigolds." (210)

Increasingly haunted by a sense of doom, on the last evening of his life, Dorian returns home, his mind the prey of truly Hebraic thoughts: "There was purification in punishment," he mused to himself. "Not 'Forgive us our sins,' but 'Smite us for iniquities,' should be the prayer of man to a most just God" (220). Seeking some sign that his resolution to be good has registered its effect on his portrait, Dorian climbs the steps to the attic schoolroom where, to his dismay, he looks upon an even more corrupted image than before.

In what proves to be a final and climactic confrontation between protagonist and antagonist, Dorian, gazing with loathing on the conscience-corrupted portrait, now, in a supreme moment of illumination, sees it for what it really is: conscience. "It had been like conscience to him. Yes, it had been conscience." Convulsed with rage toward what is now clearly seen to be his tormentor, Dorian resolves to destroy it.

> He looked round, and saw the knife that had stabbed Basil Hallward. He had cleaned it many times, till there was no stain left upon it. It was bright, and glistened. As it had killed the painter, so it would kill *the painter's work, and all that that meant*. It would kill the past, and when that was dead he would be free. It would kill this monstrous soul-life, and, without its hideous warnings, he would be at peace. He seized the thing, and stabbed the picture with it. (223, emphasis added)

Having destroyed conscience—the enemy within—Dorian through death is apotheosized in the redeemed portrait as the "visible symbol" of a new hedonism—an entirely appropriate conclusion to a hedonist romancer's quest.

That Wilde in seeking to blunt what Isobel Murray characterizes as the "hysterical" criticism of the first version of his novel[19] which had appeared in the pages of *Lippincott's Monthly Magazine* in 1890, sought to cast his conclusion in a morally acceptable light, may be inferred from the fact that he insisted to the newspapers that his novel, indeed, had what he called a "terrible moral": "All excess," he wrote in a letter to the *St. James Gazette*, "as well as all renunciation, brings its own punishment." Basil, he observed, is punished for "worshipping physical beauty far too much"; Dorian is punished for "having led a life of mere sensation and pleasure"; and Lord Henry is punished for being "merely the spectator of life."[20] Yet the resolution of the plot, as I read it, which belies this stated view, is more in keeping with Wilde's behavior toward earlier embodiments of the Charmides Self. For instance, as one will recall, he mitigated the rather harsh punishment the gods had meted out to Charmides; and in his short story, "Lord Arthur Savile's Crime," he had entirely absolved his handsome young hero who, having murdered the fat, ugly little cheiromantist Septimus Podgers, marries Sybil and flies to an idyllic country house where he leads an untroubled, guilt-free life of pagan bliss. "For them," the narrator tells us, "romance was not killed by reality. They always felt young."

Was the author of *Dorian Gray*, increasingly uneasy about the way in which his heroes invariably were extricated from their sinful pasts, and facing an increasingly hostile press and public, willing to allow romance to be killed by reality—a principle he habitually associated with the Hebraic spirit which plagued Victorian England and which begat the naturalistic novel? Perhaps so. But, in the spirit of romance, I prefer to believe that, in the end, an indulgent, albeit ironic Oscar, was moved to compose a denouement which would enable us (as well as himself) to have it both ways.

NOTES

1. I Samuel 14: 24, 27, 43, King James Bible.

2. *The Renaissance*, ed. Donald Hill (Berkeley: University of California Press, 1980), 177.

3. Oscar Wilde, *Poems and Poems in Prose*, vol. 1, ed. Bobby Fong and Karl Beckson, *Complete Works of Oscar Wilde*, ed. Russell Jackson and Ian Small (Oxford: Oxford University Press, 2000), 157, ll. 12–14. All further references to the poetry are to this edition and cited in the text.

4. I use the phrase "Hebraic spirit" and the term "Hebraism" throughout as Matthew Arnold defined them in his essay, "Hebraism and Hellenism" in his *Culture and Anarchy*. Wilde was entirely familiar with Arnold's use of these terms.

5. Richard Ellmann in "Overtures to *Salome*" in *Oscar Wilde: A Collection of Critical Essays*, ed. by Ellmann (Englewood Cliffs, N.J.: Prentice-Hall, 1969), 86, discusses Wilde's struggle in terms of Pater vs. Ruskin: "they came to stand heraldically, burning unicorn and uninflamed satyr, in front of two portals of his mental theatre. He sometimes allowed them to battle, at other times tried to reconcile them." Jan B. Gordon sees it in terms of Arnold's Hebraism and Hellenism in "Hebraism and Hellenism, and *The Picture of Dorian Gray*," *Victorian Newsletter*, no. 33 (spring 1968), 36–38.

6. Hesketh Pearson, *Oscar Wilde* (New York and London: Harper, 1946), 34.

7. Wilde's new Helen was the celebrated actress Lillie Langtry.

8. *The Picture of Dorian Gray*, The World's Classics ed., ed. Isobel Murray (Oxford and New York: Oxford University Press, 1981), 15. All further references to the novel are to this edition and cited in the text.

9. As Wilde once admitted, "it [that strange coloured book of mine] contains much of me in it. Basil Hallward is what I think I am: Lord Henry what the world thinks me: Dorian what I would like to be—in other ages, perhaps." *The Letters of Oscar Wilde*, ed. Rupert Hart-Davis (New York: Harcourt, Brace & World, 1962), 352.

10. Kiely's remarks throughout his introduction to *The Romantic Novel in England* (Cambridge: Harvard University Press, 1972), in particular, those concerning the relationship of the romance tradition to the English romantic novel are applicable to much that Wilde is doing in *Dorian Gray*.

11. "The Decay of Lying," in *Oscar Wilde, Selected Writings*, ed. Richard Ellmann (London: Oxford University Press, 1961), 8.

12. *Selected Writings*, 10–11.

13. *The Art of Oscar Wilde* (Princeton: Princeton University Press, 1967), 33–34.

14. Ellmann in "Overtures" (88), believes the "curious revival" of puritanism to have been associated in Wilde's mind with Ruskin.

15. These bizarre adventures are clearly the result of Dorian's fascinated reading of "the yellow book that Lord Henry had sent him," (125) usually assumed by readers to be J.-K. Huysmans's notorious novel, *A Rebours*.

16. "Wordsworth" in *Selected Writings of Walter Pater*, ed. Harold Bloom (New York: New American Library, 1974), 139.

17. Ibid., 137.

18. If it is possible to read Wilde's novel in terms of the internalized quest which critics have associated with such works of the High Romantics as Blake's *Jerusalem* and Wordsworth's *The Prelude*, Dorian's adventures as Charmides Self represent what Harold Bloom calls Prometheus (i.e., the first phase of the total quest which concerns, in part, in Bloom's words, "the libido's struggle against repressiveness." Although Dorian does, especially in his relations with Hetty, make an effort toward transcending or annihilating Selfhood (Blake's Spectre of Urthona), he does not make a serious and sustained effort toward the goal of the second phase or "the Real Man." See Bloom, "The Internalization of Quest Romance," in *The Ringers in the Tower* (Chicago: University of Chicago Press, 1971), 21–22.

19. Introduction to *The Picture of Dorian Gray*, vii.

20. Letter to the editor of the *St. James Gazette*, 26 June 1890 in *Letters of Oscar Wilde*, 258.

The New Woman and the Female Detective: Grant Allen's *Miss Cayley's Adventures* (1899)

JOSEPH A. KESTNER

"I knew a woman who did," said I; "and this is her story."

PERHAPS NO NOVEL PUBLISHED IN THE VICTORIAN PERIOD HAS SO memorable or so notorious an epigraph as this one from Grant Allen's famous New Woman novel *The Woman Who Did*, published in 1895.

Already known as a prolific writer about science, sociology, and travel (Cominos, 21, 231), Grant Allen (1848–1899) was to write the definitive New Woman novel about a daring individual, Herminia Barton, a Girton College graduate who has a love affair with a bohemian artist, Alan Merrick, and bears a bastard daughter, Dolores, who rejects her mother's unconventional ways; Herminia takes prussic acid in an act of defiant suicide. Despite the achievements of George Gissing's *The Odd Women* (1893) and Thomas Hardy's *Jude the Obscure* (also 1895) which exhibit dimensions of the New Woman, it is Grant Allen's *The Woman Who Did* which remains distinctive in the subgenre of New Woman fiction.

Critical focus on *The Woman Who Did* is understandable, and yet it has led to the neglect of Allen's achievements in depicting New Women in other novels. In particular, Grant Allen is justly known for his two texts which involve detection by women, written after *The Woman Who Did: Miss Cayley's Adventures*, twelve stories serialized in the *Strand Magazine* from March 1898 through February 1899 and published as a volume in 1899, and *Hilda Wade*, serialized in the *Strand* as well and published in 1900, with its final chapter written by Arthur Conan Doyle, who promised the dying Allen, his friend, he would complete the work. (On the individual installments, see Beare, 4–6.) Both works focus on independent women who engage in detection amid their professional responsibilities, Lois Cayley as journalist and typist and Hilda Wade as a nurse. Although the merits of both texts are strong, this essay will discuss *Miss Cayley's Adventures* because of the diversity of the occupations held by its protagonist and its conflation of several subgenres in its development.

By the time Grant Allen produced *Miss Cayley's Adventures*, he had already achieved distinction in the short story involving criminous activity, with such tales as "The Great Ruby Robbery" (*Strand*, October 1892) and "The Conscientious Burglar" (*Strand*, June 1892). In particular, Lois Cayley, who engages in sporadic amateur but clever detection in the stories, is part of a focus by writers on the female detective in the years preceding, noteworthy in such works as W. S. Hayward's *Revelations of a Lady Detective* (1864), Andrew Forrester Jr.'s *The Female Detective* (1864), Catherine Louisa Pirkis's *The Experiences of Loveday Brooke, Lady Detective* (1894), and George R. Sims's *Dorcas Dene, Detective: Her Adventures* (1897). An even earlier amateur detective, a seamstress, is found in Wilkie Collins's "The Diary of Anne Rodway" (1856). Of course the emergence of Sherlock Holmes by Arthur Conan Doyle in the 1880s catalyzed the genre.

It is Allen's distinct achievement to weld the New Woman novel to the detective narrative in a work such as *Miss Cayley's Adventures*. This amalgamation is signaled in the text by references to George R. Sims (269) and to Eliza Lynn Linton (113). Linton was the writer of the most famous denunciations of the New Woman in essays such as "The Wild Women as Social Insurgents" and "The Partisans of the Wild Women," published in *The Nineteenth Century* in 1891 and 1892 respectively. When the elderly Lady Georgina Fawley exclaims "I don't know what girls are coming to nowadays," Lois Cayley replies "Ask Mrs. Lynn-Linton [*sic*]. . . . She is a recognised authority on the subject" (113). Many critics, including Cunningham, Ledger, and Showalter, have discussed the emergence of the New Woman during the latter part of the nineteenth century in England, due to such factors as the increased opportunities for education for women (as with the founding of Girton College, Cambridge, in 1869), the various Married Women's Property Acts (1870, 1882, 1884), the repeal of the Contagious Diseases Acts (1886), the circulation of information about birth control, and the formation of women's organizations such as the Women's Trade Union League in 1890 or the National Union of Women's Suffrage Societies in 1897. (On the changing status of women during the nineteenth century, see the anthologies of documents edited by

Bauer, Murray, Pike, and Read.) In addition, the perfection of the typewriter around 1867, a machine crucial to *Miss Cayley's Adventures*, opened an opportunity for women to gain employment during the latter part of the century.

Allen's text engages many of the essays which debated the New Woman during the era. There is little doubt, furthermore, that interest in female detection was reignited during the 1890s by the failure of males in the detective and police forces to solve the Jack the Ripper murders of 1888. Allen had, furthermore, made his mark in the literature of crime with his renowned series of tales, *An African Millionaire* of 1897, about a rogue swindler, a prototype of several men who appear in *Miss Cayley's Adventures*.

There is one additional factor crucial to assessing Grant Allen's *Miss Cayley's Adventures*. While Lois Cayley is an amateur detective/sleuth, such behavior marks her as independent indeed, since in fact no woman was officially part of the Criminal Investigation Department (C.I.D.) until 1922 (Rawlings, 16, 151). The representation of a woman engaging in detection during the nineteenth century, therefore, constituted a profound fantasy of female empowerment. By this strategy, a woman was conceived as not only *subject* to the law but as an *enforcer* of the law. This linkage of New Woman novel with the detective novel reveals Allen's genuine ideological agenda. Grant Allen's engagement in *Miss Cayley's Adventures* with New Woman discourses begins with its title, with the stress on "adventures," for the word has two implications in the series of stories: first, the experiences of the narrator, Lois Cayley; and second, the suggestion that "adventures" implies an "adventurer" or in this specific instance, an "adventuress," a word which carries considerable ambiguity. Lois tells her friend Elsie Petheridge, "I am going out, simply in search of adventure" (5). However, in the second tale "The Supercilious Attache," in which Lois Cayley meets Harold Tillington, the nephew of the elderly Lady Georgina Fawley, to whom she is a companion, the old woman gives the word "adventures" a new inflection: "What I'm always afraid of is that some fascinating adventuress will try to marry him out of hand" she declares; Lois responds: "I don't think Mr. Tillington is quite the sort that falls a prey to adventuresses" (48). "That evening Lady Georgina managed to blurt out more malicious things than ever about the ways of adventuresses, and the duty of relations in saving young men from the clever clutches of designing creatures" (52–53).

Instead of repudiating the slur, Lois Cayley tells Harold Tillington her reason for leaving his aunt: "The world is all before me where to choose. I am an adventuress, . . . and I am in quest of adventures" (55). By the end of the second story, therefore, Grant Allen has inflected the word both in its negative aspect and in its newer application to the independence of the New Woman. When Harold dismisses his aunt's attitude, Lois refuses to see him: "I cannot—I am a penniless girl—an adventuress" (56). Even after Lois rescues Harold from a dangerous mountaineering accident in "The Impromptu Mountaineer," the fifth tale, she refuses to marry him while he is rich, although she loves him: "We are still ourselves; you rich, I a penniless adventuress" (145).

By the time she makes that statement, however, Lois has won a bicycle race and become a commission agent for an American inventor's bicycle. Her independence is established as an adventuress in the positive sense by this demonstration of the economic freedom of the New Woman. In the seventh tale, "The Urbane Old Gentleman," Lois Cayley re-encounters Lady Georgina, who informs her that Harold has encountered an "adventuress" (171). The old woman is amazed when Lois Cayley states that she herself is that woman (173). At this point, Lois has formed a typewriting service in Florence. Thus, throughout the text, the New Woman as "adventuress" is addressed.

Allen confronts the attitude of those opposed to the New Woman that she is nothing but an adventuress, a common accusation among essayists of the period. Specifically, however, amid writers who deployed such charges was Eliza Lynn Linton, referred to by name in *Miss Cayley's Adventures*. Linton, who died in 1898, was of considerable interest to supporters of the New Woman because she was so outspoken an opponent. Her name was prominent at the time of Allen's text not only because of her death but also because her memoir *My Literary Life* had been published posthumously in 1899. In debating the label "adventuress," Allen appears to repudiate a specific essay by Linton, "The Wild Women as Social Insurgents," which she published in October 1891 in *The Nineteenth Century.* Linton argues that the New Woman "does all manner of things which she thinks bestow on her the power, together with the privileges, of a man" (597).

Linton then writes: "About these Wild Women is always an unpleasant suggestion of the adventuress. Whatever their natural place and lineage, they are of the same family as those hotel heroines who forget to lock the chamber door. . . . Under the new *regime* blots do not count for so much" (601). Allen would expect his readers to know this specific passage from Linton, which is the clearest indictment of the New Woman as sexually transgressive. Although Lois

Cayley is decidedly not transgressive as is Herminia Barton in *The Woman Who Did*, her economic independence, her refusal to marry Harold Tillington for money, and her economic success on the Continent leave her open to Linton's charge, so far as opponents of the New Woman are concerned.

In fact, in the same essay, Linton observes: "With other queer inversions the frantic desire of making money has invaded the whole class of Wild Women; and it does not mitigate their desire that, as things are, they have enough for all reasonable wants" (599). After graduating from Girton, Lois refuses to be a teacher or a milliner, although she states: "As a milliner's girl; why not? 'Tis an honest calling. Earls' daughters do it now" (3), an observation directly repudiating Linton, who states: "Women who, a few years ago, would not have shaken hands with a dressmaker . . . now open shops and set up in business on their own account" (599). The fact that Lois Cayley "sets up in business" as a typist in Florence and continues that business for over a year is Allen's way of answering Linton, who herself ignores the economic imperatives which compelled women to work, however "unladylike" it might be.

Many aspects of Lois Cayley's character seem created to challenge the predispositions of opponents of the New Woman. As a "Girton girl," Lois is suspect. For instance, S. P. White, in *Blackwood's*, declares in "Modern Mannish Maidens": "The Girton girl emulates the Oxonian in the liberty accorded to her at her collegiate establishment. . . . What means this modern craze for mannish sports and mannish ways?" (252–53). George J. Romanes, writing in 1887, remarks about Girton: "When I was at Cambridge, the then newly established foundations of Girton and Newnham were to nearly all of us matters of amusement. But we have lived to alter our views" (666).

Likewise, Lois Cayley's physical strength is another challenge to opponents of the New Woman. She tells Harold Tillington: "I am a fairly good climber. . . . You see, at Cambridge, I went on the river a great deal—I canoed and sculled; then, besides, I've done a lot of bicycling," at which Harold labels her "a wholesome athletic English girl!" (50). Cyrus W. Hitchcock, the American inventor of the four-speed bicycle she will market, is impressed by her athleticism. Cayley observes: "I like to intersperse culture and athletics. I know something about athletics, and hope in time to acquire a taste for culture. 'T is expected of a Girton girl, though my own accomplishments run rather towards rowing, punting, and bicycling" (78). In the course of the stories, Cayley will demonstrate her ability at mountaineering, hunting, and above all cycling, especially in the episode of "The Inquisitive American" when she wins a race in Germany against all male opponents when she rides Hitchcock's four-speed bicycle.

The stress on cycling throughout *Miss Cayley's Adventures* is intended as a refutation of the opponents of the New Woman. Denouncing "mannish maidens," S. P. White in 1890 remarks: "What, now, shall be said of the modern popular mode of locomotion, at once a recreation and convenience to those who can afford no better—cycling? We will dismiss the bicycle from consideration, as, so far, the most enterprising of females has abstained for obvious reasons from adventuring herself thereon; though what the future may have in store in this way it is hard to say" (255). In her essay "Why Women are Ceasing to Marry" published in the same year as *Miss Cayley's Adventures* Ella Hepworth Dixon notes "the amazing changes in the social life of women. . . . Someone has boldly laid it down that it is the bicycle which has finally emancipated women, but it is certain that there are other factors besides the useful and agreeable wheel" (86).

In 1894, M. Eastwood in the essay "The New Woman in Fiction and in Fact" had noted that detractors of the New Woman had pointed to "the audacious young person who, seated astride a bicycle . . . shoots past them on the public road," but the writer continues that "if she assumes certain articles of masculine garb on occasion, it is solely on account of their superior utility; if she rides out on a bicycle it is for the purpose of strengthening her muscles and expanding her lungs for the great work she has before her": "The New Woman of today will be the woman of the future" (91). Allen's stress on bicycling in the stories "The Inquisitive American" and "The Amateur Commission Agent" emphasizes Lois Cayley's New Woman athleticism. In addition, she proves adept at climbing in the episode of "The Impromptu Mountaineer."

Grant Allen addresses another charge against the New Woman, noted in Eliza Lynn Linton's essay "The Partisans of the Wild Women" of 1892, that the New Woman travels brazenly abroad: "We will give to these restless wild creatures all the honour to which they are entitled for their mischievous interference in politics, their useless tramps abroad—which are only self-advertisements and which do not add a line to our knowledge of men or countries" (462). In *Miss Cayley's Adventures*, the protagonist travels to Germany, Italy, Egypt, India, Asia, and across Canada. In the initial tale, "The Cantankerous Old Lady," Lois Cayley overhears Lady Georgina Fawley lamenting the lack of a companion to travel abroad with her; Lois Cayley offers to do so, which initiates her subsequent "adventures."

During her global travels, Cayley has various occupations: commission agent for Hitchcock's bicycle, typist, and journalist. Cayley leaves Lady Georgina and travels alone to Germany in the third tale, "The Inquisitive American." Although Elsie Petheridge joins her in Italy, she leaves Lois Cayley at the beginning of the tenth tale, "The Cross-Eyed Q.C." Cayley then travels through Asia and Canada alone to return to England and aid Harold Tillington in repudiating accusations he is a forger. This stress on global travel marks Lois Cayley's "adventures" as entirely appropriate for a Girton girl/New Woman. In all, she remains away from England, as noted in the eleventh story "The Oriental Attendant," for three years (297). Lois Cayley labels her book her "confiding memoirs" (261), which appear to validate her status as an independent woman, at least until her marriage to Tillington at the book's conclusion. At the same time, the label of "confiding memoirs" shields the book from the "self-advertisement" indicted by Linton.

Of the twelve stories in *Miss Cayley's Adventures*, seven have a criminous or detectival element, but the point of Allen's text is to integrate all twelve tales on the basis of Lois Cayley's New Woman enterprise, ingenuity, and intelligence, whether or not these are directed at solving or preventing crime. In effect, the text subsumes the detectival genre within the New Woman narrative, a principal component of its distinction. This dual nature of the text is stressed in the first narrative, "The Cantankerous Old Lady," which appeared in March, 1898, in the *Strand*.

The beginning of the story stresses its New Woman agenda, the conclusion its detective dimension. Cayley admits that it was her mother's imprudent remarriage which drove her to be the woman she is, since she was given barely enough money to study at Girton by the stepfather. After her graduation, when her friend Elsie Petheridge suggests she teach, Cayley responds: "Did you say *teach?* . . . No, Elsie, I do *not* propose to teach" (2). In the Long Walk at Kensington Gardens, Cayley overhears Lady Georgina Fawley lamenting her need of a companion. She tells the old woman she is "a Girton girl," to which the woman replies: "What are girls coming to, I wonder? Girton, you say; Girton!" (12).

Despite this reservation, Cayley travels to the Continent with the old lady. In the train, Cayley becomes suspicious of a glib man in the compartment, who, she correctly surmises, plans to steal Lady Georgina's jewel case. She foils him by removing the steel box with the jewels from the case. It will evolve that the man, pretending to be a Count, is in reality a corrupt butler/valet named Higginson, in the service of Lady Georgina's brother Marmaduke Ashurst. This initial story links detection with the New Woman, demonstrating that a Girton girl is capable of perceptive action in and out of the university. Lady Georgina praises Cayley's "courage and promptitude" (31). The narrative also introduces the first of a string of deceiving, scheming males.

In the second story, published the following month, "The Supercilious Attache," Cayley is in Schlangenbad, Germany. This locale allows Grant Allen the opportunity to express typical later nineteenth-century contempt about Germans via the words of Lady Georgina:

> They're bursting with self-satisfaction—have such an exaggerated belief in their "land" and their "folk." And when they come to England, they do nothing but find fault with us. . . . Nasty pigs of Germans! The very sight of them sickens me. . . . They all learn English nowadays; it helps them in trade—that's why they're driving us out of all the markets. . . . They're a set of barbarians. (34)

Grant Allen's desire to contextualize the New Woman and detectival components of his text is exhibited here, as suspicions about German hegemony became very prominent in Britain during the period.

While at the spa, "a loose-limbed, languid-looking young man, with large, dreamy eyes," appears to be following Cayley and the old lady. Cayley especially notes his "superficial air of superciliousness" (36). When she describes the man's "large, poetical eye; an artistic moustache—just a trifle Oriental-looking" (40), she learns this is Lady Georgina's nephew Harold Tillington, an attache in Rome. Tillington acts the role of a supercilious man, but Cayley is impressed with his knowledge of Europe and his "epigrammatic wit, curt, keen, and pointed" (42). When he asks if she is "medieval or modern," Cayley responds that she is modern; he is from Oxford, she from Cambridge. "Thenceforth we were friends—two 'Varsity men,' he said. And indeed it does make a queer sort of link—a freemasonry to which even women are now admitted" (46), she observes.

Cayley learns that Tillington will inherit all his uncle Marmaduke Ashurst's money. In one of their discussions about marriage, Tillington observes that "a man ought to wish the woman he loves to be a free agent, his equal in point of action" (52). When he expresses his love, Lois Cayley rejects him, fearing to be construed

an adventuress merely after his inheritance. She tells his aunt, Lady
Georgina: "I am a lady by birth and education; I am an officer's
daughter; but I am not what society calls a 'good match' for Mr.
Tillington" (58). While not wishing to be construed an adventuress,
Cayley also desires independence: "I must work out my life in my
own way. I have started to work it out, and I won't be turned aside
just here on the threshold" she advises Lady Georgina (61). She
records: "Next morning I set out by myself. . . . I went forth into
the world to live my own life, partly because it was just then so
fashionable, but mainly because fate had denied me the chance of
living anybody else's" (61). "The Supercilious Attache," albeit
contains no overt detection, expands Grant Allen's evaluation of
the beliefs of the New Woman.

At the beginning of the third narrative, "The Inquisitive American," Cayley admits that parting from Tillington "left a scar . . .
but as I am not a professional sentimentalist, I will not trouble you
here with details of the symptoms" (62). If German competition is
a concern in the previous story, here it is the Americans and their
competitive spirit that are displayed in the person of Cyrus W.
Hitchcock, who has invented a four-speed bicycle that easily as-
cends hills. Declaring "an adventuress I would be; for I loved adventure" (63), Cayley states her manifesto, contrasting herself with
unmarried German women:

> I prefer to take life in a spirit of pure enquiry. I put on my hat; I saunter
> where I choose, so far as circumstances permit; and I wait to see what
> chance will bring me. My ideal is breeziness. . . . I prefer to grow up-
> wards; the frau grows sideways. . . . Adventures are to the adventurous.
> They abound on every side; but only the chosen few have the courage
> to embrace them. And they will not come to you: you must go out to
> seek them. Then they meet you half way, and rush into your arms, for
> they know their true lovers. (64, 71)

Lois Cayley has the opportunity to demonstrate this credo when
Hitchcock asks her to ride his bicycle in a contest with Germans,
who "were all men, of course" (79). When a German objects to her
competing, Cayley whips out a copy of a law which permits women
to race. Seizing the chance, Cayley competes, despite "a look of
unchivalrous dislike, such as only your sentimental German can
cast at a woman" (86). Cayley wins the race, receiving fifty pounds
from Hitchcock: "I was now a woman of means" (88). Particularly
significant in this story, beyond its cross-cultural comparison of
America, England, and Germany, are the illustrations by Gordon

Browne, some of which (66, 67, 69, 82, 86, 87), showing Cayley on bicycles competing with men and confronting German officers, underscore the agendas of the New Woman.

The American inventor Hitchcock is so impressed with Lois Cayley that he makes her his commission agent for the four-speed bicycle on the Continent. Cayley accepts his offer, "for I beheld vistas" (93). Her eagerness to make money from an American entrepreneur runs counter to the position of the detractors of the New Woman. Cayley, however, rejects Hitchcock's offer of marriage. "I set out on my wanderings . . . to go round the world on my own account" (97), recognizing "the business half of me" (99). Joined by her friend Elsie Petheridge, Cayley encounters a Mrs. Evelegh, an Englishwoman under the care of a faith healer, one Dr. Fortescue-Langley, who supposedly treats her "psychically" (107). This man dupes Mrs. Evelegh by having her wear an Indian bracelet which turns dark when her "inner self" (107) is disturbed. From her experience "in the laboratory at college" (107), Lois Cayley discovers that the maid brings the woman an india-rubber hot water bottle, the material of which contains sulfur; the rubber discolors the silver bangle.

It evolves that this man is the rogue, the Count, who had tried to steal Lady Georgina's jewels in the first tale. Cayley confronts him and tears off his fake moustache, revealing Higginson, Marmaduke Ashurst's valet/courier, who retreats confronted by the New Woman/detective. Cayley is enabled in her detection because of her education at Girton. Earlier in the same story she had encountered male trickery in the persons of two German students, Ludwig and Heinrich, who bought bicycles directly from Hitchcock to avoid paying Lois Cayley's commission, which Hitchcock pays her anyway. Yet in showing the deceit of both English and German men, the narrative reveals that the New Woman must be enterprising in whatever cultural situation she encounters.

In the fifth story, "The Impromptu Mountaineer," published in July 1898, Elsie and Lois, while on vacation, are visited by Harold Tillington, who professes his love for Lois. She nevertheless again refuses to marry him because of his potential inheritance, despite the fact she admits she loves him. She explains:

Well, because I am modern . . . I can answer you No. I can even now refuse you. . . . But *I* am modern, and I see things differently. . . . We are still ourselves; you rich, I a penniless adventuress. . . . I am a modern woman, and what I say I mean. I will renew my promise. If ever you are poor and friendless, come to me; I am yours. (144–45)

This refusal is made particularly complicated because in the course of this story, Lois Cayley rescues Harold Tillington when he falls over a precipice in the mountains.

In tracing Tillington's footsteps in order to rescue him, Lois exhibits the detectival ability to follow tracks: "the emergency seemed somehow to teach me something of the instinctive lore of hunters and savages" (133). Noting that "women are almost always brave in great emergencies" (139), Lois manages to haul Tillington up from the place of his fall. Her strength comes from her rowing at Girton, she observes (140). As in the previous story, the illustrations, especially one of Cayley descending the slope (138) and one of Harold Tillington falling (142), visualize the New Woman ideology of the text. Instead of the male rescuing the imperiled or endangered woman à la St. George, so common in the Victorian construction of genders, Grant Allen depicts the rescue of a distressed man by a strong, resourceful woman.

This enterprise is furthermore part of Lois Cayley's ability to conduct business, which proves distressing to her own aunt, who writes "to expostulate with me on my 'unladylike' conduct in becoming a bicycle commission agent" (124). Even Lady Georgina defends Lois Cayley being in business:

> What does the woman mean? Has she got no gumption? It's "ladylike," I suppose, to be a companion, or a governess, or a music-teacher, or something else in the black-thread-glove way, in London; but not to sell bicycles for a good round commission. My dear, between you and me, I don't see it. (124)

Fortified in her beliefs about economic independence, Cayley refuses to be betrothed to Tillington, despite having rescued him. Such repudiation of the romance plot is striking in this tale.

The next story, "The Urbane Old Gentleman," finds Lois Cayley in Florence, where she sets up a typewriting service with her friend Elsie. One of her clients is Marmaduke Ashurst, Lady Georgina's brother. Lois Cayley reasserts her decision not to marry Harold if he has money. However, she consents to type Ashurst's will. When Frederic Higginson, the rogue who had impersonated both a Count and a faith healer, turns up to retrieve the will for Ashurst, who has re-employed him, Cayley refuses to yield it, delivering it herself to Ashurst. Higginson had defamed without naming her to Ashurst as an "adventuress" (171), and Cayley readily admits to Ashurst she is the woman so labeled.

Ashurst has a bizarre philosophy of life which aligns religion, economics, and imperialism, showing male folly and ignorance, which Lois Cayley perceives and circumvents. "My fairy godmother's name was really Enterprise" (154) Cayley records. One illustration (160) by Gordon Browne shows Cayley at the typewriter as Ashurst sits in the client's chair, another example of the illustrations by Browne providing an ideological commentary on the narrative.

After Elsie and Lois have spent about a year in Florence in business, they go to Egypt in the episode of "The Unobtrusive Oasis." Lois Cayley has been hired by Elworthy, millionaire editor of the *Daily Telephone*, to be a roving reporter, sending "three descriptive articles a week" (181) to the newspaper. Aboard ship, the two women meet an Irish doctor, Macloghlen. Once arrived in Egypt, the three decide to visit an oasis, which requires a long camel ride. In the town, a woman whispers to them that she was captured after the fall of Khartoum (185) and sold to an Arab, whose children she has borne. Lois and the doctor contrive to effect her escape. Lois Cayley defends the right of the woman to have her children with her, despite reservations by Macloghlen. Her assertive feminism overcomes his hard-line masculine attitude that children should remain with their father.

Macloghlen nevertheless exhibits "the reckless and good-humored courage of the untamed Celt" (204) when confronted by hostile Arabs. Grant Allen had argued in his 1880 essay "Are We Englishmen?" for the *Fortnightly Review* that Celts, not Anglo-Saxons, have been the true colonizers in the Empire and the key figures in the administration of India. "The Unobtrusive Oasis" demonstrates Celtic and feminine enterprise, noting "that the English were now in practical occupation of Egypt" (204). Grant Allen shows one Englishwoman rescuing and defending another, an incident repudiating arguments about "the shrieking sisterhood" of women, as expressed for instance in the essay "Modern Man-Haters" in *The Saturday Review* (528) in 1871.

In "The Pea-Green Patrician," Elsie and Lois voyage to India via the Red Sea. On ship they encounter Lord Albert Southminster, another nephew of Lady Georgina's and hence a cousin to Harold Tillington. Southminster's courier and assistant is the rogue Frederic Higginson from previous stories. Lois Cayley spurns Southminster as a cynical clubman, declaring "He isn't a man; he's a lump of putty!" (219). Southminster admits he inhabits music halls, attends horse auctions at Tattersall's, and courts music hall performers. He tells Lois, "As a rule I don't think much of women" (229). Nevertheless, he proposes to her, claiming he rather than the other nephew Harold Tillington will inherit Marmaduke Ashurst's money. Lois rejects him, denouncing his "insulting proposal" (231) and "degrading offer" (232). The narrative presents yet another undesirable Englishman, a telling contrast with the refined, Oxford-educated Indian of the next story.

In "The Magnificent Maharajah" Lois Cayley arrives in Bombay as a successful special correspondent, where she is met by the Maharajah of Moozuffernuggar. The narrative is explicit in its critique of English racist attitudes. The captain of the ship receives the man "with true British contempt for the inferior black man" (235). Lois is impressed by the man, although she notices the incongruity of his European dress with an Indian turban. The Indian comments:

> You treat a native gentleman, I see, like a human being. I hope you will not stop long enough in our country to get over that stage—as happens to most of your countrymen and countrywomen. In England, a man like myself is an Indian prince; in India, to ninety-nine out of a hundred Europeans, he is just "a damned nigger." (240)

Lord Southminster, who has trailed Cayley to India, calls the Maharajah "a niggah . . . behaving for all the world as if he were a gentleman; it's reahlly too ridiculous" (241–42). Cayley counters by noting that the man's "ancestors were princes while ours were dressed in woad and oak-leaves, but you were right about one thing; *he* behaves—like a gentleman" (242). She concludes Southminster is "nothing more than a born bounder" (24).

In this episode, Lois Cayley goes on a tiger hunt, during which she rides an elephant and kills the tiger accidentally, drawing much acclaim. The Maharajah states he "could never have believed a woman could show such nerve and coolness" (257). "I dared not confess the truth—that I never fired at all" (261) Cayley admits in the text. This episode appears to be another charge against Eliza Lynn Linton, who in "The Wild Women as Social Insurgents" had declared:

> Free-traders in all that relates to sex, the Wild Women allow men no monopoly in sports, in games, in responsibilities. Beginning by 'walking with the guns,' they end by shooting with them; and some have made the moor a good training-ground for the jungle. (597)

The tiger shoot seems deliberately included to comment on Linton's assertion.

The final three tales of *Miss Cayley's Adventures* concentrate on a single sequence of events, involving Lois Cayley's attempts to clear Harold Tillington of charges of forgery brought by his cousin Lord Albert Southminster, who contends that Harold forged the will of their uncle Marmaduke Ashurst, whose death had been recorded at the conclusion of the previous story. This is the will that Lois Cayley typed at Florence in the sixth tale of the series. In these three tales, Lois exhibits all her amateur detection skills. It is quite possible that Grant Allen echoes the concluding trial scenes involving the titular character in Elizabeth Gaskell's *Mary Barton* (1848), who races to give testimony to save her lover. A reference to the Jubilee dates the trial to 1897. Lois Cayley travels alone through Asia and Canada to return to London.

In the tenth story, "The Cross-Eyed Q.C.," Lois Cayley is ruthlessly examined by the Queen's Counsel, who constructs her as a scheming femme fatale who has collaborated with Harold in perpetrating the fraud. Cayley discovers that her Girton education and penchant for "originality" (281) are against her. (As the 1887 essay by Romanes supposedly proves, women could not be genuinely original.) The Q.C. then labels her an "adventuress" (285, 288) after Harold's money, despite her protestations to the contrary. This summation by the Q.C. demonstrates the prejudicial male construction of women in the most glaring manner. Lois reflects about the all-male jury (shown in an illustration, 283): "The jury could never understand my point of view. It could never be made to see that there are adventuresses and adventuresses" (287). In other words, the negative connotation of "adventuress" destroys the value of her evidence. Lord Bertie Southminster wins and Harold Tillington is pursued on a charge of forgery.

In the penultimate tale, "The Oriental Attendant," the Maharajah aids Harold by having Tillington disguise himself as the Maharajah's Indian attendant. This ruse allows Harold to escape London with Lois. Together they take the train over the Scottish border, get off (at her providential suggestion) at the first town in Scotland, and convince a minister to marry them after she reveals the truth. Dressed in Indian costume, Harold, Lois writes, "folded me in his arms. I allowed him, unreproved. For the first time he kissed me. I did not shrink from it" (297). On the train journey, Harold is labeled a "nigger" (302) by a porter. Lois thus has the fantasy of transgressive sexuality with a racial Other while knowing he is in fact white. Yet even Lois reveals an element of racism: "I felt myself blush at the bare idea that I was marrying a black man, in spite of our good Maharajah's kindness" (310).

Lois Cayley foils the detective trailing them. "You can only get the better of a skilled detective by taking him thus, psychologically and humanly . . . I felt almost like a criminal" (305) she records. After the marriage, Harold Tillington turns himself in to the authorities. Lois Cayley then assumes the role of detective in order to clear her new husband: "I see a way out. I have found a clue" (317), she assures Harold. The last illustration to this chapter shows Lois delivering this statement as she holds her hands to Harold, still garbed in his Indian costume, her stance ostensibly the very image of cross-racial sexual transgression (316).

In the final tale, "The Unprofessional Detective," Lois Cayley, with the assistance of the solicitor Hayes, saves Tillington from conviction for forgery by noting discrepancies in the typed copy of the disputed will. She recognizes that although they are both typed on the same brand of machine, she made no errors on the original in Florence, while the will presented by Southminster is marked by a few mistakes. The typewriter she used in Florence also had an imperfect x, while the same letter on the copy is perfect. At Ashurst's home, Cayley finds the real will in a secret drawer of his desk. The old courier Higginson had forged the will and drawn Southminster into the plot against Harold Tillington. Because he did not actually forge the will, Southminster is allowed to leave for permanent residence in South Africa. Lois Cayley marries Harold Tillington, who in the final illustration is now shown in gentleman's street dress rather than in Indian costume. As a fugitive, Harold Tillington was an Indian in appearance; with his honor restored, he is an English gentleman.

This conclusion of the final tale raises a number of questions. Since the original will is found, Harold Tillington indeed inherits Marmaduke Ashurst's money, so Lois Cayley, despite her stated unwillingness to marry a rich man, in the end does so. The final installment has it both ways: Lois marries for love but gets the money anyway when the real will is proved in her husband's favor. In her defense, however, Lois Cayley marries Tillington when he is a fugitive who, if convicted, would never inherit his uncle's money; she supports him in his decision to turn himself in to the authorities. Mona Caird, in her essay "Marriage" in 1888, advised that a woman "ought not to be tempted to marry, or to remain married, for the sake of bread and butter" (79), and emphatically when Lois Cayley marries in so constraining a circumstance she is not marrying for money. Is Lois Cayley still a New Woman? She probably will maintain an independence of attitude, but she has no need to work or pursue a career after her marriage. Nothing is recorded about it: all her expertise as agent, typist, and journalist appears to have been subsumed by the role of wife. Pressure from the *Strand* undoubtedly compelled Grant Allen to accept narrative closure by having Lois Cayley marry Harold Tillington. In his history of the *Strand*, Reginald Pound labeled Grant Allen a "distinguished contributor" (43) to the magazine.

But was the *Strand* uneasy about the New Woman agenda, such that it is dismissed or ignored in the concluding narrative? It may well be that the *Strand* felt Allen had satisfied the demands of the unadulterated New Woman novel in *The Woman Who Did*. *Miss Cayley's Adventures* represents an amalgamation of novelistic subgenres: the detective narrative, the New Woman novel, the travel/ adventure record. That Lois Cayley marries at the conclusion is wildly in contrast with the suicide of Herminia Barton at the conclusion of *The Woman Who Did*. Nevertheless, it is possible to regard the marriage conclusion as compatible with the defense of the New Woman, since it establishes that Lois Cayley is not "unsexed," a common accusation of detractors of the New Woman such as Linton, who in her 1892 essay deployed this charge (461).

In *Miss Cayley's Adventures*, Grant Allen represents the contextualizing of New Woman ideology by exhibiting through the detectival element the functioning of the New Woman's education, originality, and freedom in a variety of circumstances—foreign travel, business relations, legal procedures. The illustrations by Gordon Browne contribute to advancing New Woman ideology by depicting Lois Cayley riding a camel, racing a bicycle, taking typed dictation, speaking with a veiled Englishwoman at an oasis, descending a mountain precipice, giving testimony in court, and holding hands with a black man, for example. Such illustrations underscore Grant Allen's ideological defense of the New Woman. Arthur Conan Doyle remembers that Grant Allen took "a certain pleasure . . . in defending outside positions" (262).

If Allen rejects the sexual permissiveness associated with the negative inflection of the word "adventuress" in *Miss Cayley's Adventures*, he advances beyond "the woman who did" to recognize its positive dimension—for "the woman who dares."

REFERENCES

Allen, Grant. "Are We Englishmen?" *Fortnightly Review* 28 (1880): 472–87.

———. *Miss Cayley's Adventures*. Illustrations by Gordon Browne. London: G. P. Putnam's Sons, 1899.

———. *The Woman Who Did*. 1895. Reprint, New York: Oxford University Press, 1995.

Bauer, Carol, ed. *Free and Ennobled.* New York: Pergamon, 1979.

Beare, Geraldine, ed. *Index to the Strand Magazine, 1891–1950.* London: Greenwood Press, 1982.

Caird, Mona. "Marriage." 1888. In *The Fin de Siecle*, edited by Sally Ledger and Roger Luckhurst, 77–80. Reprint, New York: Oxford University Press, 2000.

Cominos, Peter T. "Late-Victorian Sexual Respectability and the Social System." *International Review of Social History* 8 (1962): 18–48, 216–50.

Cunningham, Gail. *The New Woman and the Victorian Novel.* New York: Barnes & Noble, 1979.

Dixon, Ella Hepworth. "Why Women are Ceasing to Marry." 1899. In Ledger and Luckhurst, 83–88.

Doyle, Arthur Conan. *Memories and Adventures.* 1924. Reprint, London: Greenhill Books, 1988.

Eastwood, M. "The New Woman in Fiction and Fact." 1894. In Ledger and Luckhurst, 90–92.

Ledger, Sally. *The New Woman: Fiction and Feminism at the Fin de Siecle.* Manchester: Manchester University Press, 1997.

Linton, Eliza Lynn. "The Partisans of the Wild Women." *The Nineteenth Century* 31 (March 1892), 455–64.

———. "The Wild Women as Social Insurgents." *The Nineteenth Century* 30 (October 1891), 596–605.

"Modern Man-Haters." *The Saturday Review,* 29 April 1871, 528–29.

Murray, Janet, ed. *Strong-Minded Women.* New York: Pantheon, 1982.

Pike, E. Royston, ed. *Human Documents of the Age of the Forsythes.* London: Allen and Unwin. 1969.

———, ed. *Human Documents of the Lloyd George Era.* London: Allen and Unwin, 1972.

———, ed. *Human Documents of the Victorian Golden Age.* London: Allen and Unwin, 1967.

Pound, Reginald. *The Strand Magazine 1891–1950.* London: Heinemann, 1966.

Rawlings, William. *A Case for the Yard.* London: John Long, 1961.

Read, Donald, ed. *Documents from Edwardian England.* London: Harrap, 1973.

Romanes, George J. "Mental Differences between Men and Women." *The Nineteenth Century* 21 (May 1887): 654–72.

Showalter, Elaine. *Sexual Anarchy.* New York: Penguin, 1990.

White, S. P. "Modern Mannish Maidens." *Blackwood's* 147 (February 1890): 252–64.

Verbal and Other Manifestations: Further Thoughts on Ford/Pound/Ford

MAX SAUNDERS

INTRODUCTION

SCHOLARS OF MODERNISM OWE AN IMMENSE DEBT TO JOE WIESEN-farth, especially those of us working on Ford Madox Ford, on whom he has been producing a stream of pioneering and perceptive essays for forty years. More recently, and with enviable accelera-tion, he has been exploring Ford's relations with his contacts and contemporaries: not just two of the women Ford lived with, the En-glish novelist Violet Hunt and the Australian painter Stella Bowen, but also figures such as Dante Gabriel Rossetti, Henry James, Jo-seph Conrad, H. G. Wells, and James Joyce.[1] The critical and bio-graphical expertise of this work has greatly enhanced not just our sense of Ford's literary life, but of his impact on the history of mod-ernism.

This essay is prompted by that research—it's hard to think of criticism of Ford that wouldn't in some way be prompted by some-thing Joe Wiesenfarth had written—and seeks to contribute to the investigation of Ford's imbrication in modernist literary history.

The literary relations between Ezra Pound and Ford Madox Ford are now well documented.[2] But most of the discussion has come from a Poundian perspective, concerned with the lessons Pound re-iterated he had learned from Ford: the importance of writing a liv-ing language; that poetry should be as well written as prose, and so on. This, as I have argued elsewhere, has had some unfortunate consequences for the critical appreciation of Ford.[3] His poetry, gifted and moving though it often is, actually follows his own ad-vice in a way that Pound's verse rarely did, and consequently seems looser, more discursive and lower-key than Pound's dazzling, frag-mentary, allusive verbotechnics. Whereas Pound had little to say about Ford's novels. According to Ford, indeed, Pound was not the most reliable judge of prose, including his own. Ford teased him on this count, saying: "the prose of Mr. Pound is no more nor less than a national disaster."[4] And later, that: "Our distinguished colleague has always hated prose" (103); which is both ironic and self-ironic, given Pound's advocacy of "Mr Hueffer and the Prose Tradition in Verse" (15–21).

Their differing attiudes to prose can be seen in their responses to Henry James, for whom both men had the highest admiration. Ford not only wrote a one-man Festschrift for James's 70th birthday, in which he professed in the opening paragraph: "Mr. James is the greatest of living writers and in consequence, for me, the greatest of living men."[5] He also wrote novels whose conception, style, obliqueness, and subtlety can be read as forms of homage to James's aesthetics. Pound, on the other hand, wrote an essay on James in which he claimed: "Most good prose arises, perhaps, from an instinct of negation; is the detailed, convincing analysis of something detestable; of something which one wants to eliminate. Poetry is the assertion of a positive, i.e. of desire, and endures for a longer period."[6] Then in *Hugh Selwyn Mauberley* he made what he described as "an attempt to condense the James novel."[7] "Condense," despite his own assertion in the Henry James's essay that "There is no substitute for narrative-sense, however many different and entrancing charms may be spread before us."[8] The generic "James novel," despite his own assertion, also in the James essay, that "The laziness of an uncritical period can be nowhere more blatant than in the inherited habit of talking about authors as a whole."[9]

Perhaps impatience was the necessary condition of Pound's fierce energy and creativity. Whatever he was contemplating—a novel, Chinese or American history, a landscape, politics, or economics—he would home in on the fragments that seemed most significant or revelatory: exceptional moments, gists, piths, flashes. This allies him with the other epiphanic modernists: especially Proust, Joyce, and Woolf. But their epiphanies—like James's—emerge from sophisticated narrative and temporal structures, and it is those structures that Pound wanted to jettison. Even when not writing or imitating Haiku, Pound's earlier poems often have a problematic relation to narrative context. Or rather, their power is bound up with their ability to suggest a context that has been withheld, or to suggest multiple contexts. Thus the mysterious figures returning in "The Return" may—among other things—be actual gods routed in some mythical battle or hunt, ancient heroes who are like demoralized gods, modern airmen, or an allegory for the presence of past poets.[10] The Poundian "ideogramic method," or method of superposition or montage, is a quest for essences by the bracketing off of contingencies and contexts of time and place; a poetics of transcendence.

Given these divergences in attitudes to prose and narrative, it is not surprising that critical study has concentrated on the two men's sustained debates over literary principles rather than on literary influences that might be identified in particular works. The Pound annotation industry has of course not only tracked the references to Ford throughout the *Cantos*, but also noted that the tenth poem of the first sequence in *Hugh Selwyn Mauberley*, about "the stylist" who has "taken shelter" beneath a leaking thatch, refers to Ford's lying low in a ramshackle Sussex cottage.

Yet the two men were so close, not just in England before and after the war, but also in Paris in the 1920s, and they kept in close contact throughout the rest of Ford's life. I shall be arguing that the influences went deeper, and that they can be traced in at least one major work by each man:[11] first, *Hugh Selwyn Mauberley*, which owes more to Ford Madox Hueffer than has previously been recognized,[12] second, *Parade's End*, which can be seen in many ways as an analogous work to *The Cantos*.

FORD/POUND: VERBAL MANIFESTATIONS

In the second poem of the second sequence, headed "Mauberley (1920)," Pound tells us of an artist (probably Mauberley himself, as I shall henceforth assume for brevity's sake) who has drifted in and out of a romantic episode in some bewilderment:

> Unable in the supervening blankness
> To sift TO AGATHON from the chaff
> Until he found his sieve . . .
> Ultimately, his seismograph:
> —Given that is his "fundamental passion,"
> This urge to convey the relation
> Of eyelid and cheek-bone
> By verbal manifestations.

The ambiguities throughout the sequences are so intense and complexly interconnected as to have kept critics guessing, or refraining from guesswork for eighty years. So it's not surprising that it's difficult to judge the attitude toward that "fundamental passion," marked out by inverted commas like raised eyebrows for our ironic appreciation. Nor is it clear whether Mauberley's passion is being adduced as an explanation of his inability to discriminate (to sift the good from the chaff), or as an explanation of his solution to that inability: the instrument he ultimately finds,

> To present the series
> Of curious heads in medallion—

Such hermeneutic uncertainty takes people in different ways. Some might lament a lack of definiteness in the conception. To my mind the definiteness of Pound's language militates against such a view. What comes across most clearly is a complexity of sensibilities; not quite, as Leavis argued, a subtle sensibility, because part of the subtlety is the uncertain relation between Pound's sensibility and those of his personae "E.P." and "Mauberley."[13]

If we can't say exactly what Pound thinks, or wants us to think, about Mauberley, it's perhaps because Pound was using the poem to explore his ambivalences. Moral or psychological "character" isn't what's being presented in the foreground, so much as conflicting aesthetic positions and attitudes. We can see this from the way that deliberate phrase, "verbal manifestations," gets repeated in one of Pound's most important aesthetic essays, "How to Read," in the celebrated manifesto distinguishing between three modes of poetry:

> MELOPOEIA, wherein the words are charged, over and above their plain meaning, with some musical property, which directs the bearing or trend of that meaning.
> PHANOPOEIA, which is the casting of images upon the visual imagination.
> LOGOPOEIA, "the dance of the intellect among words," that is to say, it employs words not only for their direct meaning, but it takes count in a special way of habits of usage, of the context we *expect* to find with the word, its usual concomitants, of its known acceptances, and of ironical play. It holds the aesthetic content which is peculiarly the domain of verbal manifestations, and cannot possibly be contained in plastic or in music. It is the latest come, and perhaps most tricky and undependable mode.[14]

Yet there is an apparent contradiction between the two passages. Mauberley's passion is to convey the relation of eyelid and cheekbone—an essentially spatial, visual image—by "verbal manifestation," the ironic play that "cannot possibly be contained in plastic or in music." Mauberley, according to these later definitions, is confusing phanopoeia and logopoeia. It might seem an accidental echo. But I think the phrase appealed to Pound for its suggestion of something supernatural, manifesting itself in the language as a god makes itself manifest in a metamorphosis. When he echoes the passage from *Hugh Selwyn Mauberley* in canto 74, he relates it to one of the most famous images of exactly that manifestation of the divine, Botticelli's "The Birth of Venus":

> . . . cheek-bone, by verbal manifestation,
> her eyes as in "La Nascita." [15]

What has this to do with Ford? Pound may have been echoing Ford's use of the same phrase in an important pair of articles on the Imagists and Futurists, the first of which discussed and quoted Pound. In the second piece on the volume *Des Imagistes*, Ford wrote:

> on the one hand, whilst all the literary, all the verbal manifestations of Futurism are representational, and representational, and again representational, all the plastic-aesthetic products of the new movement are becoming more and more geometric, mystic, non-material, or what you will. The Futurist painters were doing very much what novelists of the type of Flaubert or short-story writers of the type of Maupassant aimed at. They gave you not so much the reconstitution of a crystallised scene in which all the figures were arrested—not so much that, as fragments of impressions gathered during a period of time, during a period of emotion, or during a period of travel. [16]

"Luini in porcelain! . . . The face-oval beneath the glaze. . . ." It would be surprising if Pound hadn't known these essays. He always took Ford's critical views seriously. In 1914 he ranked Ford as "the best critic in England, one might say the only critic of any importance" (16). Pound was helping Lewis with the Rebel Art Centre and *Blast*, and was closely involved with the questions Ford was discussing: Futurism, poetics, the relation of the verbal to the visual and the musical. The musical? One of the contrasts that has been observed in *Hugh Selwyn Mauberley* is between the lyrical investment of the first sequence, and the visual imagination of the second; as if melopoeia were being set off against phanopoeia; poetry as song against poetry as impression.

Ford is relevant here too, I suggest, because Pound could never quite settle where Ford stood in relation to these different emphases. He admired Ford's insistence that poetry should be a living language, "the speech of to-day," the poetry of the voice. "Mr. Hueffer has also the gift for making lyrics that will sing," he said, adding: "we would not be far wrong in calling Mr. Hueffer the best lyrist in England" (10). In a word, melopoeia. Yet at the same time he criticized Ford's avowed "impressionism" as hyperocular: "Impressionism belongs in paint," he wrote. And he later said of Ford's criticism: "I think Hueffer goes wrong because he bases his criticism on the eye, and almost solely on the eye" (10, 68). In another word, phanopoeia. And one way in which he makes a point against the haziness of Fordian impressionism is by giving as an example of what not to write a phrase from a poem of Ford's: "Don't use such an expression as "dim lands of peace." It dulls the image."[17] So we should not be surprised to find him echoing Ford's words elsewhere.

Even if you are persuaded that the "verbal manifestations" echo Ford's, you may feel the eyelids and cheekbones face elsewhere. But consider these passionately observed portraits from *The Good Soldier*, subtitled "A Tale of Passion," describing Nancy Rufford, with whom Edward Ashburnham has fallen fatally in love, and with whom the narrator too, in his own way, has fallen in love; and who is thought to be based on Brigit Patmore, the mutual friend of Pound and Ford, with whom Ford was in love while he was writing the novel, and dictating the opening to her.

> A turn of the eyebrow, a tone of the voice, a queer characteristic gesture—all these things, and it is these things that cause to arise the passion of love—all these things are like so many objects on the horizon of the landscape that tempt a man to walk beyond the horizon, to explore. He wants to get, as it were, behind those eyebrows with the peculiar turn, as if he desired to see the world with the eyes that they overshadow.[18]

> She had only just put her hair up, so that the carriage of her neck had that charming touch of youth and of unfamiliarity. Over her throat there played the reflection from a little pool of water, left by a thunderstorm of the night before, and all the rest of her features were in the diffused and luminous shade of her white parasol. Her dark hair just showed beneath her broad, white hat of pierced, chip straw; her throat was very long and leaned forward, and her eyebrows, arching a little as she laughed at some old-fashionedness in my phraseology, had abandoned their tense line. And there was a little colour in her cheeks and light in her deep blue eyes. (87)

> Enigmatic, silent, utterly well-behaved as far as her knife and fork go, Nancy will stare in front of her with the blue eyes that have over them strained, stretched brows. Once, or perhaps twice, during the meal her knife and fork will be suspended in mid-air as if she were trying to think of something that she had forgotten. Then she will say that she believes in an Omnipotent Deity or she will utter the one word "shuttlecocks,"

perhaps. It is very extraordinary to see the perfect flush of health on her cheeks, to see the lustre of her coiled black hair, the poise of the head upon the neck, the grace of the white hands—and to think that it all means nothing—that it is a picture without a meaning. (161)

Or this, describing the suicide of Florence Dowell, the narrator's wife:

She was a sweetly pretty woman with smooth pink and white cheeks, long hair, the eyelashes falling like a tiny curtain on her cheeks. She drank the little phial of prussic acid and there she lay—O, extremely charming and clearcut—looking with a puzzled expression at the electric-light bulb that hung from the ceiling . . . (83)

We know Pound had read *The Good Soldier* by 1923 (71). But it is hard to believe he hadn't read it earlier. He told Dorothy Shakespear on 7 March 1914 that Ford's "new novel is—as far as it has gone—above his others."[19] The editors of that letter gloss this as referring to *The Young Lovell*, published in October 1913. But it seems to me more likely to have been *The Good Soldier*, "as far as it has gone," if Ford read Pound the incomplete manuscript. Ford said he started the novel in December 1913. The first three-and-a-half chapters were published in *Blast* in June 1914, so he is likely to have written at least those by March.

Of course eyebrows are not eyelids; and Pound may not have read as far as any of these passages from *The Good Soldier* before writing *Hugh Selwyn Mauberley*. But he would have seen the following in the first number of *Blast*, in which Dowell describes Ashburnham with the same "fundamental passion" to convey the relation of facial features—indeed with a passionate intensity of observation and description that might create unease about same-sex feelings, and which may have fed into Pound's suggestion of Mauberley's ineffectual effeteness:

I had forgotten about his eyes. They were as blue as the sides of a certain type of box of matches. When you looked at them carefully you saw that they were perfectly honest, perfectly straightforward, perfectly stupid. But the brick pink of his complexion, running perfectly level to the brick pink of his inner eyelids, gave them a curious, sinister expression—like a mosaic of blue porcelain set in pink china. (26)

"Luini in porcelain . . ." It would be too facile to say that Hugh Selwyn Mauberley *is* Ford Madox Hueffer. Poundian scholarship has shown how many more prototypes are involved. He is also the type of poet Pound felt Ford had saved him from being. If anything, Mauberley is a vortex drawing in a range of Decadents, Edwardians and Georgians, and also their antitheses (like Arnold Bennett) and critics (like Pound and Ford themselves): an ideogram of the prewar literary scene. My argument is primarily that Ford loomed much larger in Pound's view of that literary scene than is usually acknowledged. And that Pound's friendship with Ford, admiration for and criticism of him, all contributed to the eventual complexity of the poem sequences in aesthetic as much as biographical terms. While Pound regularly criticized any symptoms he saw in Ford of Pre-Raphaelitism or aestheticism (such as hyperocular impressionism, insufficient willfulness, anachronism), he also praised him as offering the remedy of these things: by the clarity of his diagnostic intelligence, his Flaubertian pursuit of objectivity and style, and his telling juxtapositions of tradition and modernity. Furthermore, the critical neglect of Ford's significance has obscured what may be the most fruitful way of reading *Hugh Selwyn Mauberley*: as an attempt to combine together the three modes of poetry; juxtaposing, with ideogramic suppression of logical or narrative connection, the two sequences, the one predominantly melopoeic, the second predominantly phanopoeic, in order to energize "the dance of the intellect among words" by darting back and forth between them. Of course either sequence alone demonstrates enough ironic verbal play to qualify for logopoeic status. But it is the relation between the two that has most heightened the interpretative uncertainty. It was in his discussions with Ford, and his reponses to Ford's poetry and criticism, that Pound elaborated his Imagist project. So it is hardly surprising that *Hugh Selwyn Mauberley*, his most searching exploration to date of poetry, the literary life, and the literary world, should pay homage in various ways to his mentor.

POUND/FORD: MYTHOLOGY, COSMOLOGY, CHRONOLOGY, HISTORY

Ford's debt to Pound is even harder to demonstrate conclusively, but may be at least as significant. Pound was fond of teasing Ford for being old-fashioned, like Nancy Rufford laughing "some old-fashionedness" in Dowell's "phraseology."

> WOT you dont bloomin' see is that wot you do with ideas is just as bad for the reader's morale as wot Bridges does with langwidge. . . . No, mong, cher, you are full of suppressed forsooths and gadzookses of ideation. (58–59)

Pound felt that Ford's work was compromised by making a fetish of received ideas such as that of the "English Gentleman." "Not sure the beastly word gentleman hasn't caused more trouble in yr/ bright l'il life than all the rest of the lang," he wrote, adding, "you HAVE bitched about 80% of yr/ work through hanging onto a set of idees recues" (99–100). From another point of view, however, such a criticism was only worth making because for Pound Ford represented the attempt to escape the nineteenth century. In 1912 he had praised Ford's volume of poems, *High Germany*, saying: "Mr Hueffer is making some sort of experiment in modernity" (9).

Ford was in the army from 1915 to 1919, and wrote little. He had broken down due to what was then called "shell shock," and it took him until 1923 before he could say, to H. G. Wells: "I've got over the nerve tangle of the war and feel able at last really to write again—which I never thought I should do."[20] By then he had begun what was to be his postwar masterpiece, the tetralogy of novels about Christopher Tietjens, now known collectively as *Parade's End*.

Too much of the criticism of *Parade's End*, whether positive or negative, has concentrated on its old-fashionednesses; its preoccupation with "the beastly word gentleman"; with Tietjens as "the last Tory." These aspects are undeniable. But just as *The Good Soldier* treats its Edwardian good people with a technique that has been described as "cubist," so *Parade's End* renders the war's devastation of that Edwardian world by means of high modernist techniques.

Before embarking on *Parade's End*, however, Ford wrote one extraordinary work providing unmistakable evidence of his engagement with the "experiment in modernity" of his fellow modernists. *Mister Bosphorus and the Muses or a Short History of Poetry in Britain. Variety Entertainment in Four Acts . . . with Harlequinade, Transformation Scene, Cinematograph Effects, and Many Other Novelties, as well as Old and Tried Favourites* was published by Duckworth in 1923 in a handsome volume with woodcuts by Paul Nash. *Mister Bosphorus* is an inspired series of pastiches from poetry through the ages. It was certainly influenced by the "Circe" or "nighttown" section of *Ulysses*. It may also be responding to the parody and pastiche in "The Waste Land," though the evidence isn't conclusive as to whether Ford read Eliot's poem before finishing his own. It is certainly Ford's most thorough, spirited parody.[21] And, as Paul Skinner suggests, it can be read as in some sense a response to *Hugh Selwyn Mauberley*.[22]

By 1922–23 Ford was also well aware of Pound's progress with

The Cantos, and had read what was then canto 7, sent by Pound for comments in January 1922, with the request that Ford should "go through the enclosed with a red, blood-red, green, blue, or other pencil and scratch what is too awful," just as Pound himself had done for "The Waste Land" (63). Ford responded in minute and "mostly zoological" detail (64).

In one of the best accounts of the Pound/Ford poetic axis, Robert Hampson argues that "Pound's *Cantos* seem to have contributed something to Ford's methods in his later prose works" (117). He is discussing the generically hybrid books of the 1930s, especially *Provence* and *Great Trade Route*. But Ford's response to *The Cantos* can be traced a decade earlier, in both *Mister Bosphorus* and *Parade's End*.[23]

Mister Bosphorus is less challenging, and has a clearer narrative line than *The Cantos*. But both that narrative line, about the poet Bosphorus deciding he has to leave the war-depressed North for the regenerative Mediterranean, and its technique of pastiche of every period of literary history, have marked Poundian affinities. The modes Ford parodies are those of Pound and the Imagists rather than those foregrounded by Joyce and Eliot: classical tragedy, heroic epic, Old English, Imagist classicizing:

> BOSPHORUS: That's put the lid on! Rhyming no more
> venture-ye!
> I am dead sick of all this eighteenth-century
> Insipid metre!
>   *(Chorus, Female)*
> Bosphorus, our beautiful,
> No more in the market-place we found thee!
> Erased thy name from the tablets;
> Beside wine-purple seas, forgotten;
> The fleece unpressed;
> Cyclamens
> Faded in the autumn all unplucked by thee
> Lustre on lustre;
> Our locks ungarlanded by thee;
> Forlorn, lack-lustre!
> Forgotten the beautiful
> Singer!
>
> In the market-place sought we the Tyrrhenian laces,
> No more thy twined words;
> The clepsyhydra measured out the hours
> To the drip of its waters, never to the plucking
> Of the ivory lyre!

Forgotten the beautiful
Lyric!
On the Acropolis
Sang other poets.

HERCULES: I am of course acquainted
With the historic outlines Of Athenian poetry.
   (1st Semi-chorus, Men)
To us most painful
This short-breathed division:
   (2nd Semi-chorus, Men)
How get
Into short syllables
   (Chorus, Male)
Divinities of Argos
Devising to each,
Unnumbered destinies?
HERCULES: The slow years passing,
Take we for granted!
Ray cast now on your reasons
For seeking this sacred
Womanless Wan-waste;
Lawless, licentious,
Gold-seeking, gold-haired,
Willow-waist wantons!
ATHIS: Sudden from sea-ways
Sail swart seafarers
Merchanting manuscripts
Stripe-aye, and star-dight
Mounting the market,
Bellowing : *"Bosphorus!*
Bring Bad Mad Bosphorus'
Million-worth Manuscripts!"
HERCULES: Wherefore this wan-ness?
Manuscripts many
Doubtless in days dead
Poet did pen ye!
So from seafarers
Gold have ye gotten,
Gold in galoreness
   (1st Male Semi-chorus)
Awful! His autograph
Vaulting in value!
   (2nd Male Semi-chorus)
Dreadful! Disgusting
Degeneration!
   (Chorus)

Awfully awkward this
Alliteration.

Mister Bosphorus shows, then, that when Ford set out on his immense postwar project, *Parade's End*, he had been thinking of Pound's embarkation in quest of the modern epic. The sheer unlikeness of Ford's tetralogy and Pound's evolving epic makes one wary of facile comparisons. But there are some fundamental congruences most of which have received little notice, and deserve more detailed study than can be given here.[24]

First, like *The Cantos* and *Ulysses*, *Parade's End* is concerned with the status of the heroic and the epic in the modern world. If the awesome scale of the world war invited comparison with the heroic age, its mechanization militated against human heroics. Tietjens is a man of Odyssean intellect, surviving the war and making his way back to the woman he loves. But as in Joyce's novel, the modern epic is both heroic and mock-heroic. Pound identified three fugue-like elements in *The Cantos*:

> A. A. Live man goes down into world of Dead.
> C. B. The "repeat in history"
> B. C. The "magic moment" or moment of metamorphosis, bust thru from quotidian into "divine or permanent world." Gods, etc.[25]

There are parallels for all three in *Parade's End*. The macabre underground world of trenches and dugouts inevitably reminded combatants of the underworld. But Tietjens descends further into the world of the Dead on two occasions: when he is blown unconscious by a shell and when he is buried by another. The tetralogy is also dense with a sense of historical echoes. The prewar hysteria and violence (mad Rev. Duchemin's outburst, the assault on the Suffragettes, General Campion's car smashing into Tietjens's dogcart) have been seen as prefiguring the violence and madness unleashed in the war. The stresses of trench warfare were also notoriously conducive to sensations of the paranormal. Both Tietjens and Sylvia experience visions of the dead, as Ford himself had. But Tietjens also has a more classical "magic moment." As he walks through thistles, the flies he disturbs attract "myriads of swallows," swirling around him: "And as the blue sky was reflected in the blue of their backs—for their backs were below his eyes—he had felt like a Greek God striding through the sea. . . ."[26]

Second, the example of Dante. The debt is more marked in Pound's case, certainly. But whereas the *Inferno* begins in the middle of the journey of our life, *Some Do Not* . . . begins in the middle of a railway journey. Robie Macauley observed that the train was not only running from London to Rye, but "from the past into the future."[27] It is also, one might add, taking Tietjens on an eschatological journey. It's not that the four books of *Parade's End* correspond in a schematic way to the three books of the *Divine Comedy*. But Tietjens is in various forms of Hell or Purgatory (the line is not easy to draw) for most of the first three volumes: the psychological hell of his tormented marriage to Sylvia; the strange hells of the Western Front, bombardment, terror, shell shock, mental breakdown. In the fourth, having attained his paradisal union with Valentine, he is largely absent, but is said to be flying in an airplane above the action. This volume, *Last Post*, has sometimes seemed too removed from the others to satisfy critics. Thinking of it as *Parade's End's Paradiso* perhaps makes a new sense of its otherness.

Third, although Ford's narrative couldn't possibly be as fragmentary or ideogramic as Pound's collage, its chronology is strikingly disrupted and fragmentary. Ford was justifiably proud of his experiments, evolved with Conrad, in the "time shift." *Parade's End* uses these as intensively and disconcertingly as *The Good Soldier*, but with a different aim and effect. Whereas in the earlier novel he mimics the random rememberings of the perplexed narrator, so that temporal fragmentation mimes and produces interpretative bafflement, in *Parade's End* it enacts the struggle of the ordering intellect against the overwhelming forces of chaos and destruction. Because Tietjens's encyclopedic mind is a repository of western culture, the novels cut vertiginously from one literary or historical fragment to another. The effect is not entirely unlike that of *The Cantos*.

These three aspects all shade off into the fourth. An epic, said Pound, is "a poem including history."[28] *Parade's End* is as saturated with history as are *The Cantos*: classical history, Nordic paganism, English feudalism, Catholicism, renaissance Anglicanism, the glorious Revolution, the Napoleonic wars; individual histories, national histories, literary and cultural histories. Because the war felt like an end to history—a "crack across the table of History" in Valentine Wannop's mind—Ford wants to realise that history that the war threatened.[29]

Such a project extends beyond Ford and Pound, as the examples of Joyce and Eliot here testify. Postwar modernism is sometimes seen as subject to a *rappel à l'ordre*.[30] In Ford's case, the emphasis was more on the rappel than the ordre, perhaps. Editing the *Transat-*

lantic Review while writing *Parade's End*, he was acutely aware of, and receptive to, the range of modernist experiment. Pound was instrumental in getting the *Review* started too. Ultimately, he was only one among many influences. But the example of his "endless poem, of no known category [. . .] all about everything," must have galvanized Ford as he sat down to reorder himself and his world.

This is only an indication of a possible direction the scholarship of Ford might pursue. It may take a Joe Wiesenfarth to do the job properly.

NOTES

1. The published articles can be found in the bibliography to this volume. In addition, the essay "Ford Madox Ford, Violet Hunt, and the Battle of the Books: Sexual/Textual Hostilities" is to appear in a forthcoming volume to be entitled *Ford Madox Ford's Modernity*, edited by Max Saunders and Robert Hampson. And Joe Wiesenfarth has given papers as yet unpublished on Stella Bowen (London, 10 January 1998); on Ford's last poems—"Coda for the City" (London, 17 December 1999); and on "Portraits of the Artist: Joyce, Wells, and Ford Madox Ford" (Washington, 28 December 2000).

2. Most of the primary material is collected in *Pound/Ford: The Story of a Literary Friendship*, ed. Brita Lindberg-Seyersted (London: Faber, 1982). Page references in the text are to this volume unless otherwise indicated. The most extended critical accounts are: Camilla Bunker Haase, "Serious Artists: The Relationship between Ford Madox Ford and Ezra Pound" (Ph.D. diss., Harvard University, 1984). Paul Skinner, "Ford Madox Ford and Ezra Pound: Responses to Crisis" (Ph.D. diss., University of Bristol, 1993); Violet Cameron Skorina, "'Leaving Street': An Examination of the Relationship between Ford Madox Ford and Ezra Pound during Their Years Together in London c. 1908–1915 and the Influence of Ford's Theory of the 'Prose Tradition' upon Pound's Verse Style" (Ph.D. diss., University of Connecticut, 1979). See also: Eric Homberger, "Pound, Ford and 'Prose': The Making of a Modern Poet," *Journal of American Studies* 5, no. 3 (1971): 281–92; Robert Hampson, "'Experiments in Modernity': Ford and Pound," in *Pound in Multiple Perspective: A Collection of Critical Essays*, ed. Andrew Gibson (Basingstoke and London: Macmillan, 1993), 93–125; and Paul Skinner, "Of Owls and Waterspouts," *Paideuma* 17, no. 1 (Spring 1988): 59–68.

3. Max Saunders, "Ford/Pound," *Agenda* 27, no. 4–28, no. 1 (winter 1989–spring 1990), 93–102.

4. "Literary Causeries: VII. Pullus ad Margaritam," *Chicago Tribune* (Paris), no. 7 (30 March 1924), 3, 11.

5. *Henry James: A Critical Study* (London: Secker, [1914]), 9.

6. *Literary Essays of Ezra Pound*, ed. T. S. Eliot (London: Faber, 1974), 324n. 1.

7. *The Selected Letters of Ezra Pound*, ed. D. D. Paige (New York: New Directions, 1971), 180.

8. *Literary Essays*, 324.

9. Ibid., 304.

10. See, for example, Donald Davie, *Studies in Ezra Pound* (Manchester: Carca-

net, 1991), 35, who argues for the "phantasmal presence" of the Sapphic stanza "in or behind the first four lines."

11. I don't have space to consider other possible connections here, such as the influence of Ford's "On Heaven" on Pound, as suggested by—yes!—Joe Wiesenfarth, "The Ash-Bucket at Dawn: Ford's Art of Poetry," *Contemporary Literature* 30, no. 2 (summer 1989), 240–62; or that between Ford's remarks on classical writers in his *Outlook* articles or September 1914, and Pound's use of Propertius for his wartime exploration of the relation between poetry and imperialism. Ford describes his "great passion for the poems of Ovid," and how he has tried "to translate Ovid's case into modern terms. You see poets do not matter enough nowadays to be loved by members of Imperial houses": "Literary Portraits—LIII: The Muse of War," *Outlook* 34 (12 September 1914), 334–35.

12. Herbert Schneidau, *Ezra Pound: The Image and the Real* (Baton Rouge: Louisiana State University Press, 1969), 171–72, notes briefly that more of the work than poem X refers to Ford. I am grateful to Paul Skinner for providing this reference.

13. F. R. Leavis, *New Bearings in English Poetry* (Harmondsworth: Penguin, 1972), 104–5.

14. Pound, "How to Read," *Literary Essays*, 25. The articles were originally published in the *New York Herald Tribune Books* from 13–27 January 1929.

15. *The Cantos* (London: Faber, 1975), 446. See Peter Brooker, *A Student's Guide to the Selected Poems of Ezra Pound* (London: Faber, 1979), 217.

16. "Literary Portraits—XXXVI. Les Jeunes and 'Des Imagistes' (Second Notice)," *Outlook* 33 (16 May 1914), 682–83.

17. "A Retrospect," *Literary Essays*, 5. The phrase is from Ford's poem of 1904 "On a Marsh Road." See Ford, *Selected Poems* (Manchester: Carcanet, 1997), 35.

18. *The Good Soldier*, ed. Martin Stannard (New York: Norton, 1995), 79. Subsequent page references are to this edition.

19. *Ezra Pound and Dorothy Shakespear: Their Letters: 1909–1914*, ed. Omar Pound and A. Walton Litz (London: Faber and Faber, 1985), 316.

20. Ford to H. G. Wells, 14 October 1923, *Letters*, 154. He also wrote to Conrad: "I think I'm doing better work as the strain of the war wears off," 7 October 1923, Yale.

21. See Saunders, *Ford Madox Ford: A Dual Life* (Oxford: Oxford University Press, 1996), 2 vols., ii, 123–24. Also "Parody and Modernism in James Joyce and Ford Madox Ford," to be published in Germany in a volume of essays entitled *Modernism and the Individual Talent: Ford Madox Ford (Hueffer)*, ed. Jörg W. Rademacher.

22. Paul Skinner to Max Saunders, 12 August 2001.

23. Robert Green, *Ford Madox Ford: Prose and Politics* (Cambridge: Cambridge University Press, 1981), 123, discerns "broad similarities between patterns of thought" in Ford's work of the 1920s, and C. H. Douglas's Social Credit movement, championed by Pound.

24. An honorable exception is Paul Skinner, whose excellent "Ford Madox Ford and Ezra Pound: Responses to Crisis" (Ph.D. diss., University of Bristol, 1993) notes the shared preoccupation with history, systems of knowledge, the underworld, the heroic, as well as with genre and modes of mimesis.

25. Pound, *Selected Letters*, 210.

26. *A Man Could Stand Up—* (London: Duckworth, 1926), 205.

27. Macauley, introduction, *Parade's End* (New York: Knopf, 1950), vii.

28. Pound, *Social Credit: An Impact*, 1935. Quoted by William Cookson, *A Guide to the Cantos of Ezra Pound* (London: Croom Helm, 1985), xviii.

29. *A Man Could Stand Up—*, 13.

30. See for example Giovanni Cianci, "Tradition, Architecture and *Rappel à l'Ordre*: Ruskin and Eliot (1917–21)," in *Ruskin and Modernism*, ed. Giovanni Cianci and Peter Nicholls (Basingstoke: Palgrave, 2001), 133–54.

Feeling and Performance in Wright's *Native Son*

THOMAS H. SCHAUB

> Whereas the novel of manners presents individual thought and
> feeling indirectly through a code of usage established by social
> custom, the new Gothic novel presents individual thought and
> feeling at variance with social custom. The one emphasizes so-
> cial circumstance; the other, psychological states.
> —Joseph Wiesenfarth, *Gothic Manners and the Classic English Novel*

STRUCTURING RICHARD WRIGHT'S *NATIVE SON* IS A TENSION BE-
tween the novel's environmental or Marxist determinism, and its
commitment to individual subjectivity. In the years since the novel's publication, many readers have commented upon the conflict
between these two viewpoints, sometimes described as one between
Marxism and Freudianism, concept and feeling, and proletarian
aesthetics and those of modernist inwardness. In the late sixties, Edward Margolies saw this contradiction as a source of the novel's
failure: "Since moral responsibility involves choice, how can
Wright's deterministic Marxism be reconciled with the freedom of
action that choice implies? The contradiction is never resolved, and
it is precisely for this reason that the novel fails to fulfill itself"
(106–7). Connecting these contrary ideas and attempting their resolution on a narrative continuum, the story of Bigger Thomas develops from the inside out, from the private world of feeling to the
public world of action. Much criticism focuses upon one or another
points along this continuum, several in recent years emphasizing
Bigger's emerging freedom and self-affirmation, as against the
power of the environment to determine every aspect of his existence. This essay sets out to explore the status and character of Bigger's private world and its uneasy relationship with the Marxist
analysis of the individual in society which structures so much of
the novel.

In everyday life the relationship of determination and freedom, like the two faces of a coin, is a seamless whole that constitutes a compelling riddle each person faces, a riddle long ago dramatized by Sophocles in *Oedipus Rex*. In one degree or another, free actions within novels are always replicating this riddle, since such actions are always determined by the author, but *Native Son* might be viewed as an aesthetic form devoted to disentangling these two halves—social environment from private subjectivity–as two kinds of understanding and point of view. The two elements are inter-twined throughout the narrative of *Native Son*, but kept separate as structure and feeling.

The first of the novel's three parts focuses directly on the eco-nomic environment of the Thomas family in contrast with the envi-ronment Bigger discovers in the Dalton house. To be sure, Wright uses the two houses as contrasting images of class and race, but he also emphasizes the economic structure which unites them. The Thomas family rents from the Dalton's, but the Dalton's also pay Bigger a salary, some portion of which will return to them as rent–or would have had matters unfolded differently. This exchange relation constitutes the bare-bones schematics of capitalist organi-zation of society into landlords and renters, owners and workers, as Bigger himself recognizes when he thinks of Mrs. Dalton: "he was the hired and she was the hirer"; "she was the boss and he was the worker" (127–28).

Wright further elaborates this allegory of social structure by showing these two environments bound together into a single con-sciousness, expressed by characters from both houses, recognizable as the ideology of bourgeois capitalism. As Marx wrote in the *Com-munist Manifesto*, "Capital is a collective product, and only by the united action of many members, nay, in the last resort, only by the united action of all members of society, can it be set in motion. Capital is, therefore, not a personal, it is a social power" (Tucker, 485). The Dalton philanthropy is designed to give Bigger a start, but their assumptions are most explicitly stated by the cook Peggy when she lays out for him the gospel of hard work and opportunity for self-improvement the Daltons are generously providing him (55–56). Her view of how to succeed in the world, the central narra-tive of American opportunity, is held by all members of the society, including Bigger's mother and sister, who pester him with moralis-tic injunctions to get a job, to rise early, to make something of him-self, and reminders of their dependence upon him. This barrage, successfully inculcating Bigger with an intolerable sense of guilt, includes the especially intimidating and hurtful linkage of work with masculinity: "We wouldn't have to live in this garbage dump if you had any manhood in you," his mother admonishes him (8).

Within this economic structure and distinguishable from it, Wright establishes a psychological or psychoanalytical relation, which Robert Bone has called "a running account of Bigger's feelings" (151). Wright uses the relation between structure and feeling to show both the effect of exchange relations in every aspect of Bigger's life: from the physiological to the aesthetic, from sex for alcohol with Bessie, to physiological manifestations of fear and pinched circumstances in the way his sister chews and his mother turns her head, even to Bigger's inability, as Charles Scruggs brilliantly argues, to see the Chicago skyline as "beautiful" (91–92). This psychological dimension, then, emerges chiefly through the emotional impact which the structures of economic oppression register upon the body and mind of Bigger and others in his milieu. Bigger's recognition of these and other facts, Wright represents as thoughts interpolated through feeling: "he felt that [whites] ruled him, even when they were far away and not thinking of him, ruled him by conditioning him in his relations with this own people" (115). At this point Bigger's inwardness is an effect of social and economic environment, of his place below the lowest rung of the capitalist ladder whose highest places are occupied by white people.

The beginning of this represented inwardness is Wright's use of the rat scene, so often commented upon and described by Wright in "How Bigger Was Born," in which the cornered rat, his belly pulsing with fear, turns aggressive before Bigger kills him with a blow to the head with the frying pan. This scene initiates the novel's realm of symbolic action, which is to say that inwardness or feelings, even intuitions and emergent consciousness, are signified in this novel by the translation of the economic structure into a world of symbols which convey how it feels to experience the weight and consequences of that structure. Symbols always signify the underlying psychological and physiological complement to the Marxist critique represented in economic structure. Bigger may have only a dim sense of his role in the economic structure of society, but he is able to articulate through image and symbol how it feels to be at the mercy of that structure. He lacks conceptual grasp of Marxist totality, but he articulates feeling through image. For example, the clock's harsh ring which begins the novel and peremptorily calls Bigger to attention becomes for Bigger an image of white efficiency: "Look at the big guys. You don't ever hear of them being late, do you? Naw! They work like clocks," he tells his friends in the pool room (36). Describing the feeling of living with the fear of whites and his hatred for them, Bigger tells Gus it feels like "fire" in his stomach.

Wright's narration places Bigger's similes and images into an underlying symbolic logic of narrative events. The clock simile, just a local image for Bigger, reappears in the ticking clock at the head of Mary's bed, "its white dial glowing in the blue darkness" (88). Just as the snow which envelops him is a symbol of white space enclosing him, here the clock signifies the white face of time itself. Even before the rat appears, Bigger is awakened to this time by the ringing clock. Bigger lives within an economy of interrelated symbols. Most central to this symbolic structure is the scene of the rat and his death, for the elements of this scene are repeated throughout the novel: Bigger's attack on the rat's head is repeated in his beheading of Mary Dalton, his crushing of Bessie's head, and his attack on the head of the policeman tracking him; the newspaper in which the rat's head is wrapped reappears in the Dalton basement where Bigger uses it to hold Mary's bloody head; and later still Bigger dreams of his own bloody head embalmed in newpapers. Finally, Bigger is eventually tried and convicted in the Chicago newspapers and then burned in the frying pan of the state. Like the economic relation structuring Bigger's encounters with the Dalton's, this symbolic logic introduces into the novel the element of logical necessity within which Bigger continues to operate.

As Wright himself pointed out, the image of the rat's belly is a powerful symbolic matrix helping Wright to initiate effects throughout the novel, especially by keying Bigger's emotions and the images which express them to the novel's plot and meaning. Foremost, the belly of the rat—established as the image of hysterical fear—is then recruited by Wright to reveal the significance of Bigger's taking a job within the Dalton house. This development in effect reproduces spatially the conceptual relationship of the Thomas and Dalton families. Wright then uses the image of the rat's belly to reveal a psychological structure that embeds Bigger within the Dalton house as an allegory of the social body. Readers already know the rat to be an image of Bigger himself, but Bigger supplies an image for the hysterical fear of the rat that reappears during a conversation between Gus and Bigger. Less insightful than Bigger, Gus says that white people live "over there on Cottage Grove Avenue," but Bigger says no, they live in his stomach: "It's like fire" (21–22). Bigger has both an intuitive and physiological insight into the coherence of the capitalist system in which both he and Gus live, a recognition about the corrosive internalization of authority that is at once Freudian and Marxist. This insight, embodied in the image of fire, then becomes the axle for the central metaphors of both "Fear" and "Flight"—of heating, fanning, choking, and smothering—which in turn comprise the spokes of Wright's systematic vision carrying the novel forward to its inevitable conclusion in "Fate." The relation established by the image is made explicit in Wright's use of the word "fanwise" to describe both the spreading fire in the belly of the Dalton house, its furnace (58), and the effect of alcohol on Bigger's stomach (78); and later, in "Flight," the word is used to describe the newspapers, which "fan" the fires of hatred (386).

In the symbolic logic of the novel, then, the Dalton furnace is at once the belly of the house, which fed properly heats the rooms above, and also Bigger's stomach in which the fires of hate and fear burn red hot, and the furnace of hatred fueling the economic and racial divisions in the society at large. As Charles Scruggs has argued, connecting the furnace image with Marx's critique of capital, the "twentieth-century furnace" is a "metaphor for things once solid melting 'into air'" (88). Once Bigger is installed in the Dalton household as chauffeur and tender of the furnace, Wright has collapsed the two environments into one system, the House of Capital, itself an allegory of social structure under capitalist organization.

Installing Bigger in the basement as tender of the Dalton furnace is Wright's way of converting the Dalton house to an allegory of vertical social structure, but it also represents a relation far more circular and intimate, in which white and black live within each other's stomachs, just as the newspaper map in "Flight" represents the area of white control in black and the area of black ghetto as yet unsearched in white (245). Tracing the image of fire in this way helps explain the symbolic logic both of Mary's beheading and of her burning. Dan McCall has interpreted the brutality of these events as a "sexual violation" of Mary, but that violation has already occurred in the bedroom. Other answers have been proposed based on Wright's interest in Edgar Allen Poe. Dan McCall, Michel Fabre, and Linda Prior have drawn attention to the influence of Edgar Allen Poe's gothicism on Wright's imagination, which Fabre argues "certainly paved the way for his inordinate love of melodrama, murder stories and ghastly settings" (17). Poe's "The Black Cat," Fabre points out, was the basis for Wright's creation of a "situation in which the fire, the cat, and the obsessive guilt are linked" (18; see also McCall, 70–71). Linda Prior points out that Poe's "The Murders in the Rue Morgue" involves a victim strangled and "stuffed into the chimney, the second victim's head is severed with a razor" (53). These influence arguments are compelling, all the more so because Wright himself draws attention to Poe's gothic stories in the last sentence of his essay "How Bigger Was Born": "And if Poe were alive, he would not have to invent horror; horror would invent him" (462). Whether Poe's scenes and images were borrowed or not—and one can imagine Wright's glee in transforming Poe's black cat into the Dalton's white one—the gothic melodrama of Mary's demise has its roots in the feeling-structure of the book's symbolic logic. Feeling choked and smothered by his fear of whites, he must smother Mary. Having felt whites live in his stomach like fire, Bigger must place Mary in that fire; yet that fire—so long as it is controlled—is at the same time the fire which heats the bedrooms in the top floors of the Dalton home, where the novel's representative capitalists are asleep, warmed on the night of her death by a fire fueled in part by their daughter's body. The logical necessity of Mary's beheading becomes explicable as a de*capita*tion, a playing out of the allegory by which capitalist society undoes itself and is responsible for its own dismemberment at the hands of those it exploits. Nor are these developments only the fulfillment of premonition, as McCall argues (71); these doublings—feeling smothered and smothering; feeling fire within and burning Mary—are themselves symptoms of the social totality suffering the effects of its economic and social arrangements.

Wright thus constructs the Dalton house as an organizing device, both for the discourse of economic oppression and the psychophysiological symptoms it begets. Throughout the novel, both white perceptions of black life and Bigger's of white life may be mapped onto the vertical structure of the Dalton home, with whiteness and its associations—power, consciousness, time and space and civilization—occupying the upper floors, while blackness—to which attach the discourses of the body, the worker, the jungle, the beastly, and hell itself—occupy the basement. Thus the house is at once an economic structure and a social body, constructed by and lived through the discourses of capital, race, and class (see diagram).

Wright sustains this symbolic logic throughout "Flight." Even the image of "flight" itself has an origin in Bigger's stated wish to fly, a wish that Wright builds into the symbolic structure of which Bigger remains unaware. In book 2, he does take flight and like the skywriting airplane whose pilot he envies Bigger does write a "terrible picture of reality" to "hover" before the eyes of his oppressors (130). Further, as Bigger's temporary exultation goes flaccid under the threat of his capture, his emotions continue to be figured in the condition of the Dalton's choked furnace. The entire image-structure

Dalton House as Racial & Psycho-Economic Map of Society

Mind   Top Floor: White
                                      Bedrooms of Dalton family

"Like a god" (174)   a "great natural force" (114)
          Civilization: Whiteness (magic: 119)
                                        snow, ice and water
          Real estate   realty–reality
          Landlord   Owner
                                      Source of guilt and fear
          Capitalist time   they "run like a clock" (36, 122)
                                      white face of Mary's clock (88)

House is fed   from below
Heated by   coal furnace, by work(ers)
Live on smouldering   coals

Bigger's room

He eats in the   Kitchen

Basement

Digestion   in the Belly of the house
Food, coal   Furnace
Fire in the   Belly: spreads "fanwise" (58, 78)
                                      fear, guilt
                                      Ashes

The Body   Cannibalism: living off the social body

Primitive Negro (214)   "bottled up like wild animals" (249)

Bottom of the world: Black (150)

is brought to a halt with the extinguishing of Bigger's "fire"—all the phallic glory of Bigger's inflamed manhood—his "night stick," gun, his very life—finally out-manned by the symbolic armature of the white oppressor—snow, ice, and water. Indeed, Bigger is finally pushed from his perch atop the water tower with the phallic spray of nothing less than a fire hose spurting from behind a chimney ("the stream of water was *coming* from behind a chimney," 268, emphasis added). "Flight" ends with Bigger drenched in ice water, as if he were a dog in heat.

In this account the discourses of oppression and feeling constitute two sides of the same coin, even while they are kept identifiably distinct. Bigger's local images are given meaning within Wright's symbolic logic, itself an effortless expression of Marxist critique. Given the novel's point of view, however, the working out of that logic seems to originate in Bigger's feelings, which in turn create images that are then acted out aesthetically as plot, itself a sequential image or allegory of the psychoeconomic basis of class conflict and social history. To recognize this logic of symbolic action is also to recognize that Wright has devoted himself to representing the lived effects upon the body and emotions of those whom racism and class oppress, allowing a more abstract understanding to leach through the narrator's account of Bigger's feelings before the appearance of Boris Max who offers the analysis directly in the guise of courtroom defense. Even given this emphasis upon feeling, *Native Son* would seem to be a powerful endorsement of the Marxist understanding of Bigger's predicament and passage from ghetto to electric chair, for Bigger's feelings—even though they are given top billing—are the product of his role as black worker in a white-owned and racist society. As Craig Werner summarizes, "both politically and psychologically oriented critics have emphasized [that] Bigger's environment places crushing pressure on the development of his perceptions" (135); "Wright traces Bigger's alienation to an environmentally determined repression of thought and feeling" (134).

I have been tracing this world as the discourse of Bigger's feelings, his experience of the world's images as threatening symbols, but there are then at least three discourses threaded together within the novel: the discourse of environment, which includes the class- and race-based plot and characterization, as well as the summary by Boris Max; the discourse of Bigger's thought and feeling; and the narrator/author discourse, in which Bigger's world of particulars, of local images and thoughts, become part of the novel's imaginative and logical necessity (see Reilly, 50). As noted in the

beginning of this essay, some critics have identified the failure of
these discourses to cohere—seen especially in the distance between
Max and Bigger in the novel's final scene—as a major flaw in
Wright's novel.[1] Kinnamon characterizes this as a "failure to resolve fully his intellectual (Max) and his emotional (Bigger) understanding of black life" (*Emergence*, 143).

Most recent readings of the novel have emphasized Bigger's discourse, letting the novel's determinism and the narrative logic fall
to the background. In contrast to these dismissals, efforts to rescue
Bigger from the novel's Marxist determinism have characterized
numerous readers in the last thirty years or more. These efforts
have tried to lift out like a piece of inlay from *Native Son*'s depic-
tion of environmental determinism a narrative of Bigger's emergent
freedom and self-understanding.[2] These critics have persuasively
argued that throughout *Native Son* Wright persistently develops the
theme of Bigger's desire and need for self-expression, and that he
achieves some measure of this fulfillment not only in the last scenes
of the novel, but also in the events of "Flight" following upon Bigger's accidental murder of Mary. In this way such critics have
sought to open a fissure between Marxist doxa and Wright's vision.
Valerie Smith's "Alienation and Creativity in the Fiction of Richard Wright," is a persuasive example. In her view, Bigger learns
"to tell his own story" and this "gives him a measure of control
over his life, which releases him from his feelings of isolation." His
murder of Mary "makes Bigger less fearful of the truth" and "enables him to understand his environment more clearly" (75, 79).

Without question, these frequently brilliant readings identify in
Wright's novel an apparent intention to endow Bigger with a modest growth curve. The narrator tells us that on the morning after his
killing of Mary, Bigger is "elation filled" (107); he is "like a man
reborn" and "risen up"—like Lazarus—"from a long illness"
(111); "a new feeling had been born in him" (149). Even in the
midst of fleeing his pursuers, knowing he will be caught, Bigger
feels a pride, as Smith points out, in what he has done:

> [T]here remained to him a queer sense of power. *He* had done this. *He*
> had brought all this about. In all of his life these two murders were the
> most meaningful things that had ever happened to him. He was living,
> truly and deeply, no matter what others might think, looking at him with
> their blind eyes. Never had he had the chance to live out the conse-
> quences of his actions; never had his will been so free as in this night
> and day of fear and murder and flight. (239)

The book itself sets a baseline for this reflection in Bigger's early
question "what could he do?" (12), against which measure Bigger

has clearly come a long way. Reasonably, Smith takes this passage to suggest that Bigger has confronted the true facts of his life, that he experiences both freedom and liberation, and most important that he begins to create his life and thus to enter the world of articulation and speech that he has feared for most of his life. Smith argues that the murder of Mary gives Bigger new insight: "Because the murder makes Bigger less fearful of the truth," Smith argues, "it enables him to understand his environment more clearly" (79). To be sure, Bigger recognizes that in their blindness others only go to "the surface of things"; just as he had, those around him instinctively avoid thinking too deeply (106–8).

The entire process of Bigger's purported liberation is one of piercing through the mask, from surface to depth, from blindness to sight, from mute fear to a more articulate self-confidence, from a living death to rebirth into a life in which feelings are given expression and take form as action. "Never in all his life, with this black skin of his, had the two worlds, thought and feeling, will and mind, aspiration and satisfaction, been together; never had he felt a sense of wholeness" (240). The whole weight of the novel would seem to rest upon the inner realm of feelings seeking their natural release in the world of action and history.

We needn't reject these perceptive insights, convincingly founded upon passages in the novel that had previously been under-read, in order to question the status and meaning of such ideas as "truth," "meaning" and "freedom" as experienced by Bigger and reproduced in the criticism about his development. Gibson's view that Bigger eventually finds "freedom from the constraints of his past" assumes a fact which John M. Reilly makes explicit: that Bigger's final words "are left to stand alone without the mediation of authorial commentary" (60). Just this assumption of Bigger's managing to disentangle himself from mediation, not only from the discourse of white authority but also from authorial commentary, must be reconsidered. Surely Reilly's argument isn't that Bigger frees himself from the novel, but that Bigger's final words *coincide* with the author's point of view, and therefore require no mediating translation.

To escape mediation would require Bigger to solve the riddle posed to him near the beginning of *Native Son*. Bigger and Gus have been talking about the airplane in the sky above them, which leads Bigger to reflect, "It's funny how the white folks treats us, ain't it?" Of the two characters, Bigger is by far the more reflective, and the narrative calls attention to this interior quality explicitly: "Bigger mumbled reflectively, as though talking to himself." The two young men laugh with each other about the mystery of their predicament, but Bigger isn't really laughing: "There was in his eyes a pensive, brooding amusement, as of a man who had been long confronted and tantalized by a riddle whose answer seemed always just on the verge of escaping him, but prodding him irresistibly to seek its solution" (17). This riddle—the mystery of why whites treat blacks as they do—is virtually synonymous with an explanation of Bigger's life, with fate itself. The riddle concerns not merely the defining conditions of Bigger's life but their causes and future consequences. Wright's use of the word "riddle," which invokes the story of Oedipus and the Sphinx, suggests both the importance of solving the riddle and the futility of Bigger's efforts to escape his fate. Appearing here at the novel's original beginning, before Wright put the rat scene in front of it, the word "riddle" signals Wright's intention to establish Bigger's story within the tradition of tragic drama, but also to redefine "fate" as the consequence of social and economic forces, rather than divine predisposition. These forces may *feel* like gods to Bigger but the narrative voice throughout the novel, focused later within Max's courtroom defense, insists upon explanations within the power of society to rectify.

Knowledge of the riddle and its demands should not be confused with the discourse of "meaning." Pages earlier the narrator characterizes Bigger's repressed knowledge: "He knew that the moment he allowed what his life meant to enter fully into his consciousness, he would either kill himself or someone else. So he denied himself and acted tough." The riddle must concern something other than "what his life meant," since Bigger knows what his life means, or would, if he allowed himself to admit it. Meaning in this passage is another term for "feeling" in an identical syntax: "He knew the moment he allowed himself to feel to its fulness how they lived . . . he would be swept out of himself with fear and despair" (10). The riddle's information, on the other hand, is of a different order, because it concerns not merely Bigger's candid and felt recognition of his life's poverty, abjection, and futility, but also the secret answer to the fundamental terms of his existence. Unless Bigger were to understand those terms and escape them, his life remains mediated by and within this riddle, just as Oedipus's does, but unlike Oedipus, Bigger never attains such knowledge.

The significance of this difference between riddle and meaning becomes evident in the account of Bigger's feelings on the morning after the death of Mary Dalton. Reflecting upon his actions of the night before, he accepts the deed:

> His crime seemed natural; he felt that all of his life had been leading to something like this. . . . The hidden meaning of his life—a meaning which others did not see and which he had always tried to hide—had spilled out. . . . It was as though he had an obscure but deep debt to fulfill to himself in accepting the deed. (106)

This reflection would seem to satisfy some terms of his life's riddle: insofar as his act has made good on an earlier intuitive feeling, Bigger has fulfilled a prediction, and he now understands what awaits him in the future. But this is only to say that Bigger is well aware—in both senses—of the racial *plot* into which he has accidentally fallen and which now has him in its predictable grip.

Clearly, this accident precipitates a kind of premature ejaculate, which "spilled out." Bigger has been in an "excited" state, his hands upon Mary's breasts, kissing her, and feeling her "move toward him." As Mrs. Dalton enters the room and moves closer to the bed, Bigger "grew tight and full, as though about to explode." As Mary's body "surges" upward Bigger pushes downward. Wright has designed this scene as a killing with all the connotations of a brutal sexual rape, both of which are elements of the hidden meaning of Bigger's life. Meaning then seems to be equated with feeling given action rather than interpretation; the meaning of his life is nothing more (nor less) than his formerly repressed desire to strike out at the white world. Bigger must now contend with the issue of his violent consummation, but in no sense can his reflections upon his accident and its consequences be said to constitute a solution to the riddle of Bigger's life, despite his feeling that "he was arriving at something which had long eluded him" (106). Bessie's murder just completed, Bigger wonders "what was he after? What did he want? What did he love and what did he hate?" (240); and many pages later, now in the hands of the authorities, Bigger held "his life in his hands, staring at it with a wondering question" (310).

In many readings of the novel a kind of slippage or equivocation takes place under the cover of "feeling," but feelings produced by Capital are no less elements within the narrative of Capital once they are acted upon. It makes little sense to argue that feelings which are the result of repression become free of that repression by acting upon them. The truth of his life is performed without being understood. Perhaps this constitutes a self-realization of sorts, but one firmly within the terms of the riddle whose meaning and content remain well beyond Bigger's awareness.

Instead of solving the riddle of his life, Bigger gains at best a

kinetics of freedom. In addition, his greater understanding of others' expectations teaches him the safety of acting, the importance
of theater, of life itself as a great theater in which each actor plays
a part. Recall Bigger in the upstairs hallway of the Dalton house,
with Mary in his arms, looking desperately for the door to her bedroom; he feels "strange, possessed, or as if he were acting upon a
stage in front of a crowd of people" (84). This feeling represents a
brilliant insight of Wright's: even while Bigger is engaged in a private effort to return Mary Dalton to her bedroom without alerting
her sleeping parents he is at the same time performing what Ellison
will later term a social ritual, in which he acts a part that grips and
possesses him. Similarly, when Bigger realizes he has accidentally
killed Mary he immediately translates his private act into a public
theater: "the reality of the room fell from him; the vast city of white
people that sprawled outside took its place," for Bigger understands
his action within the discourse of the racial theater that is his life.
The next morning, when Bigger's thoughts and feelings are interpolated for the reader, we learn that Bigger collapses the two terms
"act" and "accident," embracing himself as Mary's murderer, for
the crime "seemed natural." We cannot place too much emphasis
upon the word "seemed" in this passage, nor upon the word "natural," for both signal the activity of ideology rather than freedom.
Wright peppers the text with the language of drama, of acting as
performance. Bigger "acted frightened," tells himself to "act like
you scared" and realizes that "acting in this manner was a mistake," that he had to "control himself" (100–101). Bigger thinks of
the "daring" of his "actions" and that they have created something
private "all his own," a kind room or safe home or see-through mirror from which he could look out on others without being seen. As
the morning progresses, Bigger realizes "how to act from now on.
The thing to do was to act just like the others acted, live like they
lived, and while they were not looking, do what you wanted" (106).
Told from Bigger's point of view, the narrative tries to sustain a
distinction between public acts meant to deceive or divert attention
from private thoughts and intentions: "act like other people thought
you ought to act, yet do what you wanted" but the text continues:
"In a certain sense he had been doing just that in a loud and rough
manner all his life," but it was only the killing of Mary while her
mother stood in the room that showed "how clearly it could be
done" (113). When he returns to the Dalton home, he "feels a kind
of eagerness . . . a confidence, a fulness, a freedom; his whole life
was caught up in a supreme and meaningful act" (116). No matter
what he does he is acting. It is one thing to play at being white, as

Bigger and his friends do, but to act on the world's stage—the stage managed by white power—is suddenly to draw an audience: "only after he had acted upon feelings which he had had for years would the papers carry the story, *his* story" (222). Bigger falls through one role to another, at times borrowing the scripts of others, adapting the strategies of Leopold and Loeb, for example, for his own purposes. Bigger finds himself onstage, as it were, performing a role in a social drama written long before his birth and which continues to draw large audiences in the national theater.

Throughout these developments "truth" becomes defined as what his life feels like to Bigger, now given expression in the realm of action, and the desire to make others feel what he has felt. Though leading ineluctably to his own death, this desire introduces a startling relativism into the novel, since Bigger's motivation is to intrude his "picture of reality" into the white world, "to become an idea in their minds" (130). Readers can hardly miss Bigger's rejection of others' viewpoints and explanations, or that Wright purposely takes care to describe each of these viewpoints as a "picture of reality": Bigger "had killed within himself the preacher's haunting picture of life even before he had killed Mary" (284); "Bigger knew that Max was trying to make him feel that he accepted the way he looked at things," but "he doubted that God Himself could give him a picture for that now" (346–47). Near the end of the novel, Bigger tries "to react to the picture Max was drawing, trying to compare that picture with what he had felt all his life" (427). The inviting tendency is to read Bigger's "picture of reality" as the true picture, but Bigger's viewpoint is only true to his feelings; none of these pictures has any transcendental warrant. Instead, the novel offers a battle over pictures of reality, a contest of narratives, of explanations of existence, and of history. Bigger's urge to tell, to explain himself, is the urge to win the battle of genealogy, to write his history just as the plane writes its message in the sky. Wright himself characterized his own project as "developing" a picture of Bigger (440, 442–43).

To say this we needn't deny that Bigger's accidental killing does lead to the awareness that those around him are blind, nor that this increased insight is one of the vehicles by which Wright dramatizes the workings of ideology in the lives of rich and poor alike, but Bigger's consciousness, "raised" in some degree, is still false consciousness, still within the enclosing orbit of the novel's riddle, the solution to which only the author possesses, and falls far short of the understanding Wright himself achieved. Wright describes his education as a result of "contact with the labor movement":

I became conscious, at first dimly, and then later on with increasing clarity and conviction, of a vast, muddied pool of human life in America. It was as though I had put on a pair of spectacles whose power was that of an x-ray enabling me to see deeper into the lives of men. (441)

In this as in so many other ways, as others have noted, Bigger is an allegory of Wright himself, for the novel stands as both the "solution" to the "riddle" from which Wright excludes Bigger and an aesthetic catharsis for his own emotions.

In this novel, to speak one's feelings is to become free, but again freedom in Bigger's case only means to release his feelings, as Bigger feels in his confrontation with Gus: "the hysterical tensity of his nerves urged him to speak, to free himself" (26); and to have those feelings recognized: "the impulsion to try to tell was as deep as had been the urge to kill" (308). Bigger's story is nothing if not a speech act. Despite the value given in the novel to speech and self-explanation, to act upon one's feelings is to further imprison oneself in the assumptions and expectations of society. Efforts to rebut or mitigate this conclusion have often pointed to the narrator's apparent indictment of Max on the novel's last page, "Max groped for his hat like a blind man," thus lumping Max with all the other blind figures in the novel; but it is worth pointing out that Bigger's eyes, only four pages earlier, are "wide and unseeing" (429, 425). It must be granted that the dissonant chords of the novel, just a few pages later, apparently resolve in solidarity with Bigger's "wry" smile; but this is only to grant the importance of Bigger's feelings, not his understanding. Bigger's equanimity at the book's end doesn't result from his recognizing "that he *is* what he has *done*" (Gibson, 98); but because he *feels* that what he killed for "must've been pretty deep in me to make me kill! I must have *felt* it awful hard to murder. . . ." (429, emphasis added). It is the moral relativism of this conclusion, as well as Bigger's Nietzschean transvaluation of murder, that appalls Max, his placing a value upon feeling disengaged from any universal or transcendental code or law.

Feeling—what Max calls "personality" (418)—is Wright's fundamental value, and feeling is given primary status in the novel. Though produced by economic and racial oppression, Bigger's feelings initiate the symbolic logic enclosing him and also sets in motion the novel's plot. Wright's narrator remains the faithful amanuensis of his feelings, translating them for the reader and thereby evoking sympathy for Bigger despite Wright's stated intentions to stifle liberal sentiment. Dan McCall's view—"the chief error of the third part of the novel is that it is only explanation, no longer a vital artistic effort at a full understanding" (92)—not only misses the drama of articulation which recent criticism has shown to constitute the main action of "Fate," but also fails to appreciate Wright's fealty to life as it is lived, from the inside. This theme remains vibrant to the novel's end, for Bigger's purposes are always Wright's: Bigger "wondered wistfully if there was not a set of words which he had in common with others, words which would evoke in others a sense of the same fire that smoldered in him" (364). The defense offered by Boris Max is one set of words—an explanatory vision which Wright fought to retain uncut—but they were never meant to evoke Bigger's inner life. Explanation and feeling constitute separate worlds for Bigger, as they did for Wright—perhaps for most of us. Wright saw no reason to suggest otherwise.

NOTES

1. Hazel Rowley recounts Wright's argument with Jane Newton, in whose house he was living, over Max's courtroom defense: "Jane Newton thought it overwritten and too didactic; he seemed to be cramming his own opinions into the narrative. Wright insisted he could not make these points earlier; he needed to make them, and they were best expressed by Bigger's lawyer. . . . This was, he said, his chance to say what *he* felt" (155–56).

2. In an influential essay, Donald B. Gibson has argued that most readers have failed to see Bigger's individuality, failing to distinguish him as the "representative" figure his lawyers and others in the novel make of him. He has remained "invisible" (98, 101). More recently, John M. Reilly argues that the novel's ending, in which Boris Max is unable to respond to Bigger "and the fact that Bigger's words are left to stand alone without the mediation of authorial commentary serve as the signs that in this novel dedicated to the dramatization of a black man's consciousness the subject has finally found his own unqualified incontrovertible voice" (60). James A. Miller argues that Bigger manages to escape white authoritative discourse while searching for recognition from others. In the end he must be satisfied with self-recognition.

REFERENCES

Baldwin, James. *Notes of a Native Son*. New York: Bantam, 1968.

Bell, Bernard. *The Afro-American Novel and Its Tradition*. Amherst: University of Massachusetts Press, 1987.

Bone, Robert A. *The Negro Novel in America*. 1958. Revised edition. New Haven: Yale University Press, 1965.

Burke, Kenneth. *A Grammar of Motives*. 1945. Reprint, Berkeley: University of California Press, 1969.

Callahan, John F., ed. *The Collected Essays of Ralph Ellison*. Introduced by John F. Callahan. New York: The Modern Library, 1995.

Ellison, Ralph. *Invisible Man*. New York: Vintage Books edition, 1989.

Fabre, Michel. "Black Cat and White Cat: Richard Wright's Debt to Edgar Allen Poe." *Poe Studies* 4, no. 1 (1971): 17–19.

Foley, Barbara. *Radical Representations: Politics and Form in U.S. Proletarian Fiction, 1929–1941*. Durham, N.C.: Duke University Press, 1993.

Gayle, Addison, Jr. *The Way of the New World: The Black Novel in America*. Garden City, N.Y.: Anchor Press, 1976.

Gibson, Donald B. "Wright's Invisible Native Son." In *Richard Wright: A Collection of Critical Essays*, edited by Richard Macksey and Frank E. Moorer. Englewood Cliffs, N.J.: Prentice Hall, 1984.

Kinnamon, Keneth. *The Emergence of Richard Wright: A Study in Literature and Society*. Urbana: University of Illinois Press, 1972.

———, ed. *New Essays on Native Son*. New York: Cambridge University Press, 1990.

McCall, Dan. *The Example of Richard Wright*. New York: Harcourt Brace & World, 1969.

Macksey, Richard, and Frank E. Moorer, eds. *Richard Wright: A Collection of Critical Essays*. Englewood Cliffs, N.J.: Prentice Hall, 1984.

Margolies, Edward. *The Art of Richard Wright*. Carbondale: Southern Illinois University Press, 1969.

Miller, James A. "Bigger Thomas's Quest for Voice and Audience in Richard Wright's *Native Son*." *Callaloo* 9 (1986): 501–6.

Prior, Linda T. "A Further Word on Richard Wright's Use of Poe in *Native Son*." *Poe Studies* 5, no. 2 (1972): 52–53.

Reilly, John M. "Giving Bigger a Voice: The Politics of Narrative in *Native Son*." In Kinnamon, *New Essays*.

Rowley, Hazel. *Richard Wright: The Life and Times*. New York: Henry Holt, 2001.

Scruggs, Charles. *Sweet Home: Invisible Cities in the Afro-American Novel*. Baltimore: Johns Hopkins University Press, 1993.

Smith, Valerie. *Self-Discovery and Authority in Afro-American Narrative*. Cambridge, Massachusetts: Harvard University Press, 1987.

Tucker, Robert C., ed. *The Marx-Engels Reader*. New York: W. W. Norton, 1978.

Werner, Craig. "Bigger's Blues: *Native Son* and the Articulation of Afro-American Modernism." In Kinnamon, *New Essays*.

Wiesenfarth, Joseph. *Gothic Manners and the Classic English Novel*. Madison: University of Wisconsin Press, 1988.

Wright, Richard. *Native Son*. Introduction by Arnold Rampersad. New York: HarperCollins, 1998.

A Conversation with Margaret Drabble
about Jane Austen

Emily Auerbach—Margaret Drabble

(From an interview with Emily Auerbach for a public radio documentary called "Jane Austen and the Courage to Write," February 1997)

Emily Auerbach (EA): What was your experience in reading Jane Austen? I've found that some people were forced to read her in school and hated her; others were instant fans. What about your own experience?

Margaret Drabble (MD): My experience in reading Jane Austen is probably representative of that of quite a lot of people in that I was first introduced to *Pride and Prejudice* when I was eleven or twelve and I didn't like it at all because I didn't see then that it was meant to be ironic; I took everything very seriously and literally from the first sentence on. It wasn't until I reread it about two years later that I realized the levels of irony in the book and the wit—and I loved it. Then I read my way through all of them, reread them many times, and continued to look for things in them. So since that first rather unhappy introduction, which I think was simply a question of my being too young, I haven't looked back.

EA: When you came to write novels yourself, do you think your acquaintance with Austen had an effect on how you wrote?

MD: I find my own novels are in a perpetual dialogue with Jane Austen. There are quite a number of writers who I think of perpetually when I'm thinking of plot or subject, content, moral dilemma, the scope of the novel, the possible range of the novel. It wouldn't be an exaggeration to say I think of Jane Austen nearly every day when I'm not writing and every day when I am. She's a very constant presence, and it's as though in my head there were a debate with her. I don't see her as a human being answering it. It is a debate with her as a writer, and with Virginia Woolf and George Eliot, and one or two others who mean a great deal to me and whose solutions to various formal problems in the novel continue to perplex and exercise me. So she's a very constant presence.

EA: Can you give me some sense of what that presence is—what she represents to you—and how you both are influenced by her and in some ways react against her?

MD: She was constrained to lead a fairly confined life geographically, and yet she made immense use of what was offered to her. You see in her grain of sand a whole world of implication, of moral implication far beyond the confined lives of the actual characters. I see in her the ability to use what you have to very great advantage. That in itself poses a dilemma of what do you do if you know you could stretch that canvas a little—if you know you could travel to Vietnam or Cambodia or Australia, as novelists today can do. They don't have to accept the geographical and social constraints Jane Austen faced. Offered this freedom, which should we choose? I think this is a perpetual debate for many writers today; perhaps particularly for women writers who have traditionally been encouraged to see limitation as a virtue. Now we're not encouraged to see it as a virtue. We're meant to leap beyond it, to jump over the fence and gallop away, but maybe we lose something by doing so. You lose in concentration what you gain in extent, so this is a very real problem for me.

EA: Two other contemporary writers I interviewed, Carol Shields and Kelly Cherry, said they felt Austen's use of happy marriages at the end of all six of her novels made them at times feel compelled to end their own novels with divorces.

MD: Yes, I see the happy marriage solution as not something that we can accept as easily, particularly in view of the ironies of Jane Austen's own personal situation which we now know a good deal more about than her first readers did. We do look at her solutions of marriage as being possibly ironic in some sense. I find myself in my novels arguing with her almost and saying, right, the novel ended with a marriage in her day; now it sometimes begins with a marriage and goes on from there through divorce and through a second or third marriage or through celibacy or solitude. So there's a whole new range of plots one offers. I must say that the only novel of mine that ends with a marriage is *The Realms of Gold* and I did feel compelled in the text to apologize slightly for this happy ending because I knew that feminists would object to this solution of my heroine's problems.

EA: You've worked with many writers as you edited *The Oxford Companion to English Literature*. What do you see as Jane Austen's place in the literary canon? What is it that she adds to it that wouldn't be there if she had never written anything?

MD: I think Jane Austen's place is completely assured as one of the greatest writers in the English language. There have been objectors at times, but she's always been very highly valued. I see her as the writer who introduced into the realm of the novel this intense concentration on manners and morals that in fact is an ongoing strain of preoccupation with all writers of fiction. She created the domestic novel as we know it. I know that others were writing domestic novels, but she created the flexibility of the form, the seeming lack of presumption which goes along with a great deal of formal precision. She invented the novel and made it usable by generations after it, and it is still there to be used. What she did is still something that we can draw on. So I think she is not only a highly accomplished practitioner of a form that was very new to her but she's also a continuous source of enlightenment and inspiration. In fact this very morning I was writing an introduction to Angus Wilson's novel *The Middle Age of Mrs. Elliot*, which is a wonderful play on both *Emma* and *Persuasion*, and that's a novel published in 1958 which is in a very direct relationship with Jane Austen, just as I feel myself in direct relationship with Angus Wilson's novel. And so you can see that although she is part of past, she's also very much part of our present.

EA: How do you see her humor as part of her voice?

MD: I think she's one of the funniest writers who ever wrote. I think there are sublime moments of comedy—some of them satiric comedy, some of them pure fun; moments of repartee, moments of comeback. We've all relished to the utmost Darcy's wonderful proposal to Elizabeth—the irony, the sheer ridiculousness of the situation. Austen's comic portrayals of characters like Lady Bertram or Mrs. Norris are wonderfully comic yet they always have this edge of perception and humanity—or what many would say cruelty. It can often be the same thing. I think her wit is so much part of her style, and of course it's a defensive wit. I think she had a very difficult life in the world she lived in with perceptions which extended far beyond it, and wit is a defense.

It's also an attack, a rapierlike attack on convention and absurdity. She relished absurdity, and she had a Congreve-like wit.

EA: If you think of comic characters in *Emma,* for example—Mrs. Elton and Mr. Woodhouse—how do you see them as quintessentially Austen?

MD: Mr. Woodhouse and Mrs. Elton are characters that we all know. We all know these characters because she defined and described them for us and we see them in our own lives. We all know a Mr. Woodhouse; we all know Mrs. Elton. I was looking the other day at the marvelous passage where Mrs. Elton is boasting of her barouche landau in Maple Grove to Emma, and Emma's getting more and more standoffish and huffy at Mrs. Elton's condescension. It is a wonderfully funny passage about social boasting and trying to put down the other person.

EA: Yes, today Mrs. Elton would be boasting about her relatives' Rolls Royce.

MD: Absolutely. These characteristics are permanently human. And Mr. Woodhouse is the ever-hypochondriacal father who would drive us mad in real life, yet we see him tempered by affection. I love Jane Austen's hypochondriacs. For example, Anne Elliot's sister Mary in *Persuasion* is forever feeling ill until a party comes along. We all know people like that. One of my favorite lines in the whole of Jane Austen is Kitty in *Pride and Prejudice*: when her mother tells her to stop coughing, Kitty says fretfully, "I do not cough for my own amusement." I've often said that line myself when I've seen people looking at me crossly. I think that that balance of comedy and silliness and humanity is just brilliant.

EA: Do you see yourself in some of Jane Austen's characters?

MD: I see myself in a lot of Jane Austen's characters. I see myself boasting about my children like Mrs. Bennet. We all have her bad qualities as well as her good qualities. I don't see myself as a great wit like Elizabeth, but I do see myself as occasionally unkind like Emma. So I do see bits of her heroines and bits of her less heroic characters in myself all the time.

EA: Of all novelists, she seems perhaps to provoke the most widely differing reactions—either worship or loathing. Mark Twain, for instance, defined a good library as one with no Jane Austen in it, even if it had no books. Why do you think there's been such a range of responses to Jane Austen, beginning with some of her own relatives?

MD: There have been very interesting comments over the generations. I think the Austen family didn't know whether to be proud of her or not. The historical debate has gone on between the Aunt Jane, that delightful cozy Aunt Jane who was embarrassed about writing and hid her books away and was always willing to play with her nieces and nephews, which she probably wasn't (I mean we remember Anne Elliot in *Persuasion* getting quite irritated, however patient with the children). So we see this auntlike figure, who many readers have adopted as their own aunt, on one side, and on the other side we see this infuriatingly prim irritating character whom D. H. Lawrence and Mark Twain couldn't abide. Their animal spirits rose up against this prim sexless creature. I think that Sir Walter Scott admired her and saw her as a writer who could do something he couldn't do—"I can do the big Bow-Wow strain, but I can't do what she does," he said famously; she had a realism he couldn't achieve. In the twentieth century, W. H. Auden wrote that famous Letter to Lord Byron in which he says of Jane Austen, "You could not shock her / More than she shocks me" and talks about how she reveals "the economic basis of society," which is a wonderful tribute from a male poet to a female novelist. Written in the same decade is a very interesting comment from Virginia Woolf, who is reading Austen's newly published letters which some thought revealed Jane Austen as spiteful and small-minded. Woolf had a much more interesting comment: She writes, "What I shall proceed to find out from her letters when I have time is why she failed to be much better than she was. Something to do with sex, I expect. The letters are full of hints already that she suppressed half of her in her novels. Now why?" I don't think Woolf ever answered that question. But I think it's a very challenging question. Could she have been a greater writer if her life had been different? I think our assessment of her is being constantly revised, and that's the sign of a really important writer.

EA: Why do you think Charlotte Brontë disliked Austen?

MD: Charlotte Brontë's reaction is more or less what one would expect. She found Jane Austen's work lacking in poetry; she found it lacking in passion. She found Austen's works too controlled, like a well-clipped hedge. And of course one then immediately thinks of Emily and Charlotte Brontë's evocation of the wild moorland in the north of England, which I was brought up with, rather than the delicate, southern, civilized world, in which Jane Austen was brought up with. These are the two worlds Elizabeth Gaskell contrasts in *North and South*—one being the wild north and the other being the tamed south.

EA: Why do you think so many male readers over the centuries have responded to Austen not just with dislike but with downright venom?

MD: Yes, I can see that there is a macho response to Jane Austen. I think it would be quite unfair to describe all men as anti-Austen because there have been some passionate male admirers and defenders of Austen, including W. H. Auden, Macaulay, G. H. Lewes, so it would be quite unfair to see a direct gender divide. Having said that, I do think that just as some women recoil from *Reservoir Dogs*, so some men recoil from Jane Austen. I have to admit that my own husband, Michael Holyrod, who's a truly civilized and well-read man, is not a great fan of Jane Austen. He finds Jane Austen exactly what her critics suggest—confining—and he says if only she could have gotten out of there. It somewhat stifles him and he thinks it's all much ado about nothing. We have many spirited debates about this.

EA: Comedian Dave Barry told me that he would rather watch an Arnold Schwarzenegger movie with a helicopter crashing into a jet ski than go to a Jane Austen film.

MD: Jane Austen movies take one to a realm of costume drama which is a very tricky place to be, and it even makes me long to see a bit of cops and robbers—not perhaps Schwarzenegger but *Apocalypse Now*. I do see that there is a temptation with the costume drama sensation that has happened to see her prettily in the past, which is not how I read her at all.

EA: What are some of your favorite scenes in Jane Austen?

MD: One can go on about one's favorite scenes forever. There are moments that I so love. I do think the proposal of Mr. Darcy to Elizabeth is one of the wonderful comic moments of literature. I think it's superb. There are great romantic moments, too, such as the scene in *Persuasion* where Captain Wentworth is writing a letter and there's such a moment of suspense before all is well. Moments like that are handled with such drama. There are also wonderfully tender moments, as in *The Watsons* when Emma is watching a little boy, Charles Blake, who is being neglected and so Emma asks him to dance and helps him over his embarrassment. It shows a kind of tenderness in Austen that we don't often see.

EA: Do you see Austen as a woman of courage?

MD: I see Jane Austen as a woman of courage, but I doubt that she thought about it that way. Those who have courage just perceive it as something they have to do or need to do. I doubt very much that Jane Austen sat down and said, "I'm being very brave sitting down to write this book." In fact, she had all the counterindications in that she did conceal her work, she pretended not to take it very seriously, she went along with the public view much of the time that it wasn't a serious profession. But I think that in herself she just had extraordinary confidence, which perhaps is the same thing as courage. She knew what she was doing, and she knew that she was much cleverer than most of the people around her. She had the confidence to trust her own talent and to write what she had to write. She was very careful not to offend the proprieties; her novels are almost all within the confines of the acceptable. She looks forward to the Victorian age from a coarser age. She's on the side of politeness—Sir Charles Grandison rather than Tom Jones. And yet she had this confidence to do what she had to do. There were more courageous writers than her in terms of confronting public opinion, but I think what she had was an unshakable self-confidence.

EA: But there are some bold passages. For example, Anne Elliot says in *Persuasion*, "Men have had every advantage of us in telling their own story. Education has been theirs in so much higher a degree; the pen has been in their hands. I will not allow books to prove any thing."

MD: But that is said very playfully. Anne is not rude or harsh to Captain Harville. Austen seems to want to make her point but not by causing intense irritation. She doesn't wish to shock. She simply wishes to point out with devastating clarity the situation as she sees it. It's a courage of steadfastness, and also of a kind of playfulness in which she will always use a device to make her point rather than go straight for a brutal statement about women's place, women's roles. She moves indirectly toward her route.

EA: What do you see as Jane Austen's legacy?

MD: Her legacy is much of fiction as we know it today. She created a kind of fiction, a kind of concentration on character, on the importance of the inner life, on the significance of domestic detail, the importance of human relationships which really hadn't been perceived before she perceived it. It's that aspect of her that makes one realize why George Henry Lewes called her the female Shakespeare—her extraordinary insight into human relationships and small as well as large events. I think her legacy is that she made prose fiction a vehicle for very serious speculation about human behavior.

About Joseph Wiesenfarth

WILLIAM BAKER

Born 20 AUGUST 1933 IN BROOKLYN, NEW YORK, THE YOUNGER SON of a bank official, Joseph Wiesenfarth having graduated from Bishop Loughlin High School at the age of seventeen, became a member of the Roman Catholic teaching order of Christian Brothers. He entered Catholic University of America where he subsequently was elected to Phi Beta Kappa, graduating magna cum laude with a B.A. degree in 1956. Wiesenfarth then began his career in teaching at St. Joseph's High School in Detroit, Michigan, and later lectured in English at De Salle College in Washington, D.C., while earning his M.A. from the University of Detroit (1959) and his Ph.D. from Catholic University of America (1962).

In 1970 Wiesenfarth joined the English Department at the University of Wisconsin-Madison where he taught both undergraduate and graduate courses until his retirement in 2000, rising from the rank of associate professor to professor. He served as chair of the English Department from 1983 to 1986 and subsequently from 1989 to 1992. Although nominated for the position of Dean of the College of Letters and Science in 1992, Wiesenfarth declined to be considered for the post. However, he served as Associate Dean of the Graduate School from 1995 to 1996, Associate Dean of the College of Letters and Science from 1996 to 1997, and Chair of New Directions: The Reaccreditation Project from 1997 to 2000. During his tenure at the University of Wisconsin, Wiesenfarth received a number of signal honors, among them his appointment as Hands-Bascom professorship and, later, the Nathan S. Blount chair. He also was the recipient of the Chancellor's Award for Excellence in Teaching. In 1996, he was honored with the Outstanding Achievement in Research and Scholarship award by the Alumni Society of Catholic University of America. Wiesenfarth is a founding patron of the Jane Austen Society of North America and serves on the editorial board of *Connotations: A Journal for Critical Debate* and the advisory board of *George Eliot-George Henry Lewes Studies*.

Wiesenfarth through his activities as a scholar and critic in matters relating to nineteenth and twentieth-century British and American literature, has gained both a national and international reputation. In recent years, he has lectured widely on Jane Austen, Ford Madox Ford, Stella Bowen, and others throughout the United States and in New Zealand and Australia. He currently resides with his wife, Louise, and his son, Adam, in Madison, Wisconsin.

Bibliography of Works by Joseph Wiesenfarth

WILLIAM BAKER

BOOKS AND MONOGRAPHS

Henry James and the Dramatic Analogy: A Study of the Major Novels of the Middle Period. New York: Fordham University Press, 1963.

The Errand of Form: An Assay of Jane Austen's Art. New York: Fordham University Press, 1967.

George Eliot's Mythmaking. Heidelberg: Carl Winter Universitätsverlag, 1977.

George Eliot: A Writer's Notebook, 1854–1879, and Uncollected Writings. Edited by Joseph Wiesenfarth. Charlottesville: Published for the Bibliographical Society of the University of Virginia by the University Press of Virginia, 1981.

Gothic Manners and the Classic English Novel. Madison: University of Wisconsin Press, 1988.

Ford Madox Ford and the Arts. Edited by Joseph Wiesenfarth. Special issue of *Contemporary Literature* 30 (1989).

Jack and Alice, by Jane Austen. Coedited with Laura Maestrelli and Kristin Smith. Edmonton, Canada: Juvenilia Press, 2001.

History and Representation in Ford Madox Ford's Writings. Edited by Joseph Wiesenfarth. Special issue of *International Ford Madox Ford Studies* 3 (2004).

Ford Madox Ford and the Regiment of Women: Violet Hunt, Jean Rhys, Stella Bowen, Janice Biala. Madison: University of Wisconsin Press, 2004.

ARTICLES AND CHAPTERS IN COLLECTIONS

"The Concept of 'Poetic Sensibility' in Criticism of T. S. Eliot." *Fresco* 8 (1957): 40–57.

"Art and Event in 'Ethan Brand.'" *Nineteenth-Century Fiction* 15 (1960): 249–57.

"Illusion and Allusion: Reflections in 'The Cracked Looking-Glass.'" *Four Quarters* 12 (1962): 30–37. Reprinted in *Katherine Anne Porter: A Critical Symposium*, edited by L. Hartley and G. Core, 139–48. Athens: University of Georgia Press, 1969).

"Criticism and the Semiosis of *The Good Soldier*." *Modern Fiction Studies* 8 (1963): 39–49.

"*Pride and Prejudice*: The Art of Travel." *Greater Philadelphia Council Teachers of English Newsletter* 2 (1963): 10–27.

"Stevie and the Structure of *The Secret Agent*." *Modern Fiction Studies* 13 (1968): 513–17.

"Jane Austen's Judgment." *London Times Literary Supplement* 24 (October 1968): 1210. (A Letter.)

"Internal Opposition in Porter's 'Granny Weatherall.'" *Critique* 11 (1969): 47–55. Reprinted in *Critical Essays on Katherine Anne Porter*, edited by Darlene Harbour Unrue, 103–9. Boston: G. K. Hall/Simon & Schuster/Macmillan, 1997.

"Demythologizing *Silas Marner*." *ELH* 37 (1970): 226–44.

"The Structure of Katherine Anne Porter's 'Theft.'" *Cithara* 10, no. 2 (1971): 65–71.

"*Persuasion*: History and Myth." *Wordsworth Circle* 2 (1971): 160–68.

"*Adam Bede* and Myth." *Papers on Language and Literature* 8 (1972): 39–52. Reprinted in *Nineteenth-Century Literature Criticism*. Gale Net, 2000.

"'High' People and 'Low' in *Joseph Andrews*: A Study of Structure and Style." *College Language Association (CLA) Journal* 16 (1973): 357–65.

"The Medea in *Daniel Deronda*." *Die Neueren Sprachen*, no. 2 (1973): 103–8.

"Negatives of Hope: A Reading of Katherine Anne Porter." *Renascence* 25 (1973): 85–94. Reprinted in *American Fiction, 1914–1945*, edited by Harold Bloom, 127–36. New York: Chelsea House, 1987.

"History and Myth in Jane Austen's *Persuasion*." *The Literary Criterion* 11, no. 3 (1974): 76–85.

"*Emma*: Point Counter Point." In *Jane Austen: Bicentenary Essays*, edited by John Halperin, 207–20. Cambridge: Cambridge University Press, 1975.

"Austen and Apollo." In *Jane Austen Today*, edited by Joel Weinsheimer, 46–63. Athens: University of Georgia Press, 1975. Excerpted in *Pride and Prejudice Casebook* in Scribner Literature, Novel, and Drama Series.

"Legend in *The Mill on the Floss*." *Texas Studies in Literature and Language* 18 (1976): 21–41.

"Middlemarch." *Nineteenth-Century Fiction* 30 (1976): 572–73.

"Commentary" ("*Der Neffe als Onkel* in *Middlemarch*"). *Nineteenth-Century Fiction* 30 (1976): 572–73.

"George Eliot's Notes for *Adam Bede*." *Nineteenth-Century Fiction* 32 (1977): 127–65.

"Dialectics in *Barchester Towers*." In *Trollope: Critical Studies*, edited by Tony Bareham, 36–53. London: Vision Press, 1980.

"The Greeks, the Germans, and George Eliot." *Browning Institute Studies* 10 (1982): 91–104.

"Antique Gems from *Romola* to *Daniel Deronda*." In *George Eliot: A Centenary Tribute*, edited by Gordon S. Haight and Rosmary T. VanArsdel, 55–63. London: Macmillan, 1982.

"*Middlemarch*: The Language of Art." *PMLA* 97 (May 1982): 363–77.

"George Eliot." *Dictionary of Literary Biography*. Vol. 21, *Victorian Novelists Before 1885*. Edited by W. E. Fredeman and Ira Nadel, 145–70. Detroit: Gale, 1983. Revised/reissued in *The Concise Dictionary of Literary Biography*, 1992, 183–209.

"*Middlemarch*: The Fatality of British Decorum." *Literaturwissenschaftliches Jahrbuch* 25 (1984): 205–14.

"Robert Graves, *I, Claudius* (1934)." *Der historische Roman als Bestseller und Historie Anglistik und Englischunterricht* 24 (1984): 23–24. Translated from English by Bernhard Reitz.

"The Case of *Pride and Prejudice*." *Studies in the Novel* 16 (1984): 261–73.

"*The Watsons* as Pretext." *Persuasions* 8 (1986): 101–11.

"Problems, Problems, Problems." *ADE Bulletin* 85 (1986): 40–42.

"A Woman in *The Portrait of a Lady*." *The Henry James Review* 7, nos. 2–3 (1986): 18–28.

"Violet Hunt Rewrites Jane Austen: *Pride and Prejudice* (1813) and *Their Lives* (1916)." *Persuasions* 11 (December 1989): 61–65.

"*The Portrait of a Lady*: Gothic Manners in Europe." In *Reading and Writing Women's Lives: A Study of the Novel of Manners*, edited by Barbara Brothers and Bege K. Bowers, 119–40. Ann Arbor, Mich.: U.M.I. Research Press, 1989.

"The Literary Life: A Lecture Delivered by Ford Madox Ford." *Contemporary Literature* 30 (1989): 171–82.

"Ford Madox Ford and the Arts: Introduction." *Contemporary Literature* 30 (1989): 167–69.

"The Ash-Bucket at Dawn: Ford's Art of Poetry." *Contemporary Literature* 30 (1989): 240–62.

"'Schreibe, wie du sprichst': Ford Madox Ford's Fiction." In *Mündliches Wissen in neuzlitlicher Erzahlkunst*, edited by Paul Goetsch, 137–48. Tübingen: Gunter Narr Verlag, 1990.

"The Art of Fiction and the Art of War: Henry James, H. G. Wells, and Ford Madox Ford." *Connotations: A Journal for Critical Debate* 1 (1991): 55–73.

"Fargobawlers: James Joyce and Ford Madox Ford." *Biography* (1991): 95–116. Reprinted in *Modernism and the Individual Talent*, Editor Jörg Rademacher. London: Rodopi, 2001.

"Gothic Forebears: Ford Madox Ford and the Pre-Raphaelites." *Proceedings of the Australasian Victorian Studies Association*, 131–41. Sydney: AVSA, 1992. Reprinted in *Modernism and the Individual Talent*, edited by Jörg Rademacher. London: Rodopi, 2001.

"Henry James and Ford Madox Ford: A Troubled Relationship." *The Henry James Review* 13 (1992): 172–91.

"George Eliot (Mary Ann Evans)." In *Concise Dictionary of Literary Biography*, 183–209. Detroit: Gale, 1992. Revised/reissued from *DBL 21: Victorian Novelists before 1885* (1983).

"Jane Austen's Men and Literary Tradition." In *Remembering 1992: A Collection of JASNA Illinois-Indiana Presentations*, edited by Julie L. Toleikis, 17–23. Chicago: Jane Austen Society of North America/Illinois & Indiana Chapter, 1992.

"Mythic Perspectives in George Eliot's Fiction." *The George Eliot Review: Journal of the George Eliot Fellowship* 24 (1993): 41–45.

"Excavating Pemberley." *Remembering 1993: A Collection of JASNA Illinois-Indiana Presentations*. Chicago: JASNA, 1993.

"Ford Madox Ford and the Pre-Raphaelites or How Dante Gabriel Rossetti Started the First World War." *REAL: Yearbook of Research in English and American Literature* 9 (1993): 109–48.

"Some Perspectives on George Eliot's Mythmaking." *George Eliot Review* 24 (1993): 41–45.

"The Eliot Hypothesis." *Review (Washington)* 16 (1994): 289–99.

"'Celebrating *Persuasion*.' The Jane Austen Society of North America's Annual General Meeting." *Eighteenth-Century Fiction* 6 (1994): 283–87.

"Phillip Pirrip's Afterlife, or *Great Expectations* Again . . . And Again." *George Eliot–George Henry Lewes Studies* 36–37 (1999): 70–84. A comparison of *Great Expectations* and Peter Carey's *Jack Maggs*.

"Art and Life: Henry James' Great Expectations." In *Festschrift fur Paul Goetsch*, edited by Karl Muller and Meinhard Wingkens, 275–87. Tubingen: Gunter Narr Verlag, 1994.

"The Revolution of Civility in *Pride and Prejudice* and *Persuasions*." *Journal of the Jane Austen Society of North America* 16 (December 1994):107–14.

"The Civility of *Emma*." *Sensibilities* (Jane Austen Society of Australia) 11 (December 1995): 38–54.

"The Civility of *Emma*." *Persuasions* 18 (1996): 8–23.

"The Garson-Olivier Pride and Prejudice: A Hollywood Story." In *Test und Tom im Film*, edited by Paul Goetsch and Dietrich Schuenemann, 81–93. Tubingen: Gunter Narr Verlag, 1997.

"*Northanger Abbey*: The Invention of Civility." *Persuasions On–Line* 20 (1998).

"Jane Austen's Family of Fiction." *Sensibilities* 17 (December 1998) 58–75. Reprinted in *Persuasions On-Line*, 22 (2000).

"Portraits of the Artist: Joyce, Wells, and Ford Madox Ford." In *Lineages of the Novel: Essays in Honour of Raimund Bergmeier*, edited by Bernhard Reitz and Eckart Voigts-Virchow, 179–88. Trier: Wissenschaftlichen Verlag Trier, 2000.

"Ford's *Joseph Conrad: A Personal Remembrance* as Metafiction: Or, How Conrad Became an Elizabethan Poet." *Renascence* 53 (2000): 43–60.

"Metafiction as the Real Thing." In *The Finer Thread, the Tighter Weave: Essays on the Short Fiction of Henry James*, edited by Joseph Dewey and Brooke Horvath, 235–51. West Lafayette: Indiana University Press, 2001.

"James, Henry." In *The Oxford Companion to United States History*, edited by Paul S. Boyer, 401–2. Oxford: Oxford University Press, 2001.

"Stella Bowen and Ford Madox Ford: Drawn from Life." In *Stella Bowen, Art, Love & War,* ed. Lola Wilkins, 31–37. Canberra: Australian War Memorial, 2002.

"Ford Madox Ford, Violet Hunt, and the Battle of the Books: Sexual/Textual Hostilities." In *Ford Madox Ford's Modernity,* ed. Max Saunders and Robert Hampson. London: Macmillan, 2003.

"Approaching Ford's *Joseph Conrad: A Personal Remembrance*." In *Proceedings of the James, Conrad, Ford Conference, 1999*, edited by Wieslaw Keajka. Amsterdam and New York: Rodopi, 2003. Forthcoming.

"Coda to the City: Ford Madox Ford's Poetry." In *Ford Madox Ford Studies*, edited by Sara Haslam, et al. Forthcoming.

"Emma: A Likely Story." In *Approaches to Teaching Jane Austen's* Emma, edited by Marcia McClintock Folsom. New York: MLA. Forthcoming.

Review Articles

"Robert Graves." *Contemporary Literature* 25 (1984): 93–102.

"The Eliot Hypothesis." *Review* 16 (1994): 289–99.

"The Ford-Bowen Correspondence." *Review* 17 (1995): 85–94.

"The Good Soldier on Parade." In *Review*, edited by James O. Hoge, 65–94. Charlottesville: University Press of Virginia, 1997.

"*Godot* in Stratford." *The Beckett Circle: Newsletter of the Samuel Beckett Society* 20, no. 2 (1998): 45. A review of the Stratford (Ontario) Festival's production of *Waiting for Godot*.

NOTES AND MISCELLANEOUS

"Donne's 'A Valediction: Forbidding Mourning' 1–8." *Explicator* 16, no. 7 (April 1958), no. 4.

"Graham Greene's 'The Hint of an Explanation.'" *Explicator* 30, no. 4 (January 1961), no. 1.

"Jane Austen's Judgment." *London Times Literary Supplement*, no. 3, 478 (24 October 1968): 1210. (A Letter.)

"Forum." *PMLA* 98 (1983): 90–91. (A Letter.)

"Tributes to Gordon S. Haight (1901–1985)." *The George Eliot-George Henry Lewes Newsletter* 8 (April 1986): 4.

"Ford, Ford Madox (1873–1939)." In *Encyclopedia of Twentieth-Century Britain*, edited by Fred M. Leventhal. New York: Garland Publishing, 1995.

REVIEWS

Review of *George Eliot: A Biography*, by Gordon S. Haight. *Commonweal* (7 February 1969): 597–98.

Review of *The Collected Essays and Occasional Writings of Katherine Anne Porter*. *Commonweal* (7 August 1970): 396–98.

Review of *The Saddest Story: A Biography of Ford Madox Ford*, by Arthur Mizener and of *Your Mirror to My Times*, by Ford Madox Ford, Edited by Michael Killigrew. *Commonweal* (1 October 1971): 19–20.

Review of *Henry James: The Master: 1901–1916*, by Leon Edel. *Commonweal* (17 March 1972): 44–45.

Review of *Season of Youth: The Bildungsroman from Dickens to Golding*, by Jerome Hamilton Buckley. *Commonweal* (23 May 1975): 152.

Review of *The George Eliot–George Henry Lewis Library*, by William Baker. *Literary Research Newsletter* 3 (1978): 131–34.

Review of *The George Eliot Letters*, vols. 8 and 9, by Gordon S. Haight, ed. and of *George Henry Lewes: A Victorian Mind*, by Hock Guan Tjoa. *Commonweal* (25 May 1979): 315–16.

Review of *George Eliot's Middlemarch Note-Books: A Transcription*, by John Clark Pratt and Victor A. Neufeldt, eds. *Nineteenth-Century Fiction* 36 (June 1981): 113–17.

Review of *The Life in the Fiction of Ford Madox Ford*, by Thomas C. Moser. *Journal of Modern Literature* 9 (Fall 1982): 73.

Review of *A Bibliography of Jane Austen*, by David Gilson. *Literary Research Newsletter* 9 (1984): 21–22.

Review of *Katherine Anne Porter's Women: The Eye of Her Fiction*, by Jean Kraus DeMouy. *Contemporary Literature* 25 (1984): 363–67.

Review of *The Return of the Good Soldier: Ford Madox Ford and Violet Hunt's 1917 Diary*, by Robert and Marie Secor and of *Ford Madox Ford and the Voice of Uncertainty*, by Ann Barr Snitow. *Studies in the Novel* 17 (1985):437–40.

Review of *The Language That Makes George Eliot's Fiction*, by Karen Mann. *Studies in the Novel* 17 (1985): 321–22.

Review of *George Eliot and Blackmail*, by Alexander Welsh. *Modern Language Quarterly* 47 (1986): 75–78.

Review of *Truth and Vision in Katherine Anne Porter's Fiction*, by Darlene Harbour Unrue. *Studies in American Fiction* 15 (1987): 238–40.

Review of *Fairy Tale and Romance in the Work of Ford Madox Ford*, by Timothy Weiss. *Studies in the Novel* 19 (1987): 233–35.

Review of *An Annotated Bibliography of George Eliot*, by George Levine. *The George Eliot–George Henry Lewes Newsletter* 14–15 (1989): 1–3.

Review of Claudia Johnson. *Jane Austen: Women, Politics, and the Novel. English Language Notes* 28 (1990): 77–79.

Review of *A Reception-History of George Eliot's Fiction*, by Russell J. Perkin. *The George Eliot–George Henry Lewes Newsletter* 16–17 (1990): 24–26.

Review of *In the Pride of the Moment: Encounters in Jane Austen's World*, by John A. Dussinger. *Nineteenth-Century Literature* 46 (1991): 408–10.

Review of *Ford Madox Ford*, by Alan Judd. *Style* 21, no. 1 (1993): 159–63.

Review of *George Eliot's Originals and Contemporaries*, by Gordon S. Haight. Edited by Hugh Witemeyer. *George Eliot–George Henry Lewes Studies* 22–23 (1993): 93–96.

Review of *Katherine Anne Porter at One Hundred: New Perspectives*, by Blanche T. Eerling-Koning, ed. *Analytical & Enumerative Bibliography* 8, no. 2 (1994): 153–54.

Review of *The Correspondence of Ford Madox and Stella Bower*, by Sondra J. Stang and Karen Cochran. *Review* 17 (1995): 85–94.

Review of *Ford Madox Ford: A Dual Life*, by Max Saunders. Vol. 1, The World before the War. *Clio* 26 (1996): 114–17.

Review of *The Journals of George Eliot*, by Margaret Harris and Judith Johnston, eds. *Australasian Victorian Studies Journal* 5 (1999): 162–65.

Review of *The Good Soldier*, by Ford Madox Ford. Edited by Martin Stannard. *Review* 19 (1997): 65–93.

Review of *A Collection of Letters, Evelyn* and *Lesley Castle*, by Jane Austen. *Eighteenth-Century Fiction* 13, no. 4 (July 2001): 611–16

Non-Scholarly Writings

The Meanest Animal in the Whole Wide World, with Louise Halpin Wiesenfarth (graphic artist and typographer). Madison, Wis.: The Halfpenny Press, 1973.

Plane Words, with Louise Halpin Wiesenfarth (graphic artist and typographer. Madison, Wis.: The Halfpenny Press, 1975.

Notes on Contributors

EMILY AUERBACH is Professor of English at the University of Wisconsin-Madison, where she teaches not only undergraduates but also thousands of nontraditional outreach students via radio, correspondence, and public lectures. She has published articles on Austen, Dickens, George Eliot, and others, and is the author of the forthcoming *Searching for Jane Austen*. She has collaborated with Joseph Wiesenfarth on numerous outreach projects, including an international *Jane Austen Festival* and several programs for the award-winning *Courage to Write* series of public radio documentaries on women writers.

WILLIAM BAKER is Presidential Research Professor of English at Northern Illinois University and is the author and editor of numerous books and articles on Victorian and modern literature. His most recent publications include: *George Eliot: A Bibliographical History* and *Wilkie Collins's Library: A Reconstruction*. He is the editor of *George Eliot-George Henry Lewes Studies* and coedits *The Year's Work in English Studies* (YWES).

GARETH CORDERY's dissertation on Dickens was supervised by Joe Wiesenfarth at the University of Wisconsin-Madison in the early 1970s. He is now a Senior Lecturer in English at the University of Canterbury, Christchurch, New Zealand. He has published mainly on Dickens and is currently researching the caricaturist and book illustrator Harry Furniss (1854–1925).

MARGARET DRABBLE is the preeminent British woman of letters. The author of twenty-three books including *A Summer Bird-Cage*, *The Millstone*, *The Middle Ground* and *The Witch of Exmoor*, she also edited *The Oxford Companion to English Literature*, 5th edition.

PAUL GOETSCH, professor emeritus at the University of Freiburg, has published books on Charles Dickens, Thomas Hardy, the English novel in transition (1880–1910), modern English and American drama, the short story, and Canadian literary nationalism. He has

214

also edited a number of books on orality and literacy, presidential rhetoric in the United States, and other subjects.

JOSEPH A. KESTNER studied English literature and classical languages at Columbia University. He is McFarlin Professor of English at the University of Tulsa. His most recent books include *Protest and Reform, Masculinities in Victorian Painting, Sherlock's Men: Conan Doyle, Masculinities, and Cultural History*, and *The Edwardian Detective*. He has published widely in journals such as *Poetique, Studies in the Novel, Nineteenth-Century Studies, Victorian Literature and Culture, Modern Fiction Studies*, and *Journal of Pre-Raphaelite and Aesthetic Studies*. He has lectured throughout the United States, England, and Australia. His current project involves the female detective in Victorian and Edwardian fiction. He was selected Oklahoma Professor of the Year by the Carnegie Foundation in 1993.

JAMES R. KINCAID is Aerol Arnold Professor of English at the University of Southern California. He is author, most recently, of *Erotic Innocence: The Culture of Child-Molesting* and of *Annoying the Victorians*.

IRA B. NADEL, Professor of English at the University of British Columbia, is the author of *Biography: Fiction, Fact and Form, Joyce and the Jews*, and *Various Positions: A Life of Leonard Cohen*. He has also edited Wilkie Collins's formerly lost first novel, *Iolani*, and is General Editor of *The Cambridge Companion to Ezra Pound*. His biography of *Tom Stoppard* was published in 2002.

JAMES G. NELSON, Professor Emeritus, University of Wisconsin-Madison, has written numerous books and articles on nineteenth-century British literature. His *The Early Nineties: A View from the Bodley Head* initiated a trilogy on the literary publishers of the 1890s which recently concluded with *Publisher to the Decadents: Leonard Smithers in the Careers of Beardsley, Wilde, Dowson*. Currently he is writing a book on the American poet, ghost story writer, critic and novelist, Vincent O'Sullivan, who was an intimate of Wilde, Beardsley, and other writers and artists of the 1890s.

MAX SAUNDERS is Professor of English at King's College London, where he teaches modern English, European, and American literature. He studied at the universities of Cambridge and Harvard, and was a Research Fellow and then College Lecturer at Selwyn College Cambridge. He is the author of *Ford Madox Ford: A Dual Life*, the editor of *Ford's Selected Poems*, *War Prose*, and (with Richard Stang) *Critical Essays*, and has published essays on Ford, Eliot, Joyce, Rosamond Lehmann, Lawrence, Freud, Pound, Ruskin, and others.

THOMAS SCHAUB is author of *Pynchon: The Voice of Ambiguity* and *American Fiction in the Cold War* and numerous articles, including essays on James Fenimore Cooper, William Carlos Williams, Richard Wright, and Ralph Ellison. He is editor of *Contemporary Literature*, and twice has served as department chair of the English Department of the University of Wisconsin-Madison.

ELIZABETH WINSTON is Associate Professor of English at the University of Tampa, where she teaches the nineteenth-century British novel, women's literature, and first-year writing. Her publications include essays on Oliphant, Stein, and autobiography, appearing in *Nineteenth-Century Studies*, *Mosaic*, *Biography*, and *Women's Autobiography*. An essay with Kevin Sweeney on a silent film adaptation of *Romola* was published in *Literature/Film Quarterly*. She regularly reviews for *George Eliot–George Henry Lewes Studies*. Dr. Winston was Professor Wiesenfarth's Ph.D. student between 1972–77.

Index